The Legacy of Kierkegaard

The Legacy of Kierkegaard

JOHN HEYWOOD THOMAS

CASCADE Books · Eugene, Oregon

THE LEGACY OF KIERKEGAARD

Copyright © 2012 John Heywood Thomas. All rights reserved. Except for brief quotations in critical publications or reviews, no part of this book may be reproduced in any manner without prior written permission from the publisher. Write: Permissions, Wipf and Stock Publishers, 199 W. 8th Ave., Suite 3, Eugene, OR 97401.

Cascade Books
An Imprint of Wipf and Stock Publishers
199 W. 8th Ave., Suite 3
Eugene, OR 97401

www.wipfandstock.com

ISBN 13: 978-1-61097-429-5

Cataloguing-in-Publication data:

Thomas, J. Heywood (John Heywood), 1926–.

    The legacy of Kierkegaard / John Heywood Thomas.

    viii + 258 pp. ; 23 cm. Includes bibliographical references.

    ISBN 13: 978-1-61097-429-5

    1. Kierkegaard, Søren, 1813–1855. 2. Kierkegaard, Søren, 1813–1855—Religion. 3. Christianity—Philosophy. 4. Philosophical theology. I. Title.

B4378.C5 T56 2012

Manufactured in the U.S.A.

Contents

Acknowledgments / vii

1. Kierkegaard: The Problem / 1
2. Kierkegaard and Literature / 10
3. Hegelian Aesthetic and Kierkegaard's Literary Art / 34
4. Kierkegaard and Philosophy (i) / 52
5. Kierkegaard and Philosophy (ii): Kierkegaard on Ontology / 80
6. Kierkegaard and Religion (i) / 104
7. Kierkegaard and Religion (ii): A Non-Ecclesial Religion? / 128
8. Kierkegaard on Revelation, Knowledge, and Proof / 141
9. Kierkegaard's Alternative Metaphysical Theology / 162
10. A Mature Rationalism: Kierkegaard's Reaction to Reason / 178
11. Kierkegaard and the Problem of Time / 197
12. Kierkegaard and the Problem of Death / 216
13. Kierkegaard and the Philosophy of Education / 231

Epilogue / 245

Bibliography / 251

Acknowledgments

Chapter 3 was originally a contribution to George Pattison (ed.), *Kierkegaard on Art and Communication*. London: Macmillan, 1992. It is reproduced here with permission from Palgrave Macmillan.

Chapters 8 and 9 are based on material previously published. Bloodaxe Books are to be thanks for the quotation from R. S. Thomas' poem "Reservoirs."

Finally, the author also records his gratitude to Dr. Robin Parry for the care and efficiency of his work as editor and to the Rev Blake Hemmings for transforming a typescript into a form acceptable for publication.

1

Kierkegaard: The Problem

AN AUTOBIOGRAPHICAL STATEMENT

IT IS PERHAPS APPROPRIATE to begin a study of Kierkegaard with an autobiographical statement; for of all authors, Romantics and others, he was the master of the art of using autobiography. He scandalized his contemporaries by making such intimacies of biography as his courtship and engagement the basis of a thinly-disguised novelette. Lampooned by *The Corsair*, a magazine that is often described as scurrilous but is perhaps more accurately described as the *Private Eye* of its day and the radical press of its time, he showed the versatility of his literary skill and the acuity of his sociological perception, not to mention his great courage, by engaging in battle with the satirist. Himself a satirist of power with a scholarly understanding of irony, he became increasingly serious and steadfast in his purpose, which he understood to be part of his religious mission, to be "a spy in higher service," a religious exception. My autobiographical statement is meant simply to describe the origin, persistence, and nature of my fascination with Kierkegaard.

I was born and brought up in South Wales, one of a family which on both sides had been associated with and indeed played a prominent part in the history of Welsh dissent. Naturally, therefore, my early religious life was in the context of the Congregational chapel of which my parents were members. Welsh Congregationalism perpetuated the old name of the denomination—the Independents; and independence indeed was the character of that spiritual formation which I was given. I was early taught not only the crucial importance of personal piety but also the religious responsibility of intellectual convictions and understanding. It is difficult for me to over-estimate the influence on me of the community where devout souls argued passionately about matters of faith, displaying as much sturdiness of intellect as they did conviction. By far the most significant figure was the minister who reigned supreme in his pulpit and was in fact my only minister until I was an undergraduate. In his beautiful book, *Wales*, Edward Thomas describes a minister dominating a chapel and a village but he was, in fact, rather a weak character whose power of dominance seemed to be confined to the pulpit and his oratorical performance. The character of whom I speak was very different. He was an extraordinary man of remarkable and commanding presence who was particularly impressive because of his very obvious and profound spirituality and the force of his great integrity. A stern man, he was perhaps more respected than loved and even friends would say of him that but for the grace of God he would have been a very hard man. The word "Puritan" is often used with varying degrees of the looseness that characterizes the use of such words generally nowadays, but of John Evans it is not only used correctly but is the most apt description of him. Together with the Puritan emphasis on the Bible and on the work of the Holy Spirit in effecting the communion that marks the church, his theology was also marked by a very strong antipathy towards Liberalism. Long before I ever saw the classic work of R. J. Campbell, *The New Theology*, I had heard of it as a travesty of Christian theology. Equally repugnant to this minister was the older and more persistent form of Liberalism as a critical modernism. There was, then, about him a very strange anti-intellectualism—stranger indeed this seemed to me as in my teens I used to visit him in his large study, the walls of which were completely covered with shelved books. In his way he was a learned man and yet his sermons were regular condemnations of the pride of learning and the errors of those who, he would say, with his voice rising in tones of scorn, "describe themselves so proudly as 'we critics.'" That anyone thus presumed to set himself up as a critic of the Word of God was not only anathema to him—it was to be roundly condemned lest people be led astray. Only one book did this mentor and faithful pastor ever give me to read and that was Kierkegaard's *Training in Christianity*. That alone would have made the book special but it was Kierkegaard rather than John Evans who really impressed me as I read. A lad of seventeen, I had already benefitted from the wide classical education of the grammar school and I had been familiarized with the legacy of Greece and Rome and introduced to the breadth of European literature, but I had never read prose like this. The rhetoric was spellbinding and the elaboration of paradoxes into clearly developed and strongly sustained theological argument was simply fascinating. Fascinated I was and I could not stop reading. I was then reading philosophy and I scoured the university library to find what I could. There was hardly anything of Kierkegaard's writing and what secondary material was to be found was even more disappointing. It would seem that Kierkegaard was not a figure to be taken seriously as a philosopher.

Shortly afterwards I had the very good fortune to make the acquaintance of and become friendly with another extraordinary man, J. M. Lloyd Thomas. He had been a very successful solicitor who had displayed great skill as a counsellor and so had decided to become a minister. Having been the renowned minister of the Old Meeting House in Birmingham, he had suddenly retired from public life. His retirement had been occasioned by the development of the Unitarian denomination, a name he deemed to be as misleading as it was heretical. He had become one of the leading figures in the Reunion movement associated especially with the idea of a Free Catholic Church. He had debated with Chesterton, had been a friend of Baron von Hugel and Professor Norman Kemp Smith as well as the intimate counsellor of Father Orchard. In the depths of rural Wales, whither he had retired, he pursued his literary and theological interests by contributing articles and reviews to *The Hibbert Journal*, which at that time was still edited by his friend L. P. Jacks. This indefatigable writer was one of the first to herald the vogue that Kierkegaard was about to enjoy in English letters during the fifties. Though he was aware of Kierkegaard's philosophical interests, for Lloyd Thomas Kierkegaard was first and foremost a religious thinker and indeed a prophet. To quote a bon mot from one of his letters to me—"I came to survey Kierkegaard but instead he has looked at me and left me a bundle of rags on my own doorstep." Yet he was sufficiently alive to the intellectual nature of this writing to show me that the philosophy was in the service of faith and indeed a means of articulating that faith.

The fashion of the fifties died the death of fashions but I had discovered what was to be a lifelong area of research as I became convinced that the fundamental problems of philosophy of Religion were not only raised here in the clearest fashion but illuminated too by a most subtle thinker as a matter of religious duty. There have been times when I have felt him to be uncomfortably like the Ancient Mariner's albatross as I have never been able to leave him on one side. Other interests have occupied me but they always seemed to lead back to him. I have been irritated by his cleverness and his almost deliberate obscurity and yet I have not been able to dismiss the thought as either opaque or trivial. The truth is that he haunts me as a challenge on more than one level but not least the intellectual level. More and more he seems to me an enigma. Having seen the death of a fashion, I later saw a fresh surge of interest in Kierkegaard study in the eighties, which has developed our knowledge and understanding of Kierkegaard's work quite dramatically. Despite this I describe Kierkegaard as a *problem*.

KIERKEGAARD AS A PROBLEM

That fresh surge of interest in Kierkegaard resulted in several important books—too great a number for any brief account of them to be useful; but some three themes can be picked out which help clarify what I mean.

Kierkegaard and Wittgenstein

First, there has been a good deal of interest on the part of some philosophers of religion in Kierkegaard's influence on Wittgenstein. We know that Wittgenstein found Kierkegaard interesting and illuminating and it might even be said that he admired Kierkegaard. As a research student in Cambridge I had the good fortune to be supervised for two terms by Wittgenstein's pupil, the late G. H. von Wright, who once remarked to me that he was never very sure what it was that Wittgenstein found so interesting in Kierkegaard. However, the fact of the influence is undeniable and this has led some authors to interpret Kierkegaard in the light of Wittgenstein's philosophy and to view his thought as an anticipation of those theories of metaphysics and religion which they take to have been established by Wittgenstein. To some extent I shared this tendency, as my own interpretation of Kierkegaard's philosophy of religion drew a comparison between it and the approach of linguistic analysis, but I neither argued for any connection between them or between Kierkegaard's and Wittgenstein's philosophy of religion nor defined either of them as some kind of fideism. However, after Malcolm's memoir of Wittgenstein the connection became a commonplace among historians of philosophy and there was an occasional study of Wittgenstein's debt to Kierkegaard.[1] It was left to philosophers like Peter Winch and most notably D. Z. Phillips to develop the philosophical position and approach that have been labeled "fideism."

In his first book, *The Concept of Prayer*, Phillips heralded the dominant theme of his work—that philosophy of religion was based on a mistake when it was engaged in the search for evidence to support religious assertions. For the religious man to seek empirical results which could be thought to verify his prayer is, in Phillips' view, for him to lapse into superstition. The essential task, he says, is to look at a particular piece of language and elicit from it the rules of the particular language-game it represents. This way of doing philosophy cannot be first described in the abstract and then applied to concrete problems—it is a matter of examining those problems themselves philosophically but viewing them from the inside. Philosophy of religion will make progress, he thinks, only when it recognizes that to raise the question of the reality of God is not quite the same as discussing other reality claims; God's reality is his divinity. Talk about God is not part and parcel of so much ordinary language as is talk about the material world. God's reality or existence is not a fact but part of that language-game which is my worshipping, praying, believing, obeying, and loving. It is instantly clear how Phillips came to see Kierkegaard as an ally and a guide in philosophy of religion. That attraction and inspiration I well understand and applaud. My point here is that if this is meant to be an exposition of Kierkegaard's thought then the interpretation is an extremely complex piece of hermeneutics. For it is one thing to argue, as I had done, that linguistic analysis is a very useful heuristic method to apply to Kierkegaard's philosophy but quite another to identify that with a particular philosophical position based on or exemplifying that method. For instance, the normal methods of historical investigation and explanation, which would involve the contextualization of Kierkegaard within the European culture of the nineteenth century, would seem of little use or relevance. What must certainly follow from such an interpretation is that it is quite wrong to see Kierkegaard as involved in a religious struggle which was concerned to uphold orthodox doctrine. Whether or not one comes to think that he was mistaken in this understanding of his task is neither here nor there; the fact is that this is the first and immediate impression his work makes

---

1. Cf. Gallagher, "Wittgenstein's Admiration for Kierkegaard."

and one of which he leaves us in no doubt. I emphasize my point that we are not here concerned with the question whether this kind of approach to Kierkegaard is right but rather with the way in which the possibility of such an approach resulting in this kind of interpretation shows the problem of Kierkegaard. His philosophy and his theology are clearly not separate concerns. Moreover, they are far from straightforward in the way that, however difficult the philosophy of, say, Spinoza or the theology of Calvin may be, we have in them thought-creations that are not elusive.

Understanding Kierkegaard on His Own Terms

Slightly different, though he too was later much influenced by Wittgenstein's thought, is the approach of Paul Holmer. It is more useful to look at his exposition of an approach—without reference to the later application of Wittgenstein's philosophy—to the problems of theology. In a celebrated paper, "On Understanding Kierkegaard," Holmer calls attention to the irony of there being such an immense volume of scholarship on the writings of Kierkegaard which seems "systematically oblivious to the peculiarities" of those writings and equally to Kierkegaard's own comments on them. The paper calls into question the very presuppositions of historical scholarship in connection with Kierkegaard's writing and indeed turns Kierkegaard's thought back on its interpreters. I am being neither facetious nor dismissive when I say that this kind of approach would make us aware of the canon of Kierkegaard's writings and pleads for the freedom of that "word" to speak to us and to our condition. My purpose in so describing this approach is to show that the strength of Holmer's position lies precisely in his determination to let Kierkegaard be what he himself said he was from the beginning, namely, a religious writer. Holmer's starting point is the insistence on the incontrovertible fact that Kierkegaard "presupposed a theory of knowledge which is novel and intrinsically significant."[2] Kierkegaard's quarrel, he says, is not with scholarship as such but with a kind of metaphysics of knowledge, "a quasi-argument which says that all knowledge has a unity and a meaning in totality which no single knowledge-claim has apart from the rest."[3] The scholar's "understanding" of an author's

---

2. Holmer, "On Understanding Kierkegaard," 41.
3. Ibid., 42.

writings which is a matter of exhausting the possible knowledge about the author is mythical, "an invented and contrived aim," usually defined as qualitatively different from "understanding" any particular truth-claims regarding the author or any of his works. When Kierkegaard distinguished so clearly and sharply between logic and existence it was such a view, says Holmer, that he was attacking. Moreover, Kierkegaard's "own exposition of his own point of view so described the logic and the form of the literature as to make this kind of scholarly 'metaphysics of learning' irrelevant."[4] Therefore Holmer contends that an approach to Kierkegaard must be either a matter of historical scholarship pure and simple or a critical literature which engages with Kierkegaard's argument about religion and philosophy. We do not need to follow the argument about Kierkegaard's epistemological basis for his point of view or rehearse in any detail what Holmer says about the difficulty and subtlety of this understanding of Kierkegaard. Towards the end of his paper he sets out elegantly and succinctly what is his position and his own words thus afford us a clear summary:

> What I am here arguing is that the importance of Kierkegaard's literature lies in the following: (a) it is a presentation of possibles; (b) it is a presentation of a theory about these possibles. In respect to the latter Kierkegaard argues against other theories as to how possibles are encountered, including those expressed by most historical theology, speculative philosophy and a miscellany of others. It is this theory which is Kierkegaard's own case against the kind of scholarship which argues that only by multiplying historical knowledge can one grasp the possibles. It is this which if regarded would give scholarship a more limited but fitting role. Kierkegaard may be wrong, but if so he ought to be enjoined directly. The real task of Kierkegaardian scholarship, both affirmatively and negatively, is to address this theory and judge it.[5]

As he says, if the possibilities are really offered then, of course, the task that confronts us is that of facing them ourselves. The communication is one of existence and that is why I used biblical and kerygmatic terminology to describe this approach at the outset. Holmer's plea is, in a

---

4. Ibid., 43.
5. Ibid., 51.

sense, the very simple but profoundly important one that the process of understanding should match the text.

Can We Trust Kierkegaard's Accounts of His Own Life?

If these methods of interpretation seem to make the text so unusually difficult what if the text is in fact obscured, deliberately distorted, and mythical? That is in fact the view taken and expounded by Henning Fenger in *Kierkegaard-Myter og Kierkegaard-Bilder*.[6] He challenges what he calls the official Kierkegaard scholarship as something which "depends on inbreeding for its very existence."[7] The panache of this claim is reflected in Fenger's highly metaphorical outline of the book's thesis; for, having suggested that Kierkegaard scholarship proceeds by building upon successive assumptions, he describes Kierkegaard research as "erected upon a foundation so porous that it crumbles at the very touch."[8] The thesis he advances is that Kierkegaard falsified his own history—not simply in his published accounts of his life but even in the journal he kept. Kierkegaard, he says, enjoyed suppressing, rewriting, misrepresenting, distorting, and erasing material and so leading any reader astray. He "put out snares for his contemporaries and, in the process, for posterity's historical researchers as well."[9] This is an extraordinary claim but one which has a certain initial credibility when one recalls that we are dealing with a very strange figure. Fenger's essential evidence is what he offers as a piece of detection concerning the composition of *Either-Or*. What he does is to contest both Kierkegaard's dating of its composition process and his interpretation of its significance. On the basis of material in the Papers (IV B 59 and IV A 215) he argues that Kierkegaard had in fact started writing *Either-Or* as early as 1839 and that his claim that he wrote it in eleven months was, to use his "kind" word, inexact. The first piece of material is an article which seems ready for printing, bearing the title "Postscript to Either-Or of Victor Eremita," and speaks of the manuscript having been hidden for five years, and the second is a note in a copy of *Either-Or* that the book is "the very opposite" of that collection of occasional papers which people thought

---

6. Published in English as Fenger, *Kierkegaard, the Myths and Their Origins*.
7. Fenger, *Kierkegaard, the Myths*, x.
8. Ibid., xi.
9. Ibid., 2.

had been lying in his desk. Three facts are decisive, says Fenger. First, "Copenhagen's cultural world" had expected an extensive review from Heiberg's hand of the book's basic themes and this never came. Secondly, in his ironic letter of thanks to Heiberg of March 5, Kierkegaard burned his bridges behind him as far as the Heiberg circle was concerned. Thirdly, "only now, for the first time, does the idea of connecting the aesthetic authorship with a religious one—that is, with the publication of a series of edifying discourses dedicated to the deceased hosier—arise in Kierkegaard's mind."[10] The volumes of the Journal after 1846 must be treated, he thinks, with profound and fundamental distrust, especially as the editors of the Papers have been misled by Kierkegaard to make a poetical creation the basis for establishing criteria of dating. Typical of Kierkegaard's falsification for him is the way in which Kierkegaard would have us believe that Regine was the one and only love of his life when he had been infatuated with Bolette Rørdam.

Fenger's exciting book is written with such verve and animation, if not animus, that it is difficult to convey its power. Also there is quite a wealth of historical information so that the detail of the argument will not be obvious from my summary of the book's thesis. However, my main purpose in referring to it is to illustrate the difficulty of interpreting Kierkegaard; for if Fenger is right in his view that the literature delivers only a collection of myths then Kierkegaard is indeed a problem. Without engaging in any detailed discussion of his view I must, in conclusion, say that the problem is not as difficult as this. The three decisive facts in Fenger's argument do not justify his claim. We cannot doubt that Kierkegaard was often engaged in mystification but the material does not show any *actual deception*. For Fenger's case to be proved we should need to have some clearer evidence of a rewriting of history than the material he mentions. What is so clear about this is something that is evidenced again and again in *Either-Or*, namely that Kierkegaard was very much taken up with the fashion of Romantic writing. As for the story of Regine it seems to me that the later history tells us all and that whether or not he had been infatuated with Bolette does not in any way change a story that is one of the great tragedies of history. My concern here is to deal with the material we have in Kierkegaard's writings as critically and accurately as I can in order to show what he seems to me to have bequeathed us in the different concerns of our culture.

10. Ibid., 5.

2

Kierkegaard and Literature

KIERKEGAARD AND ROMANTICISM

Kierkegaard's Romantic Context

IN THE LIGHT OF what has already been said about the difficulty of interpreting Kierkegaard it would seem that the best and safest starting point is a consideration of him at, as it were, his most basic. Whatever else he was or was not, he certainly was a writer and obviously a writer of great genius. Were he not thought to have any other significance in the history of Danish philosophy he would be remembered as the man who pioneered the use of the Danish language as a means of philosophical communication. Some months after completing his degree in July 1840, he began preparing a dissertation to be submitted for the degree of Master of Arts as well as doing pastoral training in the Royal Seminary. The dissertation was finished in May the following year and was formally submitted in June. It was the custom for academic dissertations and their defense to be completed in Latin, but Kierkegaard sought and was granted the king's permission for his dissertation to be written in Danish. Though the opinion of his examiners was that the thesis suffered from an inferiority of style, the work can now be seen to be an extremely clever composition, something of a mixture between a pastiche and a satire but yet a very scholarly, subtle, philosophical argument.

As a writer Kierkegaard was the recipient and beneficiary of different European traditions and he is thus a focus of the complexity that makes up the literature of the nineteenth century in Europe. He was as enthusiastic in his pursuit of philosophy as Coleridge—and his intellectual appetite was similarly gargantuan. Just as much as Matthew Arnold, he recognized Goethe as the master whose grasp of the meaning of life was given the kind of expression in literature that was appropriate to it. His life had, judged by the rigid code of contemporary Copenhagen society, a whiff of scandal that would put him with Byron. And if one were compassionate enough to discern the tragedy of his story then one might put him alongside Keats. It is with Keats that I would indeed link him, for he seems to me to have the same power of philosophical and theological vision of imagination. It might seem that what I am trying to say is that Kierkegaard is to be understood as a Danish Romantic. That is very much like the view taken by John W. Elrod in his book *Kierkegaard and Christendom*. Describing the age as one which saw the collapse of the nation and yet was "the golden age of literature in Danish history," he characterizes it more generally as "an age of romanticism in reaction to the Enlightenment notion that the universe is a mechanistic unity that be rationally expressed through the deductive systems of mathematics and metaphysics."[1] He continues:

> Romantic poetry, prose, drama, historical novels and hymns recover, praise, and proclaim the individual as the center of value and reality, as opposed to the Enlightenment emphasis upon the universal. Nature is also personified: it becomes a living being with whom each individual may share a personal and mystical union. This personal identification with nature appears as a symbol in literature for a dynamic and functional identity with God; at the same time, the nation becomes a leading symbol for identification with one's fellow men.[2]

Reviewing the book in *Journal of English and Germanic Philology* the following year I made the point that this only displayed the enduring but mistaken assumption that Romanticism is a single artistic and philosophical movement and that even those such as the great critic M. H. Abrams who did view it thus would not speak in the rather simplistic terms employed by John Elrod. I noted that Kierkegaard had himself

---

1. Elrod, *Kierkegaard and Christendom*, 11–12. In his "Art in the Age of Reflection" George Pattison calls attention to the way in which Kierkegaard was influenced by the moderate Romanticism of F. C. Sibbern and Poul Martin Møller (Hannay and Marino, eds., *Cambridge Companion to Kierkegaard*, 78); but Roger Poole's comment in "The Unknown Kierkegaard" is equally clear—that Kierkegaard cannot be "fitted" in to the history of German Romanticism (ibid., 48).

2. Ibid., 12.

raised the question of where he should stand in relation to Romanticism, and what that relation was remains a problem. My point was that Kierkegaard's relation to writers such as Heiberg and Andersen is not perhaps the easiest of problems to resolve, but it is a good deal easier than the problem of his relation to Romanticism and the connection he saw between that and the disintegration of real subjectivity.

It is interesting to note that Alexander Dru, who was one of the most sensitive as well as the earliest of English Kierkegaard scholars, had already in 1949 made the connection between Kierkegaard and Romanticism. In the "Introduction" to his edition of Haecker's *Journal in the Night* he remarks, "The romantics with whom Kierkegaard had most in common were the failures of the first generation whose truncated works and fragmentary thoughts were exposed in a wholly misleading perspective by the appearance of the successful and often massive 'inadequate' oeuvres that followed."[3] However, as Arthur O. Lovejoy remarks, "The word 'romantic' has come to mean so many things that by itself it means nothing."[4] Allan Rodway's remark that the when and what of Romanticism are interconnected is very apt and enlightening. He elaborates it thus:

> Romanticism grew as reform came to seem more desirable than stability . . . It was that reform movement which was sufficiently passionate to react against a whole civilization, the best and worst of it—in intention if not quite in fact . . . The negative Augustan characteristics of indifference, complacency, prudence, and cynicism had been matched by such positive characteristics as sense, science, tolerance, and wit. But all were indiscriminately labeled "Reason" and reacted against by the more extreme romantics. This "Reason" came to mean something like "calculation," and was thus very different from the "reason" sometimes evoked (with only seeming inconsistency) by the romantics themselves. That "reason" implied something like "judging by principle" rather than by convention. Romantic characteristics tended to be, negatively, fanaticism, crankiness, mysticism, and egotism; and positively, insight, daring, grandeur, exploration, and independence.[5]

---

3. Haecker, *Journal in the Night*, 22.
4. Lovejoy, "On the discrimination of Romanticisms," 6.
5. Rodway, *Romantic Conflict*, 5.

So we will need first of all to see precisely what we are talking about when we discuss Kierkegaard's context of European Romanticism. Of late there has been a greater awareness of the total social context of Romanticism as witness in Robert Ryan's book, *The Romantic Reformation*, which was a deliberate attempt to see the Romantics as religious reformers. Without such guidance it is all too easy to be misled into a discussion of mere individualism and so lose the perception of Kierkegaard's greatness, which is provided by the proper foothold of his place in literature. Though one can readily agree with Elrod that Kierkegaard was strongly influenced by his Romantic background and with Roger Poole's description of him as "trained in the school of Romantic irony"[6] the relation between Kierkegaard and Romanticism is complex. Furthermore, because Romanticism was fed by mythical philosophy it also contributed more than most literary movements to developments and currents of thought that were essentially philosophical and theological. Also, since of all European literary movements Romanticism was the least limited and confined in the geographical scope of its influence, it both inevitably touched Kierkegaard's development and assisted the worldwide impact of his work.

Criticism of romantic as of any literature is essentially the interpretation of a text and not the development of some psychological theory. Yet very often it involves the uncovering of the sources of imagery and metaphor in the artist's life; for here particularly it is true that this is what the art is meant to *express*. One is reminded that Mario Praz defines his classic study of romantic literature as a "study of certain states of mind and peculiarities of behavior."[7] Hence reference to Kierkegaard's biography is inevitable. The story of what he called his "mad upbringing" is well enough known and we need only note that this must have developed his power of imagination at a very early age and with this a very remarkable sense of excitement at the display of dialectical skill. Like many an undergraduate after him he found the study of philosophy and literature more interesting than the theological lectures he was supposed to attend and when he began keeping a journal in 1834 he had also begun to postpone the evil day of his theological examinations.

---

6. Poole, *Kierkegaard: The Indirect Communication*, 2.
7. Praz, *Romantic Agony*, xv.

KIERKEGAARD'S LITERARY DEVELOPMENT

Kierkegaard's Journal

Already then Kierkegaard appears to be a literary figure and his lifestyle would be that of a young Romantic. Reading those early entries in his *Journal* one is struck by the way in which he steeped himself in Romantic literature—Novalis, Hoffmann, and the Schlegels. The circle in which he moved was very different from that of his home. Gadding about the streets or hanging around in the cafes or attending the theatre—that was his style, not the earnest, studious behavior of his brother, whose "pharisaic eye" constantly reproached him. He seemed the perfect example of the young Romantic. Another interesting feature of the *Journal* is its revelation of a remarkable combination of theoretic and creative interest. He is concerned to find "the Archimedean point" of works of art, which quest for organic unity is the first indication of a dissatisfaction with Romanticism. Yet what the next year or two showed was a growing interest in Romanticism as he pondered more and more the theme of mythical or legendary types. He had been interested in the idea of the master-thief and was to devote a great deal of attention to the stories of the Wandering Jew, Don Juan, and Faust. All this was to lead him through aesthetics to philosophy of morals and philosophy of religion; but in the meantime he was attracted by the work of German Romantics like Hoffmann. The most important influence on his thinking at this time was J. G. Hamann, the Magus of the North, whom the great pioneer of English Kierkegaard research, Walter Lowrie, described as "the only author by whom Kierkegaard was profoundly influenced."[8] The claim seems very plausible since Hamann, a friend of Kant's and a valued critic, had tried to strangle the Enlightenment at birth. A passionate, devout, ill-disciplined, and indeed chaotic thinker, he savagely disparaged the claims of the rational intellect and the Newtonian universe.

My own reading of Kierkegaard's development sees him much more closely linked with the whole Romantic movement for two reasons. One is that this was the time of the great flowering of Danish literature—the golden age of Oehlenschlager, Grundtvig, Heiberg, and Andersen, the greatest names in nineteenth-century Danish literature.[9] Secondly,

---

8. Lowrie, *Johann Georg Hamann*, 41.

9. See Bruce Kirmmse's *Kierkegaard in Golden Age Denmark* for a detailed analysis of Kierkegaard's development in the context of Denmark's "Golden Age."

what has always seemed to me a significant fact is that when eventually Kierkegaard left Copenhagen he went to Berlin specifically to hear Schelling's lectures. The explanation of this is partly to be found in the modest but significant popularity that Schelling enjoyed amongst those thinkers in Denmark who were the advocates of Romanticism. Of these Henrik Steffens and P. M. Møller are the most important. For Steffens both German idealism and romanticism are the refined expressions of the individualistic spirit of Protestantism. The identity of individual and eternal spirit and the correlation of nature and history—themes beloved by the Romantics—are the typical motifs of this philosophy. This was the inspiration of Oehlenschlager's epic poetry and dramas. Though Møller was critical of the claims of future national greatness he developed the same philosophical motifs a generation later.

What I have been trying to depict is the development of a young litterateur who responds naturally to the Romanticism then fashionable. All of this had, as I have said, taken him away from theology and preparation for the ministry. Once again the *Journal* is very illuminating for it shows Kierkegaard uncertain about himself and his future. He had been attracted by natural science, half-envious of the way in which his cousin Peter Lund had found a niche for himself there; but he was more interested in solving the riddle of life than in finding out about the world. Theology offered no haven because he would no longer be content with the orthodoxy in which he had been raised—now that he was thinking for himself it was a tottering colossus. True to the Romantic impatience with the Enlightenment he was equally unhappy with the life of reason—rationalism, he thought, cut a pretty poor figure. All this agony of doubt must have been pretty obvious so that his father sent him on a holiday to Sjaelland to a little village on its north coast called Gilleleje. The entries of the *Journal* for this period have a distinctly Wordsworthian character. Thus he writes: "In the midst of nature where man is free from the frequently oppressive air of life and can breathe more freely the soul is readily open to every noble impression . . . Here man . . . feels that there is something higher which manifests itself in nature and before which we must bow down; he feels the necessity of giving himself up to the power which directs all things."[10] The similarities with the Wordsworth of "The Prelude" and *Lyrical Ballads* are very obvious. The opening pas-

---

10. Kierkegaard, *Journals*, 20; Kierkegaard, *Papirer* I A 68.

sage of this entry describing his mood after being in Gilleleje is even more Wordsworthian:

> ... as I stood there one quiet evening as the sea struck up its song with a deep and calm solemnity ... whilst on the other side the busy noise of life subsided and the birds sang their evening prayer—the few that are dear to me came forth from their graves or it seemed to me as though they had not died. I felt so content in their midst, I rested in their embrace, and it was as though I were out of the body, wafted with them into the ether above.[11]

However, one should not be misled into thinking that Kierkegaard was as uncritical a philosopher as Wordsworth. Already he was set on a road of self-examination that took him far beyond the emotionalism of Romantic introspection. It seems to me that he had already begun on his exploration of post-Kantian philosophy with its typically personal concerns. He read Fichte's *Vocation of Man* and it is of that work that I find distinct echoes in this passage. Fichte's own comment on that work is interesting—he was "emotionally moved only by clarity," clarity that could not fail to grip his heart. The absolute ego is the Absolute God; and yet for Fichte in the end everything "is a wonderful dream."[12] Clearly one of the things that appealed to Kierkegaard even more than the emphasis on the mystery of human experience that seems to escape thought was the way in which the philosophy stimulated by and critical of Romantic literature saw the necessity for an individual to achieve a *lebensanschauung*, a life-view that was, in Keats' words, a life of feeling rather than a life of thought alone. Perhaps the most telling entry he made in his *Journal* at this time was his declaration, "What I really lack is to be clear in my mind what I am to do not what I am to know ... The thing is to understand myself ... the thing is to find a truth which is true *for me*, to find *the idea for which I can live and die*."[13]

If I am right in discerning Fichte's influence in these reflections what we can say is that already Kierkegaard's interest in Romantic literature had kindled in him an ethical attitude that went deeper than any artistic interest. The aim of *Vocation of Man* was to emphasize the primacy of the ethical in any satisfactory account of the world so that the very opposition of action and knowing in the last quotation could have been

---

11. Ibid.
12. Fichte, *Vocation of Man*, 160–76.
13. Kierkegaard, *Journals*, 22; Kierkegard, *Papirer* I A 75.

Fichte's. Thought, he says, which is not concerned with action is worthless inasmuch as it is action that gives knowledge its purpose.[14] Action is never reducible to knowledge: the validity of knowledge is determined by a decision of the will. Equally the young Kierkegaard is concerned to screw up his courage—to act.

Kierkegaard's Early Publications

Having sketched the ideas on and of literature which the young student tried out in the privacy of his *Journal* we can now consider his earliest publications. The very first, an article in the Copenhagen *Flyvende Post*, set the pattern for so much of his main publications in that it was an anonymous publication. It bore the title "Also a Defense of Woman's Superior talents" and was a reply to an article published earlier by a fellow-student, "Woman's Superior Origin Defended." It is not the misogynistic attitude here foreshadowed that is important but the sharp wit that was in the process of cultivation. The four political articles that followed in the same newspaper in 1836 are much the same—too clever by half with more wit than judgment so that one contemporary journalist commented that he wondered what the real subject was. A couple of years later and we see that his touch is much more sure. He was still in his early years as a student and much involved in student affairs with the result that he was writing for the Students' Union. The work was a satirical play called "The Conflict between the Old and the New Soap Cellar: a heroic-patristic-cosmopolitan-philanthropic-fatalistic drama in several scenes." The interesting point about this piece is that it was seen by critics such as Karl Roos to be a parody of Goethe's *Faust*.[15] Kierkegaard's first serious work, however, was a long review article published, as he says, "against his will" and bearing the significant title "From the Papers of One Still Living." It was a polemical piece, which was a fierce personal attack on H. C. Andersen. Emil Boesen, his "faithful friend," describes it as "ably done but heavy in style and full of Hegelian expressions": Kierkegaard himself remarked that few would manage to read much of it. Considered in this light his decision to write his thesis in Danish can be seen as an attempt to harmonize these two styles which we have so far seen in his writing and to fashion for himself a style that would be at once personal and yet capable of expressing technical thought. The subtitle

---

14. S.W. II, 257ff. cf. Fichte, *Science of Knowledge*, 250, 283–86.
15. Roos, *Kierkegaard og Goethe*, 131–74.

of the review-article gives the theme—"About Andersen as a novelist with constant reference to his *Only a Fiddler*." The phrase "with constant reference" is one we shall meet again in the title of the thesis and it suggests that already Kierkegaard was one of that small band of craftsmen who are never content with performing only one task at a time. What is perhaps more telling for our present purpose is the phrase "published against his will" because he thus declares himself to be taking up an attitude fundamentally different from Andersen's. Attacking Andersen the man he is less bound to do so because a principle is at stake. However, it is Andersen the *novelist* that is the target of Kierkegaard's criticism; and that criticism is that Andersen the novelist lacks depth and honesty. There was no organizing principle in his novel: it lacked serious content. A true work of art, he says, is "the transubstantiation of experience" for "genius is not a candle which is blown out by the wind but a fire which the storm causes to flare up."[16]

We have reached the point that can be said to be the real beginning of Kierkegaard's literary career, the submission of his MA dissertation. By the time of his death the degree of MA had obviously been converted to a Doctorate so that the auction catalogue of his library refers to him as Dr. S. A. Kierkegaard. The title was "About the Concept of Irony with constant reference to Socrates." It was written in Danish and we shall come back to the matter of style, which does not at the moment concern me any more than the importance of the book as the beginning of his Hegelian critique.[17] What does concern me is the attitude to Romanticism. He approved of the Romantic emphasis on imagination and idealism but was very anxious to point out the weakness of Romanticism as liable to fall into pure emotion. It overflows the boundaries, he says, shows no discrimination, no capacity for evaluating emotion or any understanding of the way in which emotion is dependent on or derives from morality. Dreaming is an unhealthy substitute for reality and can even destroy by becoming madness or suicide. The "infinite" longing of Romantic idealism may reduce finite reality to a vanishing point. The Romantic is absorbed in his own emotions and is devoid of roots so that he has neither consistency nor continuity. He is in fact at the mercy of his ephemeral moods. It is only great artists like Shakespeare and Goethe who have been able to control irony so that

---

16. Kierkegaard, "From the Papers of One Still Living," S.V. 1, 44.
17. See Heywood Thomas, *Philosophy of Religion in Kierkegaard's Writings*, 11f.

their works afford examples of "mastered irony." The typical Romantic writer is the slave of the power that he is supposed to dominate and thus is a failure both personally and artistically. No authentic life is possible without irony but irony is only the negative way, not truth itself. The critique of Romanticism had been foreshadowed in "From the Papers of One Still Living," as Roger Poole points out: "The young Kierkegaard, much as he loathes Martensen's lectures, in which the lecturer is always about to 'go further,' is nevertheless anxious not to be counted amongst the Romantics, the 'arbitrary' or 'purposeless' Romantics so easily disposed of by Hegel in his *Lectures on Aesthetics* which Kierkegaard knew of through Prof Heiberg's lectures on aesthetic triads."[18] It is significant that the basis of that critique was moral and spiritual as much as philosophical. It is useful to elaborate this so that we can form a proper view of Kierkegaard as a writer.

Kierkegaard's Later Writings

Kierkegaard's literary career had now well and truly begun; and yet it was in a way only an abortive beginning. What gave his writing that great push to launch a sustained though short production of such large proportion was the tragic affair with Regine Olsen. The poignant tale of the long wait before proposing, the brief engagement, and the agony of the broken engagement is one of the great love stories of literary history. His flight from Copenhagen after breaking off the engagement was followed by his first major publication, *Either-Or*, written to convince Regine that he had deceived her and was a potential seducer. This was followed by a flood of other pseudonymous works—*Repetition* and *Fear and Trembling* being published in 1843 and *Philosophical Fragments* and *Concept of Anxiety* in the following year. *Either-Or* had been a big book—two volumes of 400 pages each—and these four were small books. Then came another big book, *Stages on Life's Way*, and this was followed by the masterpiece of philosophy in Kierkegaard's uniquely ironic style, *Concluding Unscientific Postscript*. Side by side with this "dialectical" authorship there was a religious one, the twenty-one discourses published under his own name. Once again the authorship might have ended; but the attack on him by the satirical weekly *The Corsair* sparked off a fresh creativity. It began with the criticism of his *Stages on Life's Way*, and in

---

18. Poole, *Kierkegaard: The Indirect Communication*, 31.

his reply to it he exposed the author and the *éminence grise* of the journal as the ambitious academic P. L. Møller. Sardonically, Kierkegaard had asked why it was that he was neglected by *The Corsair* when everyone else of any consequence was paid the compliment of being lampooned by the paper. The swift reaction, which resulted in his being made the laughing stock of the small town that Copenhagen then was, is another story that is familiar. The point for us to note is that a new period of literary activity began continuing a distinctly religious theme. In 1849 there appeared a work under a new pseudonym, Anti-Climacus, *The Sickness unto Death*, and in 1850 this was followed by *Practice in Christianity*, a work by the same pseudonym. From then on there was little until the final attack on the State Church. It perhaps should be emphasized that once more Kierkegaard felt that he was forced into publication. Having shown the Primate his *Practice in Christianity* he had expected an acknowledgement that public official Christianity was not identical with the Christianity of the New Testament; but old Mynster had given him short shrift. So Kierkegaard felt obliged to expose the error. The opportunity came with Martensen's sermon at Mynster's funeral in which he called Mynster a "witness to the truth." The attack was eventually launched, taking the form of his own broadsheet, *The Instant*. This series came to a sudden end in October 1855 when he collapsed in the street and died in hospital some weeks later.

KIERKEGAARD'S LITERARY LEGACY

Tracing his literary career as a part of his biography in this way has enabled us to see both the origins of Kierkegaard's writing and more particularly to highlight its variety. Journalist, diary writer, novelist, short story writer, author of philosophical and theological works as well as sermons, and finally a polemicist—this is Kierkegaard's legacy to literature.

Before we place this in its literary context and indicate its influence on later literature we should resume the brief discussion of his artistic achievement. His deliberate effort to learn the craft of writing and to achieve something in literature has been obvious but is all the more evident as we follow the course of his writing—his publications and his private writing. In fact the contrast between the two as he was about to launch his literary career is most instructive. The lively, direct style of the *Journal*, which is at times almost poetic, affords a marked contrast with the tortuous, stylized, and contrived manner of his writing in the earliest publications. The *Journal* is a treasure house of philosophical and theological aphorisms, of profound and extended argument—all written in a most lucid and straightforward manner. Thus he comments in 1836 on Schleiermacher and Hegel, "What Schleiermacher calls 'Religion' and the Hegelians 'Faith' is at the bottom nothing but the first immediate condition for everything—the vital fluidum—the spiritual atmosphere we breathe in—and which cannot therefore with justice be designated by those words."[19] Again there are some delightfully rhetorical passages full of perception and profundity like his thanks to Lichtenberg:

> Thanks, Lichtenberg, thanks! For having said that there is nothing so feeble as the conversation of learned literary men who have never thought for themselves but know a thousand historical-literary facts. "It is almost like a reading from a cookery book when one is hungry." Oh thanks for that voice in the wilderness of a wild bird in the silence of the night; I imagine it was written after a protracted session with one of those learned jades, which perhaps robbed him of some happy moments. Unfortunately in my copy I found a mark which disturbed me; for I already see some journalist or other going carefully through the work in order to fill the papers with aphorisms, with or without Lichtenberg's name; and that has, unfortunately, robbed me of some of the surprise.[20]

This free style of the *Journal* was what he sought to harmonize with the rather heavy style of his earliest public writing when composing his MA dissertation and so fashion a style that would be at once personal and yet capable of expressing technical thought. Obviously the personal is what he wanted to prevail and he remarks in the *Journal* that the examiners will criticize his freedom of style and the readers will have to forgive his gaiety and the fact that he sings to his work in order to lighten the task. Poetic images and play on words thus become the staple of his philosophical style.

Either-Or, the first of his published books, is a quite extraordinary collection of essays and a philosophical novel. As a novel it reflects the influence of the shape and character of the contemporary novel. Goethe's *Wilhelm Meister's Travels* was for Kierkegaard's generation

19. Kierkegaard, *Journals*, 78; Kierkegaard, *Papirer* I A 273.

20. Kierkegaard, *Journals*, 147; Kierkegaard, *Papirer* I A 122, in Kierkegaard's Writings.

the philosophical novel *par excellence*. We know that in February 1836 Kierkegaard had bought the six volumes and read them without a break. He greatly admired the work and his *Journal* shows him eagerly writing on it and, in his usual fashion, copying passages from it.[21] What excited him was the way in which Goethe had been able to write the story of a man, which was in itself the formulation of a philosophy. So it became the pattern for what is most typical of his own writing—the creation of a character who is the expression of an idea. The marvelous feature of this is that insofar as we know these characters they are not by any means mere cardboard cut-outs but people we can recognize. He did not follow Goethe exactly but created characters symbolizing *different* lifestyles or forms of life. *Either-Or* shows the "aesthetic" and the "ethical" and *Stages* the "religious." What never fails to surprise one about *Either-Or* is that it is so completely and thoroughly unified. The first part is a collection of disparate pieces—"Diapsalmata"—and the second part is the exposition of the lifestyle of the novelist. Already one is aware of the problem of reading Kierkegaard since that statement does not imply that it was an autobiographical declaration on Kierkegaard's part. The young aesthete—the romantic—has no stability and the expression is therefore chaotic—"it permits," says the pseudonymous editor, "of no single coherent exposition." More than this, as I have argued elsewhere, *Either-Or* is part of Kierkegaard's *philosophical argument* against the philosophy of system.[22] One, therefore, has the peculiar situation of a philosophical argument being conducted in a doubly extraordinary fashion—in a non-academic context as well as in a manner that seems devoid of all the usual philosophical apparatus. Yet the genius of the work is precisely that *the medium and the message are entirely as one* and constitute the revolutionary argument in that the very point of the work is that two-fold demonstration that philosophy should not be characterized by the *artificial* unity of a logical system. The same exploitation of the effect of different styles is even more obvious in *Stages on Life's Way*. To grasp the effectiveness clearly we must recall that this was the book which made so free a use of Kierkegaard's own romance, the diary there being set out having therefore a very powerfully autobiographical quality. In the diary he inserted six short stories, each written in a particular style, in which he replicates first the style of the Old Testament chronicle—"Solomon's

---

21. Kierkegaard, *Papirer* I C 72. cf. 73.
22. Heywood Thomas, *Philosophy of Religion*, 13ff.

Dream" and "Nebuchadnezzar"—then Herodotus—"Periander"—Shakespeare's King Lear on the heath—"A Leper's Soliloquy"—and the contemporary Danish novel—"A Possibility." Consequently he distances these pieces from the Diary and yet presents them as his own work.

In his philosophical and theological work Kierkegaard's method is very different. The characters in *Repetition* and *Fear and Trembling* are much more illustrations of types just as his later pieces illustrated ideas by discussing human types. A very good example of his fondness for contrast as a stylistic ploy is the publication of two books within the same month in 1844 on similar topics—at least in the sense that both were theological: *The Concept of Anxiety* dealing with the fall of man and *Philosophical Fragments* dealing with revelation. In the first Kierkegaard considers the theological problem from a psychological point of view and develops his doctrine in relation to Schleiermacher and other theologians. The irony that marked *The Concept of Irony* is once more evident: in order to destroy the contemporary theology of sin Kierkegaard has borrowed the style of a dogmatic textbook. In fact the book has a very Latin quality even in its language, that language being the very one he had rejected for his dissertation. By contrast, *Philosophical Fragments* is a book that is very Greek in its atmosphere. Socrates is the inspiration of both its problem and the method of its argument. To read the discussion with its question "How far does the Truth admit of being learned?" is to move once more in the world of the Socratic dialogues of Plato. Yet here again Kierkegaard shows himself the master of irony in that here too he uses his favorite trick of turning his enemy's weapons against him; for the Socratic style is used to convey and support an argument that is opposed to Socrates' position. Moreover, the character of Socrates undergoes a change. In Plato's dialogues Socrates' method is not to propound a thesis but rather to disprove a thesis submitted for his questioning by a sophist or a young man. Here, however, it is Socrates who propounds the thesis that is doomed to be refuted. Perhaps even more significant is the fact that the Socratic questioner is never named; but as we read we see that it is Christ. Contrast is once more evident between this slim volume and its successor, the big weighty *Postscript*. Irony too once more plays its part. To the scraps or bits of philosophy which the first volume is called this is added as a postscript that, despite its size, is called "unscientific." Contrast is evident too between the methods employed, the indirect method of *Fragments* and the direct method of *Postscript*, between the *abstract* concern with the definition of revelation and the *existential* concern of the question 'How I, Johannes Climacus, now thirty years of age, born in Copenhagen—am to become a Christian."

From 1843 onwards Kierkegaard wrote a long series of edifying discourses under his own name. There are three groups of them—"edifying," "Christian," and "godly." The edifying discourses are based on Bishop Mynster's sermons, Mynster being the most famous and fashionable preacher of the day. Here Kierkegaard's style is intimate and tender. Most of the "Christian" discourses have a very different style—gentle persuasion and argument giving way to the striking phrase, the unusual image, and the paradox. But in 1849 Kierkegaard decided to return to his favorite theme and to write henceforth for the ordinary reader. The "godly" discourses consequently use a popular style of eloquence. In 1848 Kierkegaard wrote *Practice in Christianity* which he delayed publishing until 1850. The style is full of contrasts. The gentle exposition of the invitation "Come unto me . . . and you will find rest" contrasts with the paradox that the rest is offered by the poorest of men and it involves our becoming contemporary with him and accepting him as God. Kierkegaard's purpose was to show the contrast between the bourgeois Christianity of his time and what he regarded as true Christianity. This heralded the attack on the church which concluded his literary career and in which all Kierkegaard's literary art is employed for the purpose of ridicule and invective. One brief extract will suffice to show this:

> That we are all Christians is something so generally known and assumed that it needs no proof but may even be about to work its way up from being a historical truth to becoming an axiom, one of the eternal intuitive principles with which the babe is born, so that with Christianity there may be said to have come about a change in man, that in "Christendom" a babe is born with one intuitive principle more than a human being has outside of Christendom, the principle that we are all Christians . . . We are Christians to such a degree that if among us there lived a Freethinker who in the strongest terms declared that the whole of Christianity is a lie, *item* in the strongest terms declared that he was not a Christian—there is no help for him, he is a Christian; according to the law he may be punished, that is a different thing, but a Christian he is. "What stuff and nonsense!" says the State. "What would this lead to? If once we allowed a man to declare that he is not a Christian, it soon would come to pass that all would deny that they were Christians. No, *principiis obsta*, and let

us hold fast to principles. We now have everything well tabulated, all under proper headings, everything perfectly correct—under the assumption of course that we are all Christians—*ergo* he too is a Christian. Such a conceit, which merely wants to be eccentric, one must not humor, and that's the end of it."[23]

We saw earlier how tempting it is to view Kierkegaard as a Danish Romantic and this is just as much the case when we try to locate him in the wider European literary context. True, it would be difficult to align him with the revolutionaries when for the most part his work seems remote from any political concerns; but the stress on the person and on passion as the sources of value and authentic thought seems to make him very much their man. However, only one scholar has claimed that he was influenced by such a typical French Romantic as Alfred de Musset[24] and this does seem to be stretching similarity to signify influence.[25] What is more to the point is the evidence we have that Kierkegaard was very much alive to French as well as German literature. We know that from an early age he must have been familiar with French literature since it was one of his subjects in the *artium* examinations which he successfully took in October 1830.[26] It is particularly important to remember that when Kierkegaard did not read French writings in the original he often read German and Danish translations and that in any case, as the sale catalogue of his library shows, he possessed the works of Molière and Rousseau, and the German translations of Montaigne and Pascal. In fact his library contained three German editions of Pascal's *Pensées*,[27] which is a clear enough indication of the attraction Pascal had for Kierkegaard. Also, the similarity between the two thinkers was something that was pointed out quite soon after Kierkegaard's death in an article in Copenhagen's *The Fatherland* in March 1867.[28] Several authors took up the subject including the famous Danish philosopher Harald Høffding and the Lutheran theologian H. Fuglsgang-Damgaard

---

23. Kierkegaard, *Attack on Christendom*, 107, S.V. 19, 117.
24. Tisseau, "La *Confession* de Musset et le *Banquet* de Kierkegaard."
25. Cf. Grimsley, *Kierkegaard and French Literature*, 7. Grimsley insists that he himself is not claiming any influence of the French authors mentioned on Kierkegaard but merely defining Kierkegaard's attitude to the questions raised.
26. Kierkegaard, *Letters and Documents*, 7.
27. Ktl. nos. 711–14.
28. Sundby, "Kierkegaard og Pascal."

who became Primate of Denmark. In English there was the two-volume work published by Denzil G. M. Patrick in 1947 entitled *Pascal and Kierkegaard*. Patrick was not very interested in Kierkegaard's relation to literature, though he does in fact devote some space to a discussion of Romanticism in his characterization of what he calls "the spiritual climate."[29] His conclusion is: "Our later study will bring out how significant it is that a movement which sought an immediate aesthetic unity with a divinized nature, by attuning the individual soul to it, found itself baffled, and had to express or escape its despair at its failure by means of longing or irony. This is indeed one of the main points against which Kierkegaard directed his attacks, and of which he made use in his profound psychological analyses of the conflict in the soul of man."[30]

However, as he makes very clear at the outset (p. vii) the historical analysis of Kierkegaard's life and work is meant to emphasize the offensive strategy of his Christian evangelism. Kierkegaard does not, in fact, seem to have had much awareness of Pascal when he was developing his literary skills. As Grimsley points out, the first specific reference to Pascal occurs in *Stages on Life's Way*, which was not published until 1845, and the context hardly suggests any literary connection inasmuch as it is Quidam's Diary and this is obviously inspired by Kierkegaard's own tragic love story. What is perhaps more important is that this is the only reference to Pascal in the *Works*, though there are a few references to him in the *Journal* from 1849 onwards. It is also rather surprising that of the French authors who enjoyed popularity in Denmark at that time it is Scribe who caught Kierkegaard's interest. It is, of course, true that during the very period in which his *Journal* shows him to be reading Pascal he became a very sharp critic of Scribe. The *Papers* have some dozen references to Scribe and the fact that the first is a very early entry together with the ease with which the reference is made shows that Kierkegaard concedes the admiration for Scribe shown by the Copenhagen theatregoing public. The first mention of him in the *Works* is in *Either-Or* (after *Postscript* there is no further mention) and it precedes the long analysis of *Les Premières Amours*. That analysis is, however, very revealing. Grimsley observes:

---

29. Patrick, *Pascal and Kierkegaard*, vol. 2, 6–15.
30. Ibid., 15.

Whatever its original form and purpose, the essay on *Les Premières Amours* in the first volume of *Either-Or* is plainly intended as more than an exercise in literary criticism. Kierkegaard certainly pays homage to the literary merits of the play, treating its author as a typical representative of "modern comedy," of the well-made play in which "the dramatic action becomes commensurable with the situation . . . and the dialogue audible in the transparency of the situation," so that the spectator can enjoy the play in "all its dramatic life" . . . But the main emphasis of his remark does not fall upon its literary qualities. Already . . . earlier comments had revealed his readiness to use Scribe's plays as a source of extra-literary reflection, and in *Either-Or* he discussed *Les Premières Amours* as an example of the "aesthetic" stage of existence.[31]

What attracted Kierkegaard in this little play was its ironic treatment of "romantic" love, which becomes for him the pattern of the "aesthetic" stage's tendency towards its own destruction. It is also worth observing that the play achieved that kind of treatment without any kind of moralistic tone and it would seem to me that this too was a literary technique that Kierkegaard noted for future use.

Though I have been anxious to avoid the temptation to connect Kierkegaard too easily with Romanticism I would want to stress that he was distinctly influenced by the movement. Thus he shared the exalted view of the poet, which characterized the Romantics, and indeed he shared their expanded use of the term. This is well expressed in an undated entry in the *Journal* of 1840 and the tone is very obviously Romantic:

> It is a curiously sad feeling which grips one when he sees the poetic making its appearance in the development of an individual. For the poetic is the divine woof of the purely human existence [*Existents*]; it is the cord through which the divine holds fast to existence. Therefore one could believe that they are blessed, those gifted individuals, those living telegraph wires between God and men. But this is most certainly not true. Madness is their lot; yes, and envy, lostness in short, the annihilation of their personal existence as being incapable of enduring the touch of the divine. And thus they go through the world misunderstood, neglected, criticized (can anything more ridiculous be imagined!)—yes, misunderstood, for must not everyone who understands the

---

31. Grimsley, *Kierkegaard and French Literature*, 116.

poet also undergo the same experience of being burned? And this is the glory of the world; this is the highest and best on earth: the poet—this illustrious name to which one attaches the most elevated conceptions, the most lofty expectations—and yet this is his fate: to know a thirst which is never satisfied. The poetic life in the personality is the unconscious sacrifice, the *molimina* of the divine, because it is first in the religious that the sacrifice becomes conscious and the misrelationship is removed.[32]

As we have seen, quite early in his literary career Kierkegaard criticized the Romantic readiness to be concerned with mere emotions: for him emotions had to undergo a transubstantiation. Yet as late as *Postscript* he shows the influence of this Romantic valuation of the poet when he speaks of poetry as the boundary between the aesthetic and the religious. In short, Romanticism put Kierkegaard on the way to becoming a theologian.

CONCLUSION: THE LITERARY INFLUENCE OF KIERKEGAARD

In conclusion, let me try to indicate the benefit of this legacy of literary art. As early as 1899 it was pointed out that Kierkegaard was the source for Ibsen's ideas for *Brand*. This was, M. A. Stobart insisted, "a serious poem, not a parody." Nobody who was acquainted with "the powerful and original teaching of the Danish philosopher, Søren Kirkegaard [sic]" could regard it as a mere satire on the religion that conventional Christians profess. His writings were, she points out, then untranslated into English but, "of course, easily accessible to Ibsen." "[I]n his poem *Brand* Ibsen has . . . clothed in dramatic drapery some of the tenets propounded in the neglected works of Kirkegaard [sic] . . . For the religious philosophy of this Danish thinker contained none of the usual narcotics of philosophy or the opiates of religion. Truth, for Kierkegaard, lies in Subjectivity alone. 'Subjectiviteten, Inderligheden er Sandheden.'"[33]

Stobart goes on to summarize "the Danish philosopher's melancholy figure" as the following fundamental chords:

(a) That Christianity has been annihilated by a false and specious conception of God as the deity of love and mercy.

---

32. Kierkegaard, *Journals and Papers* 1027; Kierkegaard, *Papirer* III A 62.
33. Stobart, "New Lights on Ibsen's 'Brand,'" 227–28.

(b) That by Subjectivity alone (that is, inwardness and willpower) can religious truth be reached.

(c) That the *willing* sacrifice of "All or Nothing" (*"Enten intet—Eller Alt"*) is the essential requisite of salvation.[34]

As far as I am aware, this knowledge of Kierkegaard was not used further, even as an interpretative tool for the study of Ibsen, though the Cambridge Scandinavian scholar Brian Downs tells us that the connection between Kierkegaard and Brand had been made as early as 1870. At least, it was not used again until 1914 when J. G. Robertson published an article on Kierkegaard in *Modern Language Review*, which he then edited. The article reveals a considerable knowledge of Kierkegaard's work and a keen appreciation of his significance. Robertson is mainly concerned with Kierkegaard as a literary figure and goes so far as to say that he is "the writer who holds the indispensable key to the life of Scandinavia" and "Denmark's most original man in the nineteenth century." In the meantime, M. A. Stobart had once again referred to Kierkegaard—this time devoting an article to Kierkegaard himself, "The 'Either-Or' of Søren Kirkegaard [*sic*]," commending him as the thinker best suited to the needs of the twentieth century *zeitgeist*.

Lest it be thought that I have in mind merely literary criticism when I speak of Kierkegaard's influence on literature I want to look briefly at his significance for writers of our own day. I begin with the poets. Charles Williams, who played a part in securing the involvement of the Oxford University Press in the publication of the English translation, was also responsible for introducing W. H. Auden to the work of Kierkegaard. When in 1938 Auden was discussing with Williams the publication of *The Oxford Book of Light Verse* his recent intense and profound religious experience was confirmed and deepened. This is how he described it: "Shortly afterwards, in a publisher's office I met an Anglican layman, and for the first time in my life felt myself in the presence of personal Sanctity." Consequently he "started to read theological works, Kierkegaard in particular, and began going, in a tentative and experimental sort of way, to church."[35] The very evident influence Kierkegaard exerted on Auden's work at this time was one that lasted and

---

34. Ibid.

35. Pike, ed., *Modern Canterbury Pilgrims*, 41, quoted in Lawson, ed., *Kierkegaard's Presence in Contemporary American Life*, xv.

indeed grew. The first long poem that he wrote afterwards—*The Double Man* (1941)—is full of quotations from Dru's translation of selections from the *Journal*. Critics have pointed out how the abiding interest in Kierkegaard shaped and characterized Auden's poetry ever since: it gave his poetry its distinctive character.

Before leaving Auden to continue with another poet I should briefly mention Kierkegaard's influence on Auden's prose writings. Very much in the same way as Kierkegaard, Auden made the activity of literary criticism an art form in itself, an art that is at once both passive and active. The activity is indeed that of "the dyer's hand" (the Shakespearean simile which he uses as the title for a collection of essays) but as such it imparts color as well as receives it. As William C. James points out, Auden's critical corpus is unified in large measure by a typology of heroism.[36] His discussion of individual heroes in various periods and literature is animated and controlled by a threefold typology, the triple nature of which shows its (at least partial) derivation from Kierkegaard's doctrine of the "stages" or spheres of life. That Kierkegaardian origin is most obvious in the description of the hero's exceptional authority in *The Enschafed Flood or the Romantic Iconography of the Sea*.[37] There are three kinds of hero— the aesthetic, the ethical, and the religious. Interestingly the question is raised by critics whether this Kierkegaardian outlook does not produce a dichotomy between the figure of the religious hero and any aesthetic expression of his heroism.[38] It is a vitally important question but one that is itself very much part of Kierkegaard's legacy. Strangely enough it puts me in mind of the next author on my list, my Welsh compatriot R. S. Thomas; for few writers have been so aware as he had been of the tensions that are motivations to art and that are themselves poignant songs and whose awareness has been heightened by Kierkegaard.

R. S. Thomas, the Welsh writer of English poetry, was probably the most important twentieth-century poet to be influenced deeply by Kierkegaard. As an Anglican priest in Wales, Thomas was very much aware of the interrelation of language, history, and sociopolitical aspirations. Though there are some quite fundamental and significant differences there are some striking parallels between the two national situations—not least that Wales and Denmark are two small countries

---

36. James, "Anthropological Poetics: Auden's Typology of Heroism."
37. Auden, *Selected Poems 1946-68*, 105.
38. Medina, *Reflection, Time and the Novel*, 112.

dangerously near a dominant foreign culture. Just as the smallness of Denmark was emphasized by its proximity to Germany so even more has the size of Wales been made all too evident by the thrusting nearness of England. It would be fanciful to make any comparisons between nineteenth-century Denmark and twentieth-century Wales regarding language; but there is no doubt that Kierkegaard and Thomas share a sensitivity to and a pride in their respective native tongues. Where Kierkegaard was keen to fashion a Danish prose style that would be as classical as any German literature Thomas had over the years become more and more ardent and vehement in his support of the Welsh language. With prophetic ferocity he condemns

> . . . the English
> Scavenging among the remains
> Of our culture . . . , elbowing our language
> Into the grave that we have dug for it.[39]

Though there is in Thomas' work much explicit as well as implied criticism of his fellow countrymen's religion there are other different reasons why he and Kierkegaard came to feel themselves ill at ease in their own country. At first, Thomas felt his lack of mastery of his native tongue made him an alien in the land of his fathers and of his birth. Later, despite the fact that he was now fluent in the language that was part and parcel of his craggy home, he still felt an alien. In a memorable and fierce address to the Royal National Eisteddfod on 3 August 1983 he said, "The Welsh-speaking Welshman will not only be an alien but an object of scorn in his own country." That is a tragedy that burned itself into his soul and in his last years he viewed himself as a potential redeemer of his country in the Shelley mode. This is an undercurrent that reminds me of Kierkegaard's sense of his own destiny as a "spy in higher service" whose task was to *introduce* Christianity into Christendom. Thomas' priestly work as a poet (and this was his own understanding of his poetic function rather than any conceit of my making) is that of providing his people with the vocabulary—and indeed the sensibility that this presupposes—to respond to the vision that he mediates to them. One of his characteristic turns of argument is his use of irony, which, while it need not be entirely due to Kierkegaard's influence, is certainly consistent with what was Kierkegaard's own literary art. To my mind the

---

39. R. S. Thomas, "Reservoirs" from *Selected Poems 1946–68*, 105.

dialectic between art and revelation in Thomas is itself reminiscent of Kierkegaard's life and work, his lived thought in word and action.

To select any one theme as central in Kierkegaard is a dangerous practice—my own analysis of subjectivity was obliged to recognize the interrelation of this theme with that of paradox. Yet there is an obvious sense in which Kierkegaard is preoccupied with Christ and it is very evident that Thomas' poetry comes back again and again to Christ. In language that echoes the notions of the *incognito* and the offence—those well-known features of Kierkegaard's Christology—Thomas describes our situation as a "combat" with an unknown, an "anonymous" wrestler, a combat which leaves us nursing "our bruises," "our dislocations" only to realize that we have in fact seen God. The history of Christ's earthly life is presented in his poetry with the same concrete detail and sense of ambiguity that one finds in Kierkegaard's writing, especially his more devotional ones. The choice of incarnation, the triumph in shame—these christological themes of such a work as *Practice in Christianity* are all evident in *Later Poems*.

This brings us to paradox, which is perhaps the clearest expression of the sensitivity to language of which we spoke. For Thomas the only unity of the message is that it is always "in two parts" as is the cross; and his poetic effort is that resolute attempt to elucidate the logic of paradox. The remarkable volume he entitled *Frequencies* displays this pilgrimage "beyond language" and puts one in mind of Kierkegaard's "metaphysical crotchet" in *Philosophical Fragments*. Its theme is voiced in the first poem, "The Gap"—that is, the gap between God and our articulation of his being, the assertion that "Godhead" is beyond language. I need not labor the point that there can be few more obvious manifestations of a literary legacy that is powerful in its capacity to inspire.

Angel Medina's study of the novel as communication—*Reflection, Time and the Novel*—is a useful reminder of Kierkegaard's influence on novelists. He sees Kierkegaard as one of the few exceptions to the tendency of authors and critics to treat the novel as "the proper culmination of modern rationality and of the sophisticated linguistic and literary resources available to it."[40] "Kierkegaard, the gloomy and ironic Dane" remains, he says, the model of an understanding of the linkage between communicative authenticity and rational unauthenticity.[41] Unfortunately

---

40. Medina, *Reflection, Time and the Novel*, 112.
41. Ibid., 114.

it is not at all clear that he has properly understood Kierkegaard's thought as one can see from his claim that in a nutshell "this is the unbelievable message of Kierkegaard: in contradiction we become part of each other, whether or not we are willing to accept this fact."[42] Neither, then, can one be sure that he has grasped the nature of Kierkegaard's literary art. Any discussion of these issues would take us far from our theme; but the book does usefully bring the world of the novel into focus. We can recall that Golding's explorations of man's capacity for evil and his desire to be as God himself are molded by Kierkegaard's analysis of dread and sin. Much the same kind of general comment could be made about Graham Greene; but it has also been pointed out by critics that the phenomenology of moods, attitudes, and lifestyles provided by Kierkegaard's doctrine of the stages has been very relevant for Greene as he has portrayed "cases." Finally, as Lewis A. Lawson has noted, Kierkegaard's influence on the American novel too has been significant.[43] Both Ralph Ellison's brilliant *Invisible Man* (1952) and Richard Wright's *The Outsider*, published in the same year, depend on Kierkegaardian themes to universalize the black experience. Turning to a different kind of minority group, conservative Christians have also employed Kierkegaard. John Updike is an example with his *Rabbit Run* (1961). The previous year William Styron in *Set this House on Fire* also showed Kierkegaard's influence. But the novelist who has most persistently and intensively used Kierkegaard is Walter Percy, whose fiction and nonfiction are intended to advocate an orthodox but flexible Christianity. Only spirit, he contends, can solve the problems of a materialist world. He himself has described the protagonist of his *The Moviegoer* (1961) as an inhabitant of Kierkegaard's "aesthetic mode" and in *The Last Gentleman* (1966) he describes the progression from that stage through the ethical to the religious. The ripples of the literary pond have moved very far from that remote spot where the nineteenth-century "churchyard" stone was thrown into it. The story of Kierkegaard and literature stretches on into the next century.

---

42. Ibid., 60.
43. Lawson, *Kierkegaard's Presence in Contemporary American Life*, xvff.

3

Hegelian Aesthetic and Kierkegaard's Literary Art

KIERKEGAARD, AESTHETICS, AND PHILOSOPHY

WE HAVE SEEN HOW profound the links are between Kierkegaard and the literary traditions of Europe so it is no surprise to find that his work is remarkable in showing a very unusual correlation of philosophy and literary art. There have been philosophers, like Hume, whose style displays a grace and humor that is most attractive or, like Russell, whose limpid prose has an elegant clarity or again, more rarely, a Gilbert Ryle whose writing has a directness that is almost as redolent of saddle-leather as Sassoon's. In general, however, a philosopher is more likely to show the urgent concern with clarity and the complete thoroughness of exposition that led Kant into an ugliness of style that is far removed from the beauty of his logical architectonic. It is already very clear that Kierkegaard's is a very different case from the usual. Consequently, however much interpreters may differ in their views of his work, whether they make him more of a poet than a thinker or view him as some religious polemicist who was a philosopher *malgré lui* they will agree that he was a writer. He set out to achieve a literary creation and had distinctive views of the nature of that writing. We recall his composition of a *Journal* where there is evidence of his apprenticeship as a writer and his deep interest in literature. His Students' Union lecture of November 1835—"Our Journalistic Literature"—shows how early he had developed his critical skills. The literary interest and studies of the late 1830s are well known, as is the postponement of his theological examination, which almost amounted to a desertion of theological studies. All this highlights the fact that throughout these years Kierkegaard had been developing as a writer. What I now wish to do is to show how one very important aspect of his literary art not only connects him with a particular background of philosophical aesthetics but is a clear example of his own unusual correlation of art and philosophy.

The very first publication—the anonymous article, "Also a Defense of Women's Superior Talents" in the Copenhagen *Flyvende Post*—is an exercise in wit and the later political articles in the same paper in 1836 are likewise stronger on wit than argument. This skill was developed into dramatic use of satire in his Students' Union play, *The Conflict between the Old and the New Soap Cellar: a heroic-patriotic-cosmopolitan-philanthropic-fatalistic drama in several scenes*. What is, of course, of greatest interest is his first real publication, the review-article extended into a book, *From the Papers of One Still Living* (1838), which, as its sub-title indicates, was concerned with "Andersen as a novelist with constant reference to his *Only a Fiddler*." "Published against his will," as he says, this first published work of Kierkegaard's was also his first serious effort at using his now established literary skill in the service equally of art and of a philosophy of life. I use the latter term quite deliberately and we shall have opportunity later to see how he had now understood philosophy to need this transformation. To return to the work, the content is well known—the criticism of the novelist for his lack of depth and lack of honesty in his having expressed his own self-pity as a piece of fiction. There was no serious content in Andersen's work and, unlike a genuine work of art, it lacked "transubstantiation of experience."[1] This is an interesting phrase recalling at once the idioms of sacramental theological controversy which would have been his religious background and also the kind of aesthetics to which he would have been attracted. What I mean is that we will not understand what Kierkegaard means here if we do not remember that we are dealing with a very serious young Lutheran theologian who is also an ardent student of Romantic aesthetics. Just as much as Luther's concern with the change mistakenly described as a transubstantiation so too the Wordsworthian alchemy of experience was a part of Kierkegaard's world of thought. Billeskov Jansen described Kierkegaard's originality as a writer as lying in "the art with which he combines analysis of

---

1. S.V. 1, 34.

human character and literary forms"[2] and his role in this book as that of "the philosopher-aesthetician."[3] Kierkegaard's essential criticism of Andersen's work as a novelist, then, is that it contains no life-view, which for Kierkegaard is a *conditio sine qua non*, as he says,[4] of any novelist who is truly an artist. It is a matter of light dawning on our life, an introspection that is an ideal understanding.[5] The philosophical and indeed theological context of Kierkegaard's thought is very evident if we cast our minds back a few pages in his argument to his appreciative quotation of Daub's comment about life being understood backwards by means of the idea. There, in the midst of his theological apparatus (if one may so describe his appropriation of what he read), he refers to Hegel as the creator of a succession of philosophical brick-throwers.[6] So already, in his very first book, Kierkegaard was doing several things—taking up Hegelian philosophy as an issue of debate and declaring the philosophical importance of a life-view and also protesting against the bourgeois hypocrisy of the society in which he lived. My point here is that all of this is contained within this critical development of a theory and practice of art.

Strangely little has been written about Kierkegaard's aesthetics. That comment itself is the kind of remark that John Wisdom used to refer to as the *Times* use of "seems," like the report of the Wall Street crash as, "There seems to have been a lack of confidence in the American Stock Market." Perhaps it reflects the ambiguous attitude of philosophers and the suspicious attitude of theologians to aesthetics; but George Pattison's *Kierkegaard: The Aesthetic and the Religious* remains a solitary exception to the present silence. What little there had been has appeared from the pen of Marxist philosophers like Lukacs, Benjamin, and Adorno. Bloch influenced Lukacs and led the latter to his serious study of Hegel; but Lukacs directed Bloch towards the work of Kierkegaard and also Dostoievsky.[7] Like Lukacs, Adorno was interested in Kierkegaard's work because it was an attack on Hegel and the influence of German Idealism as an intellectual influence on academic philosophy and theol-

2. Jansen, "The Literary Art of Kierkegaard," 14.
3. Ibid., 11.
4. S.V. 1, 35.
5. Ibid., 36.
6. Ibid., 31.
7. See Lowy, *Pour une sociologie des intellectuels Revolutionnaires*, 292–300.

ogy as well as on general cultural attitudes. Again, as with Lukacs, it was Kierkegaard's avowed interest in the redefinition of what was seen as real that clearly captured Adorno's philosophical imagination. Though Kierkegaard did not achieve a Marxist realism, he was, in Adorno's opinion, someone who saw the need to criticize philosophy with a view to commenting on reality—and in any case he was a force to be reckoned with because his work had spawned the other dominant materialism of our time, Existentialism. For Adorno, then, Kierkegaard is to be seen as part of a set of parallel relations: Marx and Kierkegaard were related in a similar fashion to Marxism and Existentialism, respectively.

My purpose in referring to Adorno here is not the general one of Kierkegaard's place in the history of modern thought but the more limited point that Kierkegaard had impressed him as a significant philosopher of art. Adorno's major work on Kierkegaard was in fact a study of his aesthetics. The thesis he maintains in *Kierkegaard: Konstruktion des Aesthetischen* is that Kierkegaard restricted the realm of aesthetics and by his stress on inwardness (Kierkegaard's "subjectivity") he (Kierkegaard) advocated an "objective dialectic" which he regards as depending on an abstract notion of the individual, which is the curse of the age. In passing, I may say that Marxist critics share an interesting tendency with certain kinds of theologians of being too prone to think that Kierkegaard fell prey to Hegel just as he was attacking him. It is almost as if the identification of Kierkegaard with Hamlet led them to write his intellectual biography as Hamlet's fatal duel. To return to Adorno, his argument is that Kierkegaard's central concepts form antinomies that are social in nature and origin. As he says, "All Kierkegaard's gloomy motives have good critical sense as soon as they are interpreted in terms of social critique. Many of his positive assertions gain the concrete significance they otherwise lack as soon as one translates them into concepts of a right society."[8]

Philosophy is a negative stage in Kierkegaard's development of his theology, which is a theology based on belief and not reason.[9] In that philosophy the aesthetic is not allowed any cognitive significance.[10] It is a sphere in which men live in the present, in which man is immediately what he is. The problem with Kierkegaard, for Adorno, was that

---

8. Adorno, *Kierkegaard*, 281–82.

9. Ibid., 13.

10. Ibid., 27.

he made assumptions about aesthetics that his own philosophical critique of Hegel made untenable. The basis of his aesthetics was a subject-object separation that was precisely the weakness he had identified in the Hegelian epistemology. He rejected Kierkegaard's aesthetics as an "objectless dialectic."[11]

It is not my purpose to offer any full account of Adorno's views on Kierkegaard but merely to show how difficult it is to gain a clear understanding of Kierkegaard's aesthetics. Perceptive and suggestive as Adorno's comments are, they reveal, I think, a misunderstanding of Kierkegaard's views; for he failed to keep before his mind the basic, but far from simple, ambiguity in Kierkegaard's use of the term "aesthetic." Though it is true that Kierkegaard is often concerned to point out relations between the two uses of the term so that one might say that he was mapping out the systematic ambiguity of the word, it is still the case that there are at least two different senses in which he speaks of "the aesthetic." There is first of all the normal technical sense of referring to works of art and the experience of the beautiful in artistic creation. Secondly, Kierkegaard developed a theory of the classification and description of lifestyles as being of three basic types. This is the famous doctrine of the stages, which is expounded in his works, particularly in the book, *Stages on Life's Way*. I have used the term "lifestyle" to refer to this doctrine because the Danish "stadie" has that kind of ambiguity, meaning either "stage" or "sphere." In this latter context "aesthetic" denotes the type of existence that is unreflective, amoral, and purely hedonistic. This is the kind of outlook which C. D. Broad referred to in a review of A. E. Taylor's *Faith of a Moralist*, arguing that Taylor's criticism of Ovid's hedonism as some kind of short-term policy would have been rejected by Ovid with the request that he should have further pleasures. It is because Kierkegaard was in many ways a Hegelian in his own technical view of aesthetics and yet attacked Hegel as providing nothing but an "aesthetic" view of the two higher stages on life's way—namely, ethics and religion—that the issue is so confusing and a mistake like Adorno's is not surprising.

What Kierkegaard means by this criticism is that the non-involvement characteristic of viewing a work of art is, for Hegel, characteristic of those two other languages, where in fact my involvement is an essential feature of the meaning. This is the "objectivity" for which he at-

11. Ibid., 59.

tacks Hegel so frequently and what, in rather a confusing way, he labels an "aesthetic" attitude. Why he should have chosen this term may have something to do with his considerable classical scholarship and the particular ambiguities of the root term *aisthesis*, derived from *aisthanomai*, which means "to perceive or observe or apprehend by the senses." For Kierkegaard, the way in which, according to Hegel, anything could be reduced to a spectacle to be observed posed a great threat to religion or any properly ethical life. The roots of the opposition are as much philosophical as they are passionately religious. While there can be no doubt that Kierkegaard was primarily interested in his destined task of "introducing Christianity into Christendom" he was anxious enough to point out philosophical mistakes when he saw them.

One of the most interesting features of Kierkegaard as a thinker is the way in which he is so much tied up with what one might call a nineteenth-century Reformation and yet was so thoroughly involved in the progress of philosophy. He was both part of the development of German metaphysics away from Hegelianism and, at the same time, of the development of Kantianism. In view of the current interest in Kant's aesthetics, it is perhaps strange to reflect that Kierkegaard paid no attention to this aspect of Kant's work. Schelling's positive philosophy was very obviously one inspiration of his philosophy of existence—that was why he had gone to Berlin and why he was so excited by Schelling's first lecture in the winter of 1842–43. Equally significant, in my view, is the influence of the Kantian critique of rationalism and of Kant's insistence on the actuality of existence and on the distinction between the laws of nature and the moral law.

I have already said enough about Kierkegaard's background to indicate that he belongs to that nineteenth-century world of philosopher-poets and philosopher-artists. This is important to grasp because Kierkegaard's aesthetical philosophy cannot really be detached from his essentially artistic effort in completing any particular work. We do not need to concern ourselves with the question that is often raised by scholars as a problem about his work, namely, his claim that he was from the outset a religious author. As I have already said, he seemed to find no difficulty in pursuing philosophical interests precisely when he was mounting religious protests. Sufficient for us is that he was a writer very much concerned with literature, drama, and—because of the obvious connection with opera—music. It is then as a practitioner of art that he was always a critic and a philosopher of art. This naturally leads us on to *The Concept of Irony*, which is concerned with literature, literary theory, and aesthetics as part of a wider philosophical enterprise.

THE CONCEPT OF IRONY AND HEGEL'S AESTHETICS

The Concept of Irony is often described as the most Hegelian of Kierkegaard's works.[12] After the meticulous work of Niels Thulstrup in his *Kierkegaard's Relation to Hegel* there remains not the slightest doubt in my mind concerning Mesnard's thesis, developing Bohlin's insight, that *The Concept of Irony* is itself dialectical and indeed, as Mesnard says, doubly ironic. My concern at the moment is to establish the precise significance of this for a characterization of Kierkegaard's point of view as a writer. The text displays what Stephen Dunning has described as Kierkegaard's "early talent for writing (whether in earnest or as a parody) in a Hegelian manner"[13] but what it reveals of Kierkegaard's own aesthetic theory is unclear. Consequently I am not concerned with the extent to which Kierkegaard's view of Socrates is Hegelian any more than I am concerned with the Hegelian structure of the earlier parts of the book. The use that Kierkegaard made of Hegel in this book has been carefully expounded and examined by Thulstrup[14] so that there is no need to tell the story once more and I can briefly recapitulate his conclusions. First, Kierkegaard had a rather complete knowledge of the third part of the system, the philosophy of Spirit, in general and particularly in the places and sections of it which especially dealt with Socrates and romantic irony.[15] Both in interpretations and evaluations there are a great many instances of agreement on particular points between Hegel and Kierkegaard, though there are also a great many instances of important difference. In all essential respects, says Thulstrup, "Kierkegaard knew and utilized the historical sections within the various works of Hegel that belong to the philosophy of Spirit and in so far as he shows no knowledge of the *Phenomenology of Mind*, the *Logic*, or the *Encyclopaedia of*

---

12. See Höffding, *Den Store Humor*, and Andersen, *Tider og Typer af Dansk Aands Historie*, and, of course, Himmelstrup, *Søren Kierkegaards Opfattelse af Sokrates*, as well as Geismar's *Søren Kierkegaard*. A more recent discussion is that of Merold Westphal in his "Kierkegaard and Hegel," 104–5.

13. Dunning, *Kierkegaard's Dialectic of Inwardness*, 6.

14. Thulstrup, *Kierkegaard's Relation to Hegel*, 217–61.

15. Ibid., 242.

the Philosophical Sciences his understanding of Hegel's philosophy as a whole, as system, was correspondingly deficient."[16] The conclusion that Thulstrup reaches, then, is that, despite the fact that "Kierkegaard as an experiment wished to try his hand at the role of a Hegelian history of philosophy," his own position, "which is not formulated directly or fully thought out in this work, cannot correctly be designated as Hegelian."[17] All this I accept and endorse: my aim here is to examine one of the points of agreement.

There is no doubt that *The Concept of Irony* echoes much of Hegel's theory of art and that, if Mesnard's reading of the book's purpose is right, it is itself an instance of one such agreement, namely, the theory of "substantial form." Bohlin's perception that in *The Concept of Irony* Kierkegaard had used Hegel to criticize the Romantics as well as using the latter to criticize Hegel is very important. There is, of course, the biographical importance as a means of mapping Kierkegaard's spiritual development; but of more immediate concern is the theoretical relevance.

In his critique of Romanticism, Kierkegaard advocated some kind of doctrine of substantial form that gave pre-eminence to *content* in aesthetics. The doctrine is developed by Hegel as the analysis of the relation in classical art of form to content. In this, as in his more general critique of Romanticism, Hegel took as his point of departure the conviction that the Absolute is subject. Whereas the more Romantic idealists like Schelling endorsed the general hope that art was about to bring about a new Hellenic age of glorious human expression, Hegel maintained that art could no longer be the expression of truth. The relation between this and his justification of mid-nineteenth-century art with its forecast of relativized possibilities for the future need not detain us, though there are some interesting echoes of this Platonic mistrust of art in Kierkegaard's views about the decline of Romantic aesthetics. The point to note is that Hegel's contention that the artist must become a theorist is, for him, a reflection of what had been the uniting of art and theory. *Unity* is precisely the all-important concept here and the one on which we must concentrate. What Hogarth had given as a formula "unity in variety" Hegel could accept and express systematically—"universality in agreement with particularity."[18] His theory then held that the content of

---

16. Ibid., 245. Cf. 254.
17. Ibid., 261.
18. cf. Hegel, *Aesthetics*, vol. 1, 475ff.

a classical work of art had immanent within it its own form. The meaning and the matter of its expression are fused so that *content and style together form the one organic whole.* Art demands unity so that there is a structural congruence of internal and textual, substance and form, a harmony of essence and phenomenon. The rupture of that harmony was what characterized Romanticism and signified, for Hegel, the death of art. In *The Concept of Irony* Kierkegaard had adopted and developed this view to interpret the nature of irony, which was Romanticism's prescription for art. As is well known, he proceeded to uncover the deeper significance of irony as what Hegel had called "infinite absolute negativity" and he rejected the Hegelian resolution of contradiction in a conceptual unity for a resolutely ironic dialectic of the unity of opposites.

In his "Historical Introduction" to *The Concept of Irony*, Capel asks, "Was it Kierkegaard's intention to insinuate a third alternative between Hegel and the Romantics?" and answers his question by saying, "It would appear that this correlation of opposites within the sphere of reflection is hyperbolically 'fastened together at the top' like pleasure and pain ... classicism and romanticism ... and it is Kierkegaard's curious fusion of the two which makes the total structure and design of the essay an ironic whole—a singular jest."[19] He further observes that the "apparent similarity between Kierkegaard and Hegel is posited in dissimilarity."[20] Moreover, in a lengthy note to Kierkegaard's comment in chapter 1 that he has sought himself to be "the third against each,"[21] Capel says that the phrase has several meanings which he proceeds to list and explain.[22] The interesting point is that each of them is a deliberately ironic use of Hegelian idiom and that Kierkagaard goes on similarly to involve the Hegelian dialectic of the whole and its parts. He then concludes the chapter thus: "Had I first set forth the final conception and within its particular moments assigned each of these three considerations its place then I would surely have forfeited the moment of contemplation which is always of importance, but doubly so here."[23]

Kierkegaard has made abundantly clear on this page that he is concerned to communicate with the reader; but the style and the content

---

19. Capel, "Historical Introduction," 34.
20. Ibid., 35.
21. Ibid., 183.
22. Ibid., 388.
23. Ibid., 184.

of the book make it an example of indirect communication. It is the clarification of this familiar but difficult notion in relation to Hegelian aesthetics that concerns me; and some references to Kierkegaard's indebtedness to Hegel's aesthetics will be useful. Most Kierkegaard scholars read Hegel only after reading Kierkegaard and therefore our great difficulty is guarding against the tendency to offer a hermeneutic that is based on Kierkegaard's critique and is really a travesty of Hegel's intention. Generally the response of Hegel scholars to what Kierkegaard had to say is exactly the same as the comment made by John Findlay, that Kierkegaard had misunderstood Hegel and consequently his whole philosophical undertaking was pointless as well as misguided. Philosophically, said Findlay, the picture of Hegel we thus obtain is not just wrong but misleading and useless. If then we are to read Hegel properly we must forget what Kierkegaard saw—rightly enough, in fact, and with remarkable perspicacity and prophetic insight—would be made of Hegel by others.

First, it seems to me that Hegel taught Kierkegaard the necessity of a self-understanding in aesthetics. Keats' poetry (and indeed all his writing) has much to teach us about the metaphysical and theological significance of imagination. The perception that aesthetics is ultimately metaphysical is summed up in those remarkable closing lines of "Ode to the Grecian Urn":

> Beauty is truth, truth beauty;
> That is all you know on earth
> And all you need to know.

And if that is so, then Keats would have been the first to insist with Kierkegaard on the inevitable subjectivity of this knowledge. Every aesthetic theory is an account of the relation between the resources of art and what Kierkegaard would call the point of view, the insight, or message which the artist sets out in his poem, painting, sculpture, or music. I may say a great deal about Dylan Thomas' "Do not go gentle into that good night" if I relate its biographical context in the noble death of that atheist Welsh teacher of English literature who was his father—and in particular were I to enlarge on the son's marvelous support of his mother. Yet this is only one pole of the artistic creation; and its dialectic derives from those evaluations of life and death, the hope and the fears expressed, and the tone of vital confidence that make this one of the noblest poems in the English language. It seems to me that aesthetics demand at once a sensitivity and a dispassionate intelligence that is mirrored only in philosophy of religion. Whenever the issue of that reconciliation is raised we, like Kierkegaard, have cause to be grateful to Hegel for making us aware of the problem.

Secondly, it follows that a theory of art which is self-consciously involved in its own methodology will be modest about the claims it makes for the limits of its own conceptual framework. The technology of the early part of *The Concept of Irony* may be Kantian, as Dunning says,[24] but it is as Hegelian as it is Kantian in its awareness of the limits of the conceptual framework. The very rationalism of Hegel's reservation of truth to the metaphysical interpretation of what is sensuously expressed in art meant that this expression was denied concepts as such. Too little attention has been paid in art history to the murder of artistic truth perpetrated by the notorious "German art" and its more recent successors, just as there has been too great a readiness to link Hegelianism with totalitarianism. Nor need one jump to such extreme expressions since dogmatism is not a stranger in the more technical realms of aesthetic theory. What I am saying is that Kierkegaard very obviously moved forward from an aesthetic theory to aesthetic creativity that was true to his own genius, and that both in practice and dogmatically he proclaimed that theory was, in the end, only an artificial scheme to assist understanding and must never be made the means of limiting our horizons.

Finally, I would claim that Hegel's aesthetics left an enduring mark on Kierkegaard's soul, which paradoxically saved him from the Romantic excesses of Schelling. I have always thought that Schelling's influence on Kierkegaard was a puzzle; for pervasive as it is it cannot readily or easily be squared with the very different logical and metaphysical concerns of Kierkegaard's anti-Hegelianism. What Hegel emphasized was the *requirement* of a unity between radical freedom and nature whereas what the Romantics and Schelling proclaimed was the simple fact of such unity in a metaphysic that was virtually pantheistic. For the moment I am not concerned with the success or failure of Hegel's attempt to correlate human freedom and divine creation. My point is quite simply that he saw that we not only know Nature because—as Tillich would put it in his Schellingian idiom—the logos of understanding is reflected in the logos of the world, but more particularly we know it because this is

---

24. Dunning, *Kierkegaard's Dialectic of Inwardness*, 13.

our sharing in the creative thought. Working through the destruction of Romanticism in this way was for Kierkegaard his way forward to a critique of what had become a peculiar oversimplification of this "dialectic" of divine and human creativity.

EITHER-OR

It is clear from what I have argued so far that Kierkegaard's aesthetic theory reflects the Hegelian view that there should be a unity of form and content. However, he was not prepared to relate the idea that was the content to an absolute like the Hegelian Idea. Rather he was concerned to show the variety of experience that can be expressed in art, even to the point of claiming that each particular medium could perfectly embody only a single idea. Notwithstanding this claim, the achievement of a work of art that illustrates the theory of substantive form is once again repeated in *Either-Or*. There is a good deal of aesthetic theory in the first volume of this work and it is difficult to know just what we need to consider. The basic nature of the book clearly does raise a problem and it is sufficient to say that it is a contrast between an ethical view of life and a life-style and attitude that is consciously non-ethical. There are two authors—the young man A who writes the first volume and the ethicist B who is the author of the letters to A in the second. The book's title indicates the decision or choice that confronts A—and also the reader; and inasmuch as the very theme has that self-involving character the double reference to the hero of the tale and the reader (that is, *any* reader) is crucial. Yet the first volume seeks to express a consistent as well as a self-conscious view of life that is non-ethical. As Kierkegaard himself remarked later, in his "Glance at a contemporary effort in Danish Literature," "There is no didacticizing; but this does not mean that there is no thought-content . . . to think is one thing and to exist in what has been thought is something else . . . here the existing is in thought and the book or work has no finite relation to anyone."[25] What is then very significant is the literary character of the book, there being a very obvious contrast between the amorphous collection of papers that is found in the first part and the consistently sober pattern of the letters addressed by B to A which make up the second part. The very form of the writing thus reflects the contrasting life-styles expressed. The use of Romantic con-

---

25. Kierkegaard, *Concluding Unscientific Postscript*, 1, 254; S.V. 9, 213.

vention of "discovered" papers is interesting but what the editor, Victor Eremita, has to say about the form of the book is more significant.

> Then I tried to arrange the papers as well I could. In the case of those written by B this was fairly easy. Each of these letters presupposes the one preceding, and in the second letter there is a quotation from the first; the third letter presupposes the other two.
> The arranging of A's papers was not so simple. I have therefore let chance determine the order . . . Since many of the aphorisms have a lyric form, it seemed proper to use the word *Diapsalmata* as the principal title . . . I have left the arrangement of the individual aphorisms to chance. That these individual expressions often contradict one another seemed quite natural, since each one of them belongs precisely to an essential mood.[26]

That *Either-Or* is meant to be a contrast of life-styles and attitudes is something that we, as readers of the book, gather only after reading the "novel," which in its multiform character seems diverse rather than united. Essential to that unity in multiplicity is the fact that the book has no ending. The pseudonimity of *Either-Or* is, as A. Hannay says,[27] elaborate and far-reaching. Moreover, as I have argued before,[28] there was to *Either-Or* an underlying philosophical as well as a religious purpose; for—despite its quite apparently amorphous structure and its possible reading as having an ethico-religious purpose in that Assessor Wilhelm is given the last word, which is an ethic that hints at a theistic morality—the work was in its subtle way a comment on the current debate about logic and philosophy.

INDIRECT COMMUNICATION

I come at last to indirect communication and I can make my point quite simply. It is that if one wanted a single illustration of how utterly extraordinary Hegel's influence was on Kierkegaard—as at once positive and negative—this is perhaps one of the best. Without attempting a full analysis of the concept I can say two things. First, as I suggested some years ago in a review of Oden's *Parables of Kierkegaard*,[29] such an

26. Kierkegaard, *Either-Or*, 1, 7; S.V. 2, 13.
27. Hannay, *Kierkegaard: A Biography*, 174–75.
28. Heywood Thomas, *Philosophy of Religion in Kierkegaard's Writings*, 13ff.
29. Heywood Thomas, Review of "Parables of Kierkegaard," 368.

analysis proves to be anything but easy because the concept is far from simple or univocal. Secondly, in all Kierkegaard's references to it there is a constant and consistent emphasis on the way in which it is part and parcel of both the theory and practice of communication in particular contexts. I may add that any full analysis of the theme of indirect communication would have to consider both the theoretical problem of what kind of indirectness we are considering and also the specific historical context of each piece of writing mentioned. This is one of the most noteworthy features of the late Roger Poole's significant work, *Kierkegaard: The Indirect Communication*, where he distinguished two indirections—the "aesthetic" and the "reduplicated." He also maintains that one of the key ideas of the indirect communication which links the two is evident from the early pages of *Concluding Unscientific Postscript*.[30] There Johannes Climacus speaks of the necessity of the reflection which realizes the suitable expression of thought—what might be called a purely aesthetic, that is, a stylistic matter—being followed by a second. That second—the "reduplicative" indirection—involves the author in a different relation to the communication. This, says Roger Poole, is a reduplication between written text and lived expression where "the indirection takes on its hitting power."[31] His discussion of this as a matter of literary theory confirms me in my insistence on the systematic ambiguity of this concept of indirect communication. Even more telling is the very illuminating suggestion that "one published work after another amounts to little less than an extended commentary on Thorvaldsen's sculptures."[32] This element of indirect communication he finds particularly evident in *Discourses at the Communion on Fridays* where he sees Kierkegaard as actually making use of the sculptures as homiletical aids. They illustrate the contrast between what is seen and what is not seen. This was something that Thorvaldsen had established, especially by his famous statue of the Christ with arms outspread in welcome and the subscription "Come unto Me." Roger Poole has given a very full description of the statues and by his careful analysis of the spatial tensions they create[33] establishes his theory that Thorvaldsen, who was not known for

---

30. Poole, *Kierkegaard: The Indirect Communication*, 158–59.
31. Ibid., 159.
32. Ibid., 245.
33. Ibid., 238–41.

his piety, produced "in the contrasts of the Vor Frue Kirke an essential theological conundrum."[34]

The problem that I am trying to discuss was doubtless recognized by Kierkegaard and indeed it is equally certain that he saw this as part of a general problem about religious art. My original interest in it was aroused by a casual remark of his describing the tension in such religious art as *hymnody*—the greater the concern with poetry the less significant the religiousness expressed. It is not only patriotism that leads me to recall some notable examples in the rich heritage of Welsh hymnody which establish the contrary; but I must admit that this serves only to highlight the aptness of this exaggeration. The discussion of the problem as seen in his own authorship is perhaps a useful, though modest, beginning. To return to the precise theme of indirect communication I can say—again without embroiling myself in large issues of interpretation—that, wherever we want to draw the lines between the two kinds of communication, Kierkegaard was himself very much aware of the *distinction* between direct and indirect communication. Those who are familiar with the work of earlier generations of Kierkegaard scholars will recall how Torsten Bohlin was anxious to distinguish what he regarded as the "real Kierkegaard" from the artificial construct of his philosophical theory of paradox. For Bohlin the authentic message was to be found only in that profound expression of passionate Christian devotion of the heart as distinct from what he repeatedly calls the contradictory intellectualism of the theme of paradox, going so far as to call the latter unchristian.[35] The corollary of this is that it is only in the devotional literature with its direct communication of Christian truth that Kierkegaard's authentic communication is to be found. As I have argued against Bohlin's theory as destructive of the unity of Kierkegaard's thought so I would now reject it as making nonsense of the intention, structure, and efficacy of the writings. The one thing that is now clearer than ever to me is that Kierkegaard succeeded as a philosopher of religion precisely because he was able to *exploit both direct and indirect communication*. His genius was indeed to effect what was, in the main, the consistently indirect communication *demanded* by his subject matter. I insist on the philosophical nature of this activity because in Kierkegaard's view it is only thus that the philosophical case could be established. Contrary to what

---

34. Ibid., 243.
35. Bohlin, *Kierkegaards Dogmatiska Aaskaadning*, 219.

is often said, Kierkegaard has quite a lot to say about the issues that concerned the natural theologian and the biblical theologian of his day. The issues of proof from reason, from experience, or from history are there for anyone to see. The dubitability of sources and the relation between faith and history concerned him as much as a Strauss or a Clausen. Yet time and again Kierkegaard reminds us that he is not really trying to *explain* what Christianity is. There were times when he had to proclaim it as a gospel and still others when he had to proclaim it and show it. Nor does that little catalogue exhaust either the multiplicity or the subtlety of the authorship. As I said earlier, I do not think that Fenger's account of Kierkegaard in his *Kierkegaard: The Myths and Their Origins* is anywhere near true; but surely his argument can only get off the ground because Kierkegaard was such a self-conscious writer. So it is strange that until the publication of George Pattison's *Kierkegaard's Upbuilding Discourses* hardly any attention had been given to his own examination of the problem of communication and so little recognition of the fact that it was clearly in the classical tradition of aesthetics. I mean that in the years leading up to that lengthy discussion of communication in 1847[36] he had been reading Aristotle, as is clear from the 1845 comment that a "new science must be introduced: the Christian art of speaking, to be constructed *admodum* Aristotle's Rhetoric and equally the marginal reference to Aristotle's connection of the art of speaking and the media for awakening faith with probability."[37]

I am very conscious of my failure to say anything much—let alone all that needs to be said—about indirect communication. But I hope that I have shown how from his earliest effort at saying what he had in mind Kierkegaard developed this as both an example of what art was and indeed as an art form of some novelty as well as of urgent relevance. At the very end of his lectures on the dialectic of ethical and ethical-religious communication he reverts to a point he had made earlier,[38] the distinction between communicating something as an art and communicating something as a science. Under the title "The Direct Method and the Indirect Method" there is a series of assertions one of which is, "First of all comes what I have called genuine art-communication: it is indi-

---

36. Kierkegaard, *Papirer* VIII, section 2 B 79–89; Kierkegaard, *Journals and Papers* 649 I, 267–308.

37. Kierkegaard, *Papirer* VI A 17, 19; Kierkegaard, *Journals and Papers* 627–28.

38. Ibid., 272.

rect or at least essentially indirect," and in the margin he wrote, "Here again it is naturally the error of the modern period that all communication is direct, that it has forgotten that there is such a thing as indirect communication."[39] The assertions begin with the distinction between communication of knowledge and communication of capability, which is parallel to that between communication of a science and that of an art. Kierkegaard's point then is that as the ethical is a matter of doing something, knowing how to behave and actually creating a piece of behavior or action so its communication must be indirect. To be ethical and equally to be religious is to learn the relation between my beliefs and my life of hope, the relation between what is true and my life of courage. That is not coming to know something in the way in which information is given one in the Teletext news (i.e., simple propositional information) but is more like the *art* of a newspaper or—better—that of the visual impact of television news. It is a matter of getting one to believe, hope, and feel in a certain way. This is the kind of function of moral language, which was, in the 1940s, much noticed after the work of Stevenson. It is clearly not tied to an emotive theory of ethical meaning and is not so here. These days considerably more attention is being paid to the *art* of the New Testament literature and the point of what I am saying is that Kierkegaard called attention to the necessary connection between this and the purpose expressed by the Johannine author—"These things were written that you might have life and have it in greater abundance."

One final point I would make is that—as I was reminded by Bohlin's German translator Katz—Kierkegaard does break through to a very distinctive *directness* in his Christian authorship. It would take too long to try and unravel the indirectness of his homiletical authorship, where someone like T. H. Croxall over-simplifies, I think, the meaning of Kierkegaard's phrase "one without authority," seeing it as simply a reference to his lay status.[40] Yet it is quite clear that the "attack" on Christendom was born of the conviction that a direct communication is possible, that words can be found which do more than half-reveal the soul within. The situation of the Christian church in mid-nineteenth-century Denmark was something capable of a "direct" expression and that truth was capable of direct communication. The interesting thing,

39. Kierkegaard, *Papirer* VIII2 B 89; Kierkegaard, *Journals and Papers* 657, vol. 1, 308.

40. Croxall, *Kierkegaard Commentary*, 288.

however, is that even here the essential difference between art and science to which he has referred is preserved. There is a *response involved* because the truth communicated is the self-involving truth of subjectivity. That is exactly the point of the famous "Whosoever thou art . . . by not attending public worship—thou hast one guilt the less on thy soul."[41] "For Self-Examination" and "Practice in Christianity" are very instructive phrases when one thinks of this problem of Kierkegaard's literary art. Yet what becomes very clear too is the distinctly anti-Hegelian thrust of this "direct" communication. No longer is the truth of religion to be found by pushing beyond the realm of belief to the higher reaches of abstract thought. It is in the life and works of love that a person finds the truth of his faith. Hence Kierkegaard's identification of Christian communication with martyrdom.

What I have tried to argue is that there is a very important sense in which Hegelian aesthetics both influenced Kierkegaard as a writer—theoretically and practically—and remained for him a matter of the most profound significance. Furthermore the "indirect communication" theme and method that express this were, from the beginning, a means of combating the unfortunate effects of Hegel's popularity. Then the issue of a direct communication is to be recognized and my contention is that while that does indeed complicate the issue it does not alter in any significant way the truth of the theory I have outlined.

41. Kierkegaard, *Attack upon Christendom*, 59; S.V. 19, 76.

4

Kierkegaard and Philosophy (i)

KIERKEGAARD A PHILOSOPHER?

IF KIERKEGAARD IS A problem as a literary figure and man of action his status as a philosopher is even more problematic. It is only prejudice or dogmatism that can refuse to allow him the title of philosopher; for the fact that he was not an academic should trouble no historian of philosophers and the religious inspiration of his work should not make him less of a philosopher than it does, say, St. Thomas Aquinas. I do in fact accept Kierkegaard's own view of his work; that he was from the beginning a religious author. However, that seems to me to be rather an ambiguous description and certainly it leaves all kinds of things as open possibilities. Hence, as I say, it is merely dogmatic to claim that he cannot be a philosopher. Also I have always been very impatient of those strangely dismissive apologies so beloved of those scholars who tell us that he was only "a kind of philosopher" or a philosopher *malgré lui*. I could not match Kierkegaard's own wit but I can imagine how he would turn Molière on such pronouncements. Clearly, the use of unusual literary forms does pose difficulties, but these should not be more than or indeed different from those we encounter in reading the work of someone like Sartre or Lessing. The language of Spinoza is not easy nor the style of Wittgenstein anything other than the barrier to early understanding he meant it to be. If Kierkegaard's way of writing is extraordinary, volatile, and vivacious this should not worry us unduly. That a text is difficult to follow and the sentences convoluted is not something so very unusual in philosophy that it should make us wonder whether what we are reading is philosophy.

It may be thought that I am tedious in my lengthy protestations but I do feel keenly this slight not so much on one's own philosophical judgment but on the philosophical legacy of this genius. Rather than rehearse some tedious catalogue of such disparagement or apology let me say that I am all too clearly aware of the way in which Kierkegaard does not fit comfortably into our formal categories of philosophers. I appreciate that he is very much the poet, but it is significant that one of the greatest and earliest of Kierkegaard scholars, E. Hirsch, discusses at length the transition from poet to thinker. The point is that this kind of assessment is only a half-truth. The basic difficulty with regard to any philosophical evaluation of Kierkegaard is that his whole outlook and output, as we have said, are religious. In his case this means that he was hardly ever concerned with questions that obviously find their place in a tradition of philosophical debate. Thus his first work is more obviously literary than philosophical and his engagement with the problem of Cartesian doubt takes the form of a novel. Later, what he ironically calls "Philosophical Fragments" deals with ontology only with reference to the nature of Christian facts. What one needs to appreciate is that his work is essentially polemical and as such it is directed towards the legacy of a particular kind of philosophy, the Hegelian, and similarly employs philosophical argument for the purpose of exposing what he saw as the bankruptcy of that philosophical legacy. There are in Kierkegaard's writings several basic problems and different kinds of problems; but all of them relate to the task he had taken upon himself: that of introducing Christianity into Christendom. Essentially his problem was to clarify the confusion that had been generated by the way in which a Hegelian orthodoxy had given bourgeois religiosity the kind of credibility which confirmed its self-deception. Not to see this in quite this way is to dismiss his protests against established religion as either extremism which might or might not have developed into a mature Catholicism or else as a one-sided and perhaps heretical sectarianism, and his protests against philosophy as mere irrationalism. However, if one does try to define this fundamentally religious problem in all its intellectual perplexity then I think that one begins to see too that Kierkegaard's philosophy was always a leitmotif of that religious truth, not indeed part of it but what helped to purify it.

THE PHILOSOPHICAL CLIMATE OF KIERKEGAARD'S DENMARK

The better to appreciate Kierkegaard's philosophical intention and achievement we must consider briefly the philosophical climate of Denmark in his time. In 1741 the Norwegian author Holberg, then a professor at the University of Copenhagen, published his fantasy novel, *The Subterranean Voyage of Niels Klin*, criticizing the narrowness of his age and the religious fanaticism then prevalent. A hundred years later Kierkegaard found himself in a similar situation and his philosophy is born of that radical dissatisfaction. As we have seen, he had been attracted by Romanticism, with its more-than-artistic significance, but he had come to the conclusion that it offered no way forward, a realization that left him in despair. The despair was compounded by his growing suspicion that the solution and remedy offered by Hegelianism was equally to prove a failure. He greatly admired the distinguished literary critic, dramatic author, and philosopher J. L. Heiberg, the main exponent of Hegelianism in Denmark. In 1833 Heiberg had published a little work, *Of the Importance of Philosophy for the Present Time*, where he showed that the Hegelian philosophy puts in their place the contradictory ideas of which the era suffered. The philosophy of Hegel and the poetry of Goethe are the miracles of the age, reconciling the ideal and the real. What Hegel's system offered was an organization of the seeming chaos that resulted from the different ideas about art, religion, science, and politics. It would not be too much to say that, however much Kierkegaard admired Heiberg, he had always harbored the suspicion that all this was too good to be true.

Someone who, in a way, took on Heiberg's mantle and by his position as a lecturer in systematic theology was very well able to influence Kierkegaard was the brilliant young theologian H. L. Martensen. His two main works on dogmatics and ethics were translated into English, as was the book on Boehme. A superficial reading of them leaves one feeling perplexed at Kierkegaard's critical comments on him. Essentially, however, what Martensen sought to do was to apply the Hegelian method to theology. As already indicated, he had, too, a devotion to the mystics, Boehme and Eckhardt. Consequently he saw the experience of God, the Christian faith no less, as the root of all knowledge and so all theory of knowledge was for him theology not philosophy. The characteristically Hegelian slant was seen in what he then envisaged as the possibilities open to the thinker, a speculative dogmatics constructed from the acquisition of faith, a total system. Kierkegaard followed Martensen's work very closely and more and more came to regard him as his intellectual *bête noir*.

To round out the picture we can mention three other figures, two of whom were more or less intimately connected with Kierkegaard; Treschow, Sibbern, and Møller. Niels Treschow was born in Norway but became professor of philosophy at Copenhagen before returning to Norway in 1813 to the newly founded University of Christiana in Oslo. A thorough Romantic, he saw a profound unity in nature. Creation was for him a long and shadowy process, the result of imperceptible transitions rather than observable change. Both in his cosmology and his general philosophy his Romanticism led him to oppose the dominance of some Platonic idea: the idea, he said, cannot exhaust the individual. The individual in all its particularity is as significant as the general common characteristic. Indeed individuals are the sole reality and each of them contains an inexhaustible richness.

F. C. Sibbern succeeded Treschow in the chair of philosophy at Copenhagen and outlived Kierkegaard. In 1833–34 Kierkegaard followed the course of lectures he gave on the philosophy of Christianity. In 1838 Sibbern published a book on Hegel's philosophy, *Bemaerkningen og Undersolgelsen, fornemmelig betraeffende Hegels Philosophie, betraget in Forhold til vor Tid* (Remarks and Investigations, Mainly Treating Hegel's Philosophy, Considered in Relation to our Time), where he emphasizes that Hegel neglects the Cartesian doubt. As well as pointing out the way in which Hegel actually made assumptions, regarding them as self-evident, Sibbern pointed out the futility of Hegel's attempt to abrogate the principle of contradiction, this being assumed in the very negation of the principle. Sharing the Romantic vision of the cosmos Sibbern nevertheless did not countenance an *a priori* system of nature: for him creation goes on indefinitely. Life is a continuous evolution. Sibbern and Møller represent the significant Danish influence on Kierkegaard, as the latter's library testifies. It may also be true that Sibbern had envisaged Kierkegaard taking up an academic career.

P. M. Møller was probably the thinker who got closest to Kierkegaard and to whom Kierkegaard himself was most devoted as he surveyed "the harbor of merchandise" that Copenhagen still was. A theologian, Hellenist, talented poet, Møller had been Professor of Philosophy at the

University of Christiana in Oslo in 1826, returning to Copenhagen in 1831 where he was Professor Extraordinary until his untimely death in 1838. How profound an influence he was on Kierkegaard's development can be gauged from the various drafts even more than from the final form of the dedication to Møller of *The Concept of Anxiety*. What is of particular interest is that early in his career Møller had greatly admired Hegel's philosophy, which he had taught in Oslo. However, he showed a suspicion similar to Sibbern's and came to feel that the individual tended to disappear in the progress of the dialectic. In the Hegelian system, he says, the individual is only "an imperceptible movement of the wave in the ocean of speculation."[1] We gather that Møller was a colorful character who exercised as great if not greater influence on his students by his conversation than by his lectures: clearly there was much in his breadth of cultural outlook and, perhaps more, his character, with which Kierkegaard resonated so that he really was "the trumpet" that sounded his soul's challenge. Møller expounded his philosophy in some articles and in a host of aphorisms. What we see there is a kind of Romantic Platonism for which the individual has an indestructible kernel, the idea of the individual. True personality is not to be found in the ephemeral worldly appearance: the truth of the individual is the progress of his eternal ego. One other very characteristic theme is Møller's stress on the concept of loyalty (*Redelighed*). One can well imagine the power of these recollected lessons when Kierkegaard received from Sibbern Møller's dying message to him.

KIERKEGAARD'S PHILOSOPHICAL DEVELOPMENT

Returning to our topic, there are several different kinds of problems facing us. The MA dissertation as Kierkegaard's first work of published philosophy is a complex work: as serious an evaluation of Romanticism as Hegel's *Phenomenology of Spirit*, it actually exemplifies his basic philosophical attitude in the way in which he has composed this superb critique of Hegel. Then *Either-Or*, a work where the philosophy is even more heavily disguised, has a very clear formal thesis about the nature of philosophy. In his *Journal* Kierkegaard sets it out with the kind of logical precision that one finds in Wittgenstein, "Tautology as the highest principle of thought."[2] The philosophy becomes more concerned with

---

1. Møller, *Efterladte Skrifter*, vol. 5, 72.
2. Kierkegaard, *Journals*, 405 (II B 177) referring to Kierkegaard, *Either-Or* 1, 30; S.V. 2, 39.

matters of religious faith as the formal characterization of the religious stage now distinguished is undertaken in *Fragments*. So one could go through the whole Kierkegaard oeuvre and sketch the architectonic of problems relating to a philosopher's standpoint, life as different spheres of existence, the relation of knowledge to truth and salvation and of history to faith, and that most intractable difficulty, sin.

Kierkegaard and Kant

It may seem surprising if I say that what I have so far set out as the characterization of Kierkegaard's work is what makes me link him with Kant. However, the centrality of freedom of the will to the whole of Kant's philosophy made him see the nature of morality as concerned with the kingdom of ends and produced both his profound agnosticism and his moving awareness of the mystery of sin. Also one of the reasons why I began by placing Kierkegaard in the context of Romanticism is that both Bertrand Russell[3] and George Santayana[4] held the opinion that Kant was the father of Romanticism. Jerry Gill was probably the first to attempt a comparison between Kant and Kierkegaard.[5] Similarity of details is, however, not my claim. Rather it is that though Kant, who was neither a sage nor a saint but a professional philosopher, would not have warmed to Kierkegaard as a man or a thinker, finding his passion uncomfortable and his irony and sarcasm recklessly dangerous, he would have recognized a similar outlook. Both are aware of the way in which the basic certainties for which we pant are granted only as postulates, that pure reason has its limits, and that sin discloses the need to work out a new kind of rationality. It is a theme that antedates his reading of Kant; for interestingly what Kierkegaard thought about rationalism was bound up with his theological reading. Thus he makes the point that a careful analysis of what is said by "rationalistic dogmaticians" reveals that for them an essentially Christian position is, at base, nothing but a philosophical statement which, however, only results in the contradiction that this is something of which man cannot be convinced without Christ's appearance.[6] Rationalism, he came to believe, was confusion. It represented the

---

3. Russell, "Dr. Schiller's Analysis," 645.
4. Santayana, *Egotism in German Philosophy*, 11–20, 54–64.
5. Gill, "Kant, Kierkegaard and Religious Knowledge."
6. Kierkegaard, *Journals and Papers* 1304, I A 29.

union of Christianity and philosophy, the result of which was confusion of language.[7] The various epigrammatic references to philosophy made in the *Journal* of 1836 and 1837 show Kierkegaard becoming impatient with the emptiness of the contemporary philosophy.[8]

Kierkegaard's Deepening Concern with Philosophy

As we have seen, in 1835 Kierkegaard was looking for a truth, an idea. For which he could "live and die." He thought he would not find that in orthodox Christianity and consequently may have felt driven all the more to what he regarded as its opposite, *viz.* philosophy. In any case, some of the earliest entries in the *Journal* and the *Notebook* show that his concern with philosophy was deepening in the year immediately preceding his Gilleleje sojourn. He himself says in the statement of supplication (*Eksamens-petitum*) to the faculty of Theology of Copenhagen University, which he made on 2 June 1840, that philosophy had been his main interest.[9] This is indeed very clear from the *Papers* relating to the winter of 1873. Thus we know that he bought Erdmann's *Lectures on Faith and Knowledge* in November of that year, almost as soon as it had been published, and had finished reading it by mid-December.[10] One possibly very significant aspect of this reading which cannot be estimated with any kind of precision is the emphasis Kierkegaard would have found there on Schelling, the latter's *Vorlesungen uber academische studier* together with Hegel's *Phenomenology of the Spirit* and *Encyclopaedia* being the recent works which Erdmann treats. Schelling's importance for Kierkegaard is a matter to which we shall return; but for the moment the significant thing to note is the methodological issue that Erdmann treats.

It is very interesting that he raises the question of the methodological or disciplinary classification for his problem: is the problem of faith and knowledge a problem in theology or one to be located in philosophy? In a manner that is indeed very reminiscent of Schelling he answers his question by saying that it belongs to neither but is in

---

7. Kierkegaard, *Journals and Papers* 3246, I A 98.

8. Kierkegaard, *Journals and Papers* 3248-55.

9. Thulstrup, ed., *Breve og Akstykker*, 8.

10. See Kierkegaard, *Papirer* II C 38-49; Kierkegaard, *Journals and Papers*, 5271-73, 1972, 5278, 2250-52, 772; cf. Kierkegaard, *Papirer* II A 193; Kierkegaard, *Journals and Papers*, 5274.

fact one that is the concern of philosophy of religion. Already, it seems to me that Kierkegaard had found the Archimedean point in relation to the problem he had identified in Hegel's treatment of religion, and in particular, Christianity. What it amounts to is the perception that even for a thinker who followed Hegel's understanding of the course of philosophy's history and the nature of its enterprise there had to be the recognition that thinking about faith and the practice of faith are not one and the same thing. Furthermore, without repeating the arguments of Hirsch,[11] and Thulstrup's more judicious estimate,[12] we can mention the impact on Kierkegaard of Erdmann's discussion of his crucial problem, *viz.* the position of faith relative to knowledge. In November and December 1837 Kierkegaard followed and paid particular attention to Martensen's lectures on speculative dogmatics, which, incidentally, would have been his introduction to the history of philosophy. There is no doubt, as Thulstrup says, that Martensen had also read Erdmann's work.[13] So, Thulstrup says, "Kierkegaard became aware that in speculative thought both rationalism and supranaturalism were judged to be vanquished positions, vanquished together with Kant." Thulstrup's conclusion is that Kierkegaard was at odds with both aspects of the double trend in Erdmann;[14] the inclination in the first place to assign faith a lower position than knowledge and in the second place the anxiety to maintain a continuity between faith and knowledge so that there could be a transition from the lower to the higher sphere. Already there appears in Kierkegaard's development a growing understanding of the necessity for philosophy to recognize that issues of faith have to be dealt with on their own terms; and surely it cannot be wrong to see in this the surviving influence of Kant's insistence on limiting knowledge "to make room for faith." Equally there is a growing understanding that philosophy ignores faith at its own peril.

More than a year before this (September 1836) Kierkegaard had been greatly impressed by his discovery of J. G. Hamann's work.[15] It is clear from the *Journal* that during these two years Hamann became a significant influence on Kierkegaard's philosophical development.

11. Hirsch, *Kierkegaard-Studien*, II, 535–36.
12. Thulstrup, *Kierkegaard's Relation to Hegel*, 124–27.
13. Ibid., 125.
14. Ibid., 127.
15. See Kierkegaard, *Papirer* I A 100; Kierkegaard, *Journals and Papers*, 1539.

Thus an entry of 1838 shows him reviewing the progress of modern philosophy by means of a reference to Hamann: "To what extent is there an element of correspondence between Hamann's deep *personal protest* against the reality-significance [*Realitets-Betydning*] of existence [*Tilvaerelse*] and the genuinely serious *doubt* in modern philosophy."[16] How much Hamann influenced Kierkegaard is not my present concern. The great Walter Lowrie gave it as his opinion that Hamann was "the only author by whom Søren Kierkegaard was profoundly influenced."[17] Yet, in spite of the fact that he never abandoned this position he was obliged to admit in his pamphlet on Hamann that it was one that had "perhaps more truth than evidence on its side."[18] It is not necessary for us to struggle with Hamann's obscurities to grasp the way in which this powerful genius—critic of Kant and admirer (avowed successor?) of Socrates—confirmed in Kierkegaard's mind the conviction that philosophy should take a more existential turn away from the rationalism which predominated. Thought and life should, in his view, be a much more subtle dialectic. As he was to write in a note after reading Erdmann, "the incommensurability of life is inaccessible to the abstract dialectic developing through the thought-knots of necessity."[19]

Through Martensen's lectures, his own reading of Erdmann and, doubtless, his connection with Poul Møller and F. C. Sibbern, Kierkegaard acquired such knowledge as he had at this time of Hegel's philosophy. What he had read in Erdmann did not make him warm to that philosophy and it is evident that he was looking elsewhere for inspiration. Some days before he ceased to attend Martensen's lectures he read I. H. Fichte, whose monograph on *Speculation and Revelation* had appeared in a Danish version that year. Not much mentioned before this time, Fichte now becomes a figure of importance, filling Kierkegaard with a kind of intellectual hopelessness: he felt that he would never achieve anything and yet he was confirmed in his dissatisfaction with the Hegelianism he had encountered in Erdmann. This dissatisfaction was to be expressed in two contexts prior to what can be regarded as the beginning of his published critique of Hegel in *Either-Or, viz.* his very first book, *Af en endnu livendes Papirer (From the Papers of One Still*

16. Kierkegaard, *Papirer* II A 214 n.d. 1838; Kierkegaard, *Journals and Papers*, 1544.
17. Lowrie, *Kierkegaard*, 164.
18. Lowrie, *Johan Georg Hamann*, 4.
19. Kierkegaard, *Papirer* II C Nov. 7, 1837; Kierkegaard, *Journals and Papers*, 5272.

Living) and the Master's dissertation, *The Concept of Irony*. What is important is not so much the argument as the fact that it is an engagement with Hegelianism and, to that extent, a deliberately philosophical enterprise. That his knowledge of Hegel was hardly extensive or even accurate is obvious from the reference made on the first page of *From the Papers of One Still Living* to Hegel's "great attempt to begin with nothing." This was a matter that occupied Kierkegaard consistently during these years so that, as we shall see, he returned to it later—then with a much more clearly negative evaluation. In 1838 he was perhaps more concerned with what had been done with Hegel, having in mind the "endless series of bricklayer's helpers who took from Hegel the philosophical building stones from hand to hand."[20] The lack of precision with regard to Hegel's actual claim displayed in these references is not really important. Rather the important point is that in 1838 Kierkegaard was concerned with the nature and scope of philosophy and that this concern continued into the next decade and beyond. It is also worth noting that even as early as this Kierkegaard showed a respect for Hegel (heightened indeed by the disdain he felt for Hegel's followers), which, despite his profound and passionate rejection of Hegel's philosophy, he never lost.

During the period that follows this Kierkegaard would have been very largely occupied with the composition and later the defense of his Master's thesis, *The Concept of Irony*. The philosophical purpose of this work, Kierkegaard's main contribution to aesthetics, is something I noted briefly in my *Philosophy of Religion in Kierkegaard's Writings*[21] and I would simply add that what Kierkegaard does is to launch a *philosophical* attack on both Romantic irony and Hegelianism. The influences on that attack cannot be traced here, but there can be little doubt that they lie in the German philosophy that might be broadly called anti-Hegelian.[22] This philosophical enterprise and the developing sense of a position in philosophy are, to my view, much clearer in the thinking of the years following *The Concept of Irony*. He had fled the scandal which his broken engagement would have caused and gone to Berlin, the very choice of refuge showing the seriousness of his philosophizing. There he attended various lectures and his eager interest in Schelling's is obvious from the enthusiastic letters he wrote to his friend Emil Boesen and to

---

20. Ibid., 2.
21. Heywood Thomas, *Philosophy of Religion in Kierkegaard's Writings*, 11f.
22. Cf. Heywood Thomas, "J. G. Fichte and F. W. J. Schelling."

F. C. Sibbern during the winter of 1841. In January 1842 he wrote to Boesen that he had written "a major section of a piece of 'Either-Or.'"[23] Significantly only a month later he wrote expressing his "disappointed expectations of Schelling";[24] and three weeks later, announcing his intention to leave Berlin and return to Copenhagen, he says bluntly, "Schelling talks endless nonsense both in an extensive and an intensive sense."[25] However, as I have suggested, it was Schelling's lectures on the philosophy of revelation that inspired his developing ideas about existence, as is clear from the well-known expression of excitement at hearing Schelling's first lecture. I would emphasize the importance of not being misled by the disappointment but of rather bearing in mind that he had expected to hear something quite specific from Schelling. The care he took in making fair copy of his notes is indication enough of the importance he attached to those early lectures.[26] The one point that is clear about their *influence* is that after his delight in hearing the word "reality" in the second lecture he expected the positive philosophy Schelling proposed to develop to be some kind of a philosophy of existence. This, I believe, was the support and inspiration he wanted for writing *Either-Or*.

Either-Or

Whatever this semi-biographical account has established it is clear that *Either-Or* had a philosophical purpose. Ronald M. Green's suggestive contribution to the volume of essays on *Either-Or* Part II argues that *Either-Or* can be described as a deliberate re-creation and re-presentation of Kant's epistemological and ethical position in his first two *Critiques*.[27] For our present purpose we do not need to *identify* the philosophical ancestry if one can so describe it but simply note that such discernible philosophical features support the point just made. It seems to me that this purpose weighed so much with Kierkegaard as a writer that in 1843 he made several philosophical notes in his own copy of *Either-Or*.[28] Thus

---

23. Kierkegaard, *Breve* No. 62, *Journals and Papers*, 5548.

24. Kierkegaard, *Breve* No. 68, *Journals and Papers*, 5551.

25. See Kollegie til Schellings Forelaesninger I Berlin, Pk 4 Laeg 4 in Kierkegaard Arkivet C. (Items in the Royal Copenhagen Library Archive.)

26. Kierkegaard, *Breve* No. 62, *Journals and Papers*, 5548.

27. Green, "Kierkegaard's Great Critique."

28. Kierkegaard, *Papirer* IV A 214–17, 221–23, 231, 234, 238, 241; Kierkegaard,

he says "Possibly no one suspects that *Either-Or* has a plan from the first word to the last, since the preface makes a joke of it and does not say a word about speculation."[29] The complexity of that plan is indicated by the next *Journal* entry, which says that he had omitted the narrative which he had begun as a *form* for *Either-Or*. What we make of the decision to write a philosophical pastiche rather than a philosophical novel proper is another matter that need not concern us here; what matters is that the several different concerns motivating this literary composition were all philosophical. This much is clear from the later *Journal* entry of 1845 which comments on the relation between *Either-Or* and the *Stages*, contrasting the two "competing components," *viz.* the aesthetic and the ethical, in *Either-Or* with the three of *Stages*, the religious being the third.[30]

At the risk of oversimplifying this point about the philosophical purpose of *Either-Or* I want to emphasize that this was generally to criticize Hegel and that Kierkegaard's sojourn in Berlin had given him a clear vision of where the Hegelian philosophy needed to be attacked. In 1837 and 1838 both Poul Møller and Sibbern had offered sharp criticism of Hegel. Doubtless these publications in the journal *Maanedskrift for Litteratur* influenced Kierkegaard's developing thought and so it was, I suggest, that Kierkegaard grasped that logic was in fact the Achilles heel of Hegelianism, something that Victor Kuhr pointed out in his important monograph on the principle of contradiction.[31] In volume XIX of the journal, Sibbern argued against Hegel that the principle of contradiction holds universally and that any denial of that is self-contradictory; something that Hegel should have recognized.[32] Here is what could be described as the key inspiration of the aim of *Either-Or* as Kierkegaard himself describes it:

> My particular concern with the whole of *Either-Or* is: that it should be quite clear that the metaphysical significance at the bottom of the whole work leads everything back to the philosophical essay: Tautology as the highest principle of thought; that is to say (how many will understand it) if the principle of contradiction

Journals and Papers, 5627–36.
29. Ibid., 214, 5629.
30. Kierkegaard, *Papirer* VI A 41; Kierkegaard, *Journals and Papers* 5803.
31. Kuhr, *Modsigelsens Grunsaetning*.
32. Sibbern, *Maanedskrift for Litteratur*, 425–26.

is true (and that is expressed in "either-or"), it is the scientific expression for mediation, and is the only unity in which it can be resolved, the only way in which the system is possible. It would not be aesthetically correct to write a treatise on the principle of contradiction in this work and so it is expressed personally—but the same thing seen from a speculative point of view (if one does not wish to "go further") is the apotheosis of tautology.[33]

The importance of logic for Kierkegaard is a matter to which we shall return later. Here what matters is that he uses its very formalism to gather the various philosophical themes he wished to pursue in his writing.

KIERKEGAARD AGAINST PRESUPPOSITIONLESS PHILOSOPHY

Discussing Kierkegaard's rather Romantic rejection of Romanticism we saw how his philosophy was an opposition to the Idealism that had gone hand in hand with Romanticism, which similarly grew out of the Idealist tradition. It is time to start characterizing that philosophical position. One aspect was the argument that it was wrong to suppose that one could build a system of philosophy without assuming anything as a beginning: philosophy could only begin with some definite presuppositions. Hegel had maintained that the only thing he required as a basis for his system was a purely undetermined notion of Being. This claim is ridiculed by Kierkegaard in the "dialogue" between Socrates and Hegel, "Scene in the Underworld,"[34] Socrates replying to Hegel's claim that he begins with nothing by saying that perhaps Hegel does not begin at all! The point very obviously is that philosophy without assumptions is an impossibility.

In the same year (1845) Kierkegaard completed the *Unscientific Postscript*, which makes this same point again and again.[35] His contention is that Hegel's so-called presuppositionless beginning is a deception. If the system comes after existence, then it does not begin "immediately" as the Hegelians claimed it did. No existential system is possible, says Kierkegaard, and moreover, no logical system may boast of an absolute beginning. Hegel's system looked plausible enough; but when one exam-

---

33. Kierkegaard, *Journals*, 405; Kierkegaard, *Papirer* II B 177.
34. Kierkegaard, *Papirer* VI A 145; Kierkegaard, *Journals and Papers*, 3306.
35. See Kierkegaard, *Postscript*, 1, 116–22, 163–64; S.V. 9, 94–100, 124.

ined it one discovered that it was based on a mistake and that it derived its power from a confusion. The basic mistake we have shown already is the idea that a presuppositionless beginning was possible. There are bound to be presuppositions, and Kierkegaard makes quite clear that he starts with some assumptions about man—that he is a synthesis of being and knowing, and a synthesis of time and eternity.

Not content with this general criticism, Kierkegaard identifies the confusion that gives the system its vitality. This is the idea of *transition*. Like Trendelenburg, Kierkegaard shows that Hegel's doctrine identifies real change with the dialectical method so that in fact Hegel imports change and movement into his logical construction. Kierkegaard accepted the Aristotelian dictum that real change is first grasped through the sense: it is a factor that is given and which cannot be generated by thought alone. He therefore agreed with Feuerbach that the apprehension of change as such is the achievement of the understanding acting in cooperation with the senses. The negative implications of this doctrine are what Kierkegaard stressed, namely that logic cannot deal properly with change and that no existential system is possible. But he did not deny the positive side of the doctrine and so tacitly affirmed an empirical epistemology. So far we have only repeated Kierkegaard's own statement of his position vis-à-vis Hegel. Modernizing his language we may perhaps understand the point he wants to make somewhat better.

In emphasizing the fact that Hegel's method is logical and that his system is logical Kierkegaard is calling attention to the fact that Hegel thought that he could make *a priori* claims about the structure and the composition of the world. The point is therefore that if these propositions are *a priori* their truth or falsity is independent of what the world is like. An empirical proposition's truth or falsity, on the other hand, is determined by experiential evidence, so that an examination of a state of affairs is relevant to its establishment. A true *a priori* proposition is necessarily true and a false one necessarily false. No state of affairs can make the first false or the second true. Therefore, if Hegel claimed that his system could give us information about the structure of the world then his system was not *a priori*. But since it was, then the claim that it gave information about the world was false. Moreover, the point about the necessity of assuming existence follows from this. For if the metaphysician has claimed to show that, for instance, freedom or individual existence is unreal then it follows that the appearance of such reality, which he has granted, must also be unreal. To put it differently, we cannot be in Plato's cave looking at shadows if the outer world is unreal. "Matter does not exist," says the metaphysician, "because matter is logically impossible." But if "matter is logically impossible" is true then "the appearance of matter is logically impossible" is also true. And if we are going to talk about individual existence then this must be assumed at the outset and cannot be established within the deductive framework.

"SUBJECTIVITY IS TRUTH"

What I have just been arguing would put Kierkegaard firmly in the empiricist tradition; and, to a large extent, I think that is correct. Certainly, he was more of an Aristotelian than a Platonist and we shall see how this works out in his ontology. To give this kind of discussion too great a prominence would in fact misrepresent Kierkegaard's greatness as a philosopher. He does not fit easily into any textbook tradition of philosophy or indeed into some neat classification of those who declare themselves critics of Philosophy. He has regularly been hailed as a notable member of the great line of irrationalists; and, misrepresentation though this is, in an odd way it has reminded us that his great contribution to Philosophy was to show the limitations of a rationalist philosophy. By his very analysis of reason he showed both his devotion to Reason and the kinds of reasons which the heart has and of which Reason has no knowledge. If John Wisdom could sum up Wittgenstein's great achievement as his having asked the question whether one can play chess without the Queen so one can say that Kierkegaard's greatness was his grand assertion that "subjectivity is truth." If my understanding of this slogan is right then the main implication of this as regards philosophy is that philosophy is something specifically humane. He commends Socrates as a subjective thinker, that is, one who *lives* his philosophy. According to Kierkegaard, Socrates finds the world of essences and possibilities worthwhile only in so far as it works for his own moral perfection. Behind his irony and maieutic method lay a personal regard for the truth, not only as an objective fact, but also as a practical principle that should make a difference in our life. His paramount concern was for the way his hearers related themselves to the truth and were changed by it in their manner of existence. Hence the subjective thinker, says Kierkegaard, is led to communicate truth indirectly so as to provoke personal reflection and appropriation on the part of the potential learner. A subjective thinker like Socrates is not content with the movement of thought in the order of essence and possibility. He is constantly putting his theories to the test of actual existence, which alone is the supreme court. A knowledge of possibilities is not as perfect as the apprehension of actual concrete being, and in the sphere of human existence actuality is found only in contingent existence and not in some Platonic essences.

Before we proceed to interpret this description of the subjective philosophy let us briefly indicate how this philosophy understands rationality, a matter to which we shall return. Kierkegaard's description of rationality is indeed unusual. He rejects equally the extreme anti-intellectualism which makes some kind of immediacy or revelation supreme and also the intellectualism which would make God, freedom, and immortality almost the productions of reason. He defends a third view which he himself does not work out in any detail but simply puts forward as being better than either of these ivory castles. He maintains that rationality cannot be replaced, that there is no substitute for logicality, while also insisting that reason has its limits to go beyond which a person has to make "the leap." This leap he would describe as something essentially human and not an instance of animal faith as Santayana does. To have interests was, for Kierkegaard, human, and to have interests was to be motivated to make a leap of faith.

The question that Kierkegaard puts to himself from the beginning of his published work is that of the relation of philosophy to the person's own existence. There has been a long tradition that philosophy is a study that can only be successfully pursued if we block out all emotion and passion. It is a "cold" subject that deals with proofs and arguments. Kierkegaard took up this tradition and turned this whole way of looking at philosophy upside down. And he was right in doing so. For we can appreciate today how wrong it is to expect the philosopher to be engaged in proving things. The idea may die hard; nevertheless, proof and demonstration are antiquated words in philosophy. And if it is wrong to imagine that philosophy aimed at presenting theorems it is surely equally wrong to imagine that the philosopher is "all head and no heart."

John Wisdom spoke of the philosopher as the "animal in which the scientist vanishes into the logician—not to mention the poet and the psycho-analyst."[36] It is the way in which the scientist vanishes into the poet that Kierkegaard saw so clearly and put forward as his description

---

36. Wisdom, "Moore's Technique," 145.

of the philosopher. Seeing this, he saw that the old way of doing philosophy would not do because such interest in everything except human beings and the human situation blinded it to the fact that first of all in philosophy we must always be prepared to give language its cash value in terms of concrete situations.

Again his scientific examination of the place of reason in human existence might be described as halfway between Kant and Wittgenstein. The recognition, startling to all Hegelians, that there were limits to reason's operation was indeed, like Kant's critique, meant to safeguard religion; but in Kierkegaard's, too, it was no less sound because of that. The way it did so was, however novel, because for the first time in modern thought it was suggested that here was an area of meaning with its own logic that was different from that of other areas whose claim to meaning was recognized. The importance of this could be described as a clarification of Kant's great claim about his first critique: it emphasized that we should not think of this particular area in terms of the others. To continue the comparison, unlike Kant Kierkegaard had no special interest in science; but he was as impressed as the next man by the advance of science and to that extent was very much the modern man. However, he puts a great divide between religion and science: religion has a meaning but it is not that of science. Also it is just as different from the other source of knowledge for his contemporaries, namely, metaphysics. Following Kant against Hegel he emphasizes the close connection between religion and morality; but he applies Kant's insights to show that religion is not reducible to morality.

LINKING PHILOSOPHY WITH EXISTENCE

On this relation of philosophy to existence it is thus necessary, I think, to distinguish between what motivated Kierkegaard's thinking and what could be said to be the grammar of philosophy as he expounds it. That is, there is no denying what I have said more than once; that Kierkegaard's philosophy is born of a religious interest and purpose and is therefore set out in the context of such an argument. However, what is not always clear is that what he has to say about philosophy is often something of a more general interest. The point I am expounding at the moment is the general one about philosophy rather than its relation to the nature of religion and in particular of Christianity. The first thing Kierkegaard shows in this linking of philosophy with life or existence is the necessity for phenomenological description in philosophy. Though this had indeed been practiced, in a very limited fashion, by someone like Descartes, what Kierkegaard appreciates and clarifies so well is how in this initial task the philosopher's approach is, in a very real sense, neutral. In his account of what it is to live a life of emotional stimulus, to live a life of moral principle, to recognize that there is a point at which morality, like hedonism, appeals to something else he was so obviously neither undermining nor supporting any of their attitudes. His question in *Either-Or* as he *shows* the alternatives is not whether they are right or wrong but precisely what they are. This very obvious or elementary sense was what he had in mind when he said to his teacher Sibbern that he sought "a philosophy of existence."[37]

When one recalls Hegel's *Phenomenology* the difference is clear and telling; for in that work Hegel sought to trace the process of experience from mere sensation to absolute knowing, the way in which consciousness can become aware that as Spirit it holds the vision of reality within itself. With Kierkegaard phenomenology is a much more modest affair and the philosopher at this point has indulged in no large-scale interpretation which will be some –ism or other. Now I am far from saying that Kierkegaard saw philosophy in the same way as Husserl did; but I do contend that long before Husserl he had summoned the philosopher "back to the facts." The first thing we need to do is to describe, and that means starting where we are and recognizing the facts for what they are. It was precisely because he set out the facts of religious behavior that he progressed so successfully to the analytic task of defining the meaning of religious statements.

The linking of philosophy with life or existence clearly means more than this. Even granted that nobody had quite managed to portray the panorama of life as Kierkegaard did, it was nothing new for philosophers to concern themselves with features of everyday experience. Yet perhaps this is the telling point; for surely there is a world of difference in atmosphere between Locke's *Essay on the Human Understanding* and Kierkegaard's *Concluding Unscientific Postscript*. I deliberately choose an empiricist example to show that the point has nothing to do with a reference to concrete experience. To be graphic at the risk of being very imprecise and perhaps equally misleading, let me describe the difference as that between a world of fantasy and a world which is open

---

37. Kirmmse, ed., *Encounters with Kierkegaard*, 217.

to those pressing calls of life's tasks, life's destiny, and life's meaning. If Kierkegaard is right then the difficulty with so much philosophy is that it does not appreciate the way in which its analysis is conducted within a certain framework and that the conceptual items and scheme it offers are not somehow magically derived from the analysis. To go back to that amusing little dialogue from the *Journal* ("Scene in the Underworld") in which Hegel and Socrates meet, this is a point he pressed home when talking of the way in which philosophy necessarily involves presuppositions: and it was a point to which he returned in the more technical context of the discussion of logic and movement. It is because there are metaphysical beliefs that control our thinking that we make our choice between one kind of analysis and another. Putting the matter crudely, what I think Kierkegaard shows is that philosophy is indeed neither a presuppositionless nor a value-free inquiry and that its concern is precisely with those very beliefs that motivate our whole thinking.

This is why I believe that, for all his agnosticism and all his polemics against the fashionable philosophy of his day, his view of philosophy was positive and not negative. He is, to my mind, the real heir to Kant's *Prolegomena to Any Future Metaphysics*. His philosophical ambition, after he had reconciled in his own mind his youthful opposition of Christianity to philosophy, was to work out a philosophy of existence when he had come to understand existence as a life of Christian faith. It was nothing short, then, of producing a metaphysical theology when neither aspect of the enterprise was, in his view, to be treated in the manner of the established tradition. We shall return to the issue of metaphysical theology but for the moment we stay with the problem of characterizing this philosophical outlook and method.

FREE WILL

I have deliberately avoided attempting a chronological account of Kierkegaard's comments on philosophy; for this not only raises at all points the problem of his *persona* as author but all too often leads one into difficult issues of interpreting the nature of his development. Leading on, then, from what has just been said, we can consider the way in which Kierkegaard tackles free will, a traditional problem of metaphysics and morals.

First of all, it perhaps needs to be said that another instance of his rejection of Hegelianism is his strongly Kantian understanding of the nature of morality, something which might not be appreciated because of the apparently non-Kantian character of his famous notion of the "teleological suspension of the ethical." The Kantian "mode" of Kierkegaard's view of ethics was so strong that it is visible even in the polemical writings of his final year. Thus he says in *The Instant*: "The difference between a genius and a Christian is that a genius is nature's extraordinary, no man being able to make himself a genius, whereas a Christian is freedom's extraordinary, or, more precisely, freedom's ordinary, for though it is found extraordinarily seldom, it is what everyone ought to be."[38]

What we ought to be is what we are free to be: this Kantian theme remained a guiding principle of Kierkegaard's thinking in contradistinction to Hegel's, whether he considered personal or social morality or the nature of ethico-Christian existence. However, the point that needs to be emphasized here is that no sooner is Kierkegaard launched on his career as an author than he is dealing with the philosophical issue of freedom. *Either-Or* is more obviously a novel in an extravagantly Romantic mode than a piece of moral philosophy. Yet the very drama of what story we can make of the two parts centers on the issue of choice and so is concerned with free will.

Freedom in Either-Or

Either-Or was a work which, Kierkegaard tells us, he not only wrote in Berlin but perhaps had even gone to Berlin to write: "When I left 'her' I begged God for one thing, that I might succeed in writing and finishing *Either-Or*."[39] His correspondence with his friend Emil Boesen and with his teacher, Sibbern, gives us a clear picture of the feverish activity that marked his sojourn in Berlin, a punishing program of reading capped by a furious program of writing. It is clear from this correspondence that he was deliberately working on the composition of different styles of writing. In a long letter of 16 January 1842 to Emil Boesen, much of which is taken up with his agonized sense of absence from Copenhagen (and especially Regine), he says that he has again written a major section of a piece, "Either-Or." Strange as it may seem, the very groans of the letter reveal the way in which he was working out his philosophical

---

38. Kierkegaard, *Attack upon Christendom*, 159; S.V. 19, 178.
39. Kierkegaard, *Papirer* X5 A 146; Kierkegaard, *Journals and Papers*, 1843.

problem as well as his love-story, as when he blurts out, "Did I not tell you in my very first letter that forgetting her is still out of the question?" Just as he speaks of himself as "a bad husband" who could remain such so the section of *Either-Or* that he was writing presented an aesthetic defense of marriage. Alastair Hannay makes a very enlightening point regarding this by connecting it with the discussion by Kant and Fichte of the problem of how nature and duty are combined in love and marriage.[40] Interestingly he also connects it with the criticism Kierkegaard had made of H. C. Andersen that his work lacked that transubstantiation of experience which is what a life-view is:

> what had just happened, what he had done to Regine, had merely given him more of that experiential basis... Far from escaping the thought of marriage, marriage was now something he could think rather than endure. No longer having it in prospect, he could now do the Hegelian thing and look at it in retrospect, but not exactly in the Hegelian way, since he had no real reason to suppose that marriage itself was not "valid" and could be surpassed; it was simply that it would not do for him, and so there must be some way of seeing that marriage is a task for which not all are fitted... because they are over mature or too *little* natural.[41]

In passing it is worth noting how this illustrated the consistency of Kierkegaard's philosophical attitude from 1838 onwards. E. Hirsch was one of the earliest scholars to give this proper recognition, though it was something pointed out by Georg Brandes who described the M.A. dissertation as "the true point of departure for Kierkegaard's authorship."[42]

What we have seen here is the deliberately philosophical context and purpose of *Either-Or*. The importance of the work, then, as a discussion of the issue of freedom is not simply the emphasis on choice, which is as it were the work's symphonic theme, but the way in which the necessity of choice is described. The hedonism of Part 1's aesthete is no cardboard cutout or caricature. Completely without a moral purpose, the aesthete is yet neither a stranger to moral awareness nor unfamiliar with moral principles. The life-style he represents is one supremely concerned with pleasure, one in which morality and religion are recognized as possibilities with which he has no energy to be con-

---

40. Hannay, *Kierkegaard, a Biography*, 166–67.
41. Ibid.
42. Brandes, *Søren Kierkegaard, En Kritisk Fremstilling in Grundriss*, 187.

cerned, taken up as he is with the attractions of present pleasure. The subtle phenomenology of the aesthete's moods, which is delineated in *Either-Or* Part 1, need not concern us here as we fasten on the progress as it were of the story.

To the young aesthete who becomes troubled by the tragedy and boredom of the aesthetic life Assessor William urges the remedy for all this, which is to be found in choice. The Socratic "Know thyself" is a prescription that yields first place to "Choose yourself." I want to suggest that here we find Kierkegaard reacting to the Kantian notion of autonomy as the mark of ethical practice and also to the view of moral freedom in the classically Aristotelian tradition. The very name of the pseudonym, Victor Eremita, shows how this notion was for him a personal problem, how to understand the dimly perceived religious obligation to renounce marriage in favor of a solitary life. The Kantian, not simply Hegelian, characteristic of the ethical as the universal is clear enough in Assessor William's recommendation of marriage as an ethical ideal. The end of ethical activity is to become a self that is not merely a personal self but a civic self. That universal end is the self's because the self chooses it.

The problematic nature of this universality reveals a most profound feature of Kierkegaard's treatment of the autonomy of ethics. In Kant it had been a mark of what made ethics the limit of human possibility, that ideal being a kingdom of ends. The story of the aesthete, however, shows a humanity which ends with a glimpse of what makes that autonomy itself questionable, there being edification in the thought that as against God we are always in the wrong. Even a superficial reading of *Either-Or* shows Kierkegaard filling out Kant's concept of ethical autonomy. Though Kant later speaks of the conflict that is endemic in the situation of passion, his initial description of morality and moral experience is that we are rationally aware of the categorical imperative. While taking up the insistence on the autonomy of choice which is what transforms an aesthetic existence into an ethical one Kierkegaard shows that the young poet's ethical problem is not a simple choice between A and B which is his own free choice but rather the choice of the ethical which is an obvious matter of autonomy. The profundity of the analysis lies in the description of the choice he has to make, the choice of despair. This is also reminiscent of such Romantic poetry as Elizabeth Browning's "How do I love thee?" inasmuch as the story shows the choice.

As well as this development of Kant's theory into a phenomenology of moral development, Kierkegaard offered a very Aristotelian account of the absolute choice of oneself as the transition from the aesthetic to the ethical life. He had substituted "Choose thyself" for the Socratic "Know thyself" because knowledge of oneself was more of a presupposition than an expression of ethics. If the injunction that I choose myself seems strange and not merely ambiguous, it is precisely because one ignores the very concept of voluntary action which Kierkegaard borrows from Aristotle, whose *Nicomachean Ethics* he was reading in 1842.[43] Later the Aristotelian notion of potentiality becomes a basis of the critique he offers of Hegel's doctrine of motion; but here it can only be said to be latent in his thinking.

It would seem to me that his early view of ethics as we see it in the Papers is a very Kantian notion of ethics as duty. By the time he was writing *Either-Or* he had effected that transubstantiation of experience of which he had spoken in *From the Papers of One Still Living* and seen the self's freedom to be related to the necessity and the possibility he knew in himself. The persistent emphasis on duty in all Assessor William's remarks, including the religious reference at the end of Part 2, would not blind us to what Kierkegaard shows in the story of *Either-Or* as a whole. A *Journal* entry of 1840 suggests this deepening of the Kantian view of ethics we have been considering: "When the individual has given up every effort to find himself outside of himself in existence, in relationships and the environment, and then after this shipwreck turns towards the highest, the absolute increases not only in fullness for him after the vacuum but also in the responsibility which he feels he has."[44]

The way in which this thinking finds its expression in *Either-Or* as both a story and a work of art is something that highlights this notion of the exercise of freedom as that choice which creates ethics as personal morality. Ethics is seen as a teleological movement and this is the specifically human teleology. It has often been said that Kierkegaard brought the human person into philosophy. Perhaps few aspects of his work better illustrate the truth of the remark than this deliberately Aristotelian

---

43. See the reference to Aristotle's comment on voluntary action in Kierkegaard, *Papirer* IV C 20; Kierkegaard, *Journals and Papers*, 112.

44. Kierkegaard, *Journals and Papers*, 1026; Kierkegaard, *Papirer* III A 26.

conception of ethics which he employs as he demonstrates the more obvious ways in which the remark could be understood.

Before leaving *Either-Or* to consider what Kierkegaard says about freedom in the more theological context of *Concept of Anxiety* it will be useful to note the very significant comparison drawn by Ronald M. Green between *Either-Or* and Kant's *Critique of Pure Reason*.[45] After noting some obvious parallels between Kant's mode of argument and Kierkegaard's, Green proceeds to show more persuasive parallels. *Either-Or*'s concern with aesthetic-romantic-ethical existence contains an un-contested element like the fact of intuition in Kant's first *Critique*: this is first love. Thus William's advice to the young man involves demonstrating that the real meaning of first love is disclosed in marriage. Even clearer, argues Green, is the parallel between William's argument and Kant's position in the *Critique of Practical Reason*. He concludes that "it is no exaggeration . . . to describe *Either-Or* as a deliberate *re-creation* and *representation* of Kant's epistemological and ethical position in his first two *Critiques*."[46]

Freedom in Concept of Anxiety

The Aristotelian notion of possibility already seen in *Either-Or* is immediately prominent in the argument of *Concept of Anxiety*. Having returned to Copenhagen in 1842 Kierkegaard had busied himself with reading Trendelenburg and Tennemann; and he noted the latter's translation of *kinesis* as "change." This became the starting point for his own view of transition, developed in *Concept of Anxiety*, as the notion of "qualitative leap."

Underlying the book's argument, it could be said, is Kierkegaard's hierarchical understanding of the three "stages"; for the psychology to which its subtitle refers is that of a development from a simple life based in whatever pleasure or joy history offers through a transtemporal existence to one in which the self is related to a transcendental goal. In this it would seem that Kierkegaard is attempting some kind of phenomenological account of what the moral life is, as Kant had delineated it in terms of a good will, which also has to recognize that there is a call to holiness of will. The challenge which Assessor William puts before the

---

45. Green, Ronald M. "Kierkegaard's Great Critique: *Either-Or* as a Kantian Transcendental Deduction," 139–53.

46. Ibid., 153.

young aesthete of acknowledging the necessity of an act of will pictures morality in a thoroughly Kantian fashion.

Here in *Concept of Anxiety*, however, Kierkegaard wants to illumine the concept of sin by relating it to such an act, thus offering an account of freedom that carries the logic of Kant's *Groundwork* beyond the argument of *Religion within the Limits of Reason Alone*. In its way *Either-Or* had accepted the position with which Kant starts in the latter work, namely that morality does not require any external warrant; but the autonomy of ethics did not for Kierkegaard imply that the ethical exhausted the possibilities of man as spirit.

Because he held this somewhat paradoxical position we would misread the "doctrine" of the stages were we to see the three spheres as a simple progression in which the higher presupposes the lower. Though it is true to say that for Kierkegaard neither the aesthetic nor the ethical sphere is self-sufficient it is also true that neither logically nor historically does the ethical presuppose the aesthetic and the religious the ethical.

Yet Kierkegaard had made it clear even in *Either-Or* that the choice of one's self "in its eternal significance" takes one beyond the ethical, where blame as much as praise relates to what it is that I know that I have done or can be shown to have done and for which, then, as I look back I must say that I am responsible. The subject of *Anxiety* was thus, as he says, the psychology of sin inasmuch as it was the possibility of sin, which remained a problem when both ethics and dogmatics had had their say.[47]

As is often the case, the way in which Kierkegaard sets out his argument is both full of historical reference and convoluted. However, it seems to me that the nub of the issue that he wants to confront is how it is that when we talk of ethics we find ourselves driven to use the concept of sin which, to use his graphic metaphor, shipwrecks ethics. It was the account that he would give of this which for him charted the map of freedom in ethics. That this is no fanciful way of describing the human condition is revealed as much by the complexities of the decision to go to war in Iraq and its manifold and horrendous consequences as by the great tragedy of the hydrogen bomb that ended the Second World War. The sobering confession of the scientists involved in this latter event is haunting—"We have known sin."

---

47. Kierkegaard, *Concept of Anxiety*, 21–23; S.V. 6, 119–21.

What has just been said about the *map* of freedom in ethics brings us back to what is said at the beginning of *Anxiety* about the "dizziness of freedom" and the picture there suggested of perilous altitude. Should we be content to live our lives as governed by what Kierkegaard would have called the "simple" problems of a psycho-physical existence, freedom is an equally simple issue. In regard to that we could say, as Richard Price did, that we know not what other explanation of behavior we need beyond saying that it is the action of someone or other—and that is its cause. However, when we appreciate that freedom, as Kierkegaard says, "does not arise out of anything" then its infinite character is clear to us and we see our task as achieving a self-consciousness through freedom. That self-consciousness he understood not as a mere psychological state or a simple matter of epistemology: it is the process of achieving "spirit." Such a phenomenology of morals reveals a certain hollowness in the traditional mode of discussing freedom as if we were looking for some underlying cause behind the known causal nexus of events. For Kierkegaard, the knowledge of freedom is the kind of thing that Ovid described as the predicament of his pursuing the worse when he approved of the better. That is how Kierkegaard understands knowledge of freedom, which is an active understanding of that task which is ours by nature. In both *Either-Or* and *Concept of Anxiety* he develops this view of the self as being true only in the act of absolute choice.

Because we are talking of an absolute choice we have gone beyond talking of choosing this or that good and we can see that St. Paul describes our predicament more accurately than Ovid when he cries, "Who shall deliver me from the death of this sin?" Here is the truth of Kierkegaard's paradox, which is so often dismissed as either a conceit or a simple self-contradiction, that sin presupposes itself.

Equally it shows that it is no simple *reductio ad absurdum* of hedonism that he offers in his analysis of the futility to which he sees the aesthetic life leading. Such may have been A. E. Taylor's rejection of hedonism as a self-defeating outlook in *Faith of a Moralist*, which elicited C. D. Broad's comment that to such advice the pagan poet would respond only by asking for more wine and further lascivious pleasure. Kierkegaard's point is that the boredom lays bare the contradiction between saying that I should pursue pleasure and the fact that whatever constitutes that pleasure what I do is making a choice that is *mine*, a contradiction between the external and the internal. While emphasizing the cruciality of my sense of my own freedom he sees ethics as finally leading to something more than a simple choice of certain policies and the unconstrained pursuit of such policies. As his analysis of ethics as freedom links ethics to a transcendent idea it leads him to see the nature of temptation in those terms: tempted, I am still anxious though I have not in fact performed evil. The idea of goodness suggested by *Either-Or* and made clear by *Concept of Anxiety* is one of a life-achievement that is found to be strangely a gift rather than the product of effort. This is once again the Pauline concept of grace that St. Paul expressed by disclaiming any credit for goodness freely chosen and fulfilled by saying that it is the work of Christ in him.

CONCLUSION

This account of the way in which Kierkegaard resolved the metaphysical problem of freedom might suggest that what he sought to achieve in philosophy was the advocacy of a Christian philosophy. Even if one could say this it will be clear that this advocacy was so remarkably subtle an epistemological and metaphysical effort that it is philosophy far removed from any form of the dogmatism that marks a doctrinally controlled philosophy whatever the controlling persuasion may be. Moreover, it hardly needs to be said that the last thing such a philosophy would be is a system. There can be no doubt that he philosophized as a man of faith and sought to achieve a philosophy after Christianity.

Nothing, however, could be clearer than that he would reject any understanding of the Christian faith *as* philosophy. That would for him be guilty of a double error: the betrayal of faith as something primarily for thought rather than life and the grievous misunderstanding of philosophy as results instead of dialectic. That condemnation and rejection had been one of the philosophical purposes of *Postscript*. However, he wanted faith to inspire philosophy without trying to produce proofs; and this intuition that philosophy was not a matter of proof surely is one of the ways in which he can indeed be said to be a thinker ahead of his time. One could say that in his understanding of the relation of theology to philosophy he sought to bring us back to our life-situation: it is a question of the philosopher's own attitude to ultimate problems. He would hold that every true philosopher takes morality and religion seriously. Part of his genius was the clarity of his perception that however intellectual a process philosophy (of necessity) is, it cannot pretend that life is a matter of cool reflection from which the passion of the free choice of religious faith is absent. "To think about existential problems," he says, "so as to leave out passion is not to think about them at all, is to forget the point that one indeed is oneself an existing person." Very significantly he goes on to say that the subjective thinker "is not an ethicist even if he is also an ethicist but is also a dialectician and is himself essentially existing."[48]

If he was thus inspired by his Christian faith and vocation to clarify the nature of philosophy itself, he was equally inspired to clarify its independence from faith. Handmaiden it might be, but it has its own proper concern. Neither did life, he thought, need the sanction of philosophy for its living. Beneath these two points lies his resistance to any attempt at defining "reasoning" uniquely. With a remarkable prescience he marked the limits of logical reasoning and the important difference between the kinds of reasoning in which one is engaged in the different contexts of life. Where a Hume had emphasized the importance of passion *against* reason, Kierkegaard showed the importance of passion *in* reason, which meant a more human understanding of what philosophy is.

---

48. Kierkegaard, *Postscript* 1, 351; S.V. 10, 52.

5

Kierkegaard and Philosophy (ii)
Kierkegaard on Ontology

METHODOLOGICAL ISSUES IN DISCERNING KIERKEGAARD'S ONTOLOGY

IN THE VOLUMINOUS LITERATURE on Kierkegaard, that is still growing, there is little discussion of the wealth of purely ontological thinking that he left. His stature as a philosopher is clear to anyone who reads the *Postscript* or *Stages on Life's Way*, and there have been several interpreters who have drawn attention to this. However, even when, as Heidegger, they reinforce Kierkegaard's achievement as an existential thinker, they tend to neglect Kierkegaard's interest in some of the more technical problems of philosophy.[1] Part of the reason for this is that these nuggets of gold are buried deep in unlikely places, like the discussion of sin. Another part of the reason is that these discussions are scattered throughout his works and papers, especially the latter.

Here what I hope to achieve is not by any means a full discussion of the topic of ontology but rather a further demonstration of the philosophical heritage bequeathed by Kierkegaard. What I have already said will also make it clear that the incompleteness of this discussion is due not merely to limitations of scholarship but also to the fact that, as may be expected, Kierkegaard was not interested in developing systematically ideas that he grasped clearly and used effectively. It also explains why

---

1. Kierkegaard's influence on Heidegger is less significant than one might expect. See Caputo, "Heidegger and Theology" and Blattner, *Heidegger's Temporal Idealism*, 60–61.

what I shall do will be for the most part to reconstruct rather than to expound or interpret. It is necessary to find out what exactly Kierkegaard said before we can explain what he meant. The relevant material is not too difficult to find since there are sections of the published works where the topic is clearly a theme in the discussion and it is not difficult to find the material in the Papers. There is a great deal of material in the Papers that has not yet received any attention from scholars.

In this connection there is one point about the interpretation of Kierkegaard's work that must be mentioned before proceeding further. However valid in other cases may be the method of setting out a philosopher's doctrine on any subject by gathering together all the references to this from the various parts of his work, this cannot be applied in any straightforward fashion to Kierkegaard.

First, there is the problem posed by the nature of the material we are dealing with in the Papers. This is not the same kind of evidence as the published works because Kierkegaard did not intend anyone to read these private notes. At first sight, this does not seem a particularly difficult problem; for, it might be argued, the notebooks of any philosopher would be exactly the same. However, they are not exactly the same since Kierkegaard claimed that his life-work was in a sense to be an enigma. I am certainly not suggesting that there is no value in what we glean from the Papers but simply emphasizing the need for sympathy and imagination in our use of this material.

Another reason is that the remarks that would be bundled together might be made by different members of Kierkegaard's little band of pseudonymous authors, and so the problem of the relation of Kierkegaard himself to his pseudonyms is also here involved. Indeed, one could say that the whole question of the Kierkegaard authorship is raised here, and in particular the question of Kierkegaard's interpretation of his own authorship. Though I accept Kierkegaard's interpretation of his writings as being, from the beginning, religious, I do not think that this makes any real difference to an interpretation of his thought on this subject. What might make such a difference is one's views on the question of whether Kierkegaard's thought is a unity or not. Yet even this does not present too serious a difficulty since Kierkegaard did in fact indicate his acceptance of the works which are most relevant here, namely *Philosophical Fragments* and *Concluding Unscientific Postscript*, as is clear from "A First and Last Explanation" in the latter work.² To this extent we are in no doubt about Kierkegaard's mind, and we are also sure that this was a basic theme of his philosophy. In *Papirer* VIII1 A127 Kierkegaard records, in 1847, his conviction—"Even if I achieve nothing else I nevertheless hope to have very accurate and experientially based observations concerning the conditions of existence." It is his fundamental disagreement with Hegel. For him Hegel, like Plato, though not in the same way, accepts the assumption of an identity or immediate unity of being and thought. This was then the point at which Kierkegaard felt that Hegel's philosophy had to be refuted. That this was no simplistic attack on Hegel will be evident. It has all the subtlety and a good deal of the opaqueness of Hegel's own thought. We shall see that logic and existence are distinguished in a variety of contexts and there are very different uses made of the thesis that existence cannot be reduced to a concept.

KIERKEGAARD'S BASIC CRITICISM OF HEGEL

Kierkegaard's first attack on Hegel is seen in the dissertation on the concept of irony with reference to Socrates.³ The conclusion to which he there came was that philosophy ends with the same presupposition with which it began. Hegel's assumption is of a unity of thought and reality. Basically Kierkegaard's attack can be understood as his having asked the question whether the Hegelian reality is not merely an ideal reality. Hegel, he argues, starts not by asking about the reality of any specific thing but by abstract enquiry into reality in general, "not nearly so difficult a problem as it is to raise and answer the question of what it means that this definite something is a reality." This must be the point of departure for any philosophy since the definite something is that from which abstract thought abstracts. But the difficulty lies in bringing this definite something and the ideality of thought together, by penetrating the concrete particularity with thought. "Abstraction simply cannot concern itself with such a contradiction, since abstraction expressly pre-

2. Kierkegaard, *Postscript* 1, 625ff.; S.V. 10, 285ff.

3. See Kierkegaard, *Concept of Irony*. This was pointed out by Himmelstrup in *Søren Kierkegaards Opfattelse af Socrates*, 299, though Himmelstrup also thought that there was a different understanding of Socrates in the *Postscript*. For a further discussion of this see Hirsch, *Kierkegaard Studien*, Vol. II, 586–602, and Bejerholm, *Meddelelsens Dialektik*.

vents it."[4] This plea on behalf of the more difficult task of philosophy is interesting, raising as it does the question of Kierkegaard's "existential philosophy."

It would be useful to point out here that an appreciation of Kierkegaard's achievement in revolutionizing philosophy's understanding of its relation to life does not commit us to any facile contrast between philosophy and experience. There were indeed occasions when Kierkegaard urged that one should be something rather than think about it; but that is a different story, and it is worth remembering this. In order to show Kierkegaard's interest in ontology and his contribution to it I shall not complicate the issue by discussing what he has to say about time. So I hope that we shall appreciate that the distinction he makes between logic and existence is not a piece of mere religious rhetoric.

A convenient starting-point is the crucial doctrine of Hegel's *Logic* that there is an identity of thinking and being. Hegel's claim is that it is the very nature of our thought to imply an identity of thinking and being, "And thus when we study Thought . . . we study Absolute Being . . . The two sides, Being and Thought, must come equally forward: and come in synthesis with the antagonism between the two overcome."[5] This is what Kierkegaard rejects on the ground that as long as we remain in the realm of pure thought the difference between them cannot be seen.

Kierkegaard's criticism is not a sceptical challenge. No more than Hegel did he doubt that the object of thought was real. His contention is that Hegel does not see that there is a problem as it were within being itself, namely, the relation of being in the conceptual sense to being in other senses of the term. Being, he said, may be differentiated inwardly by its own modalities.[6]

The problem of the relationship of thought to being then cannot be understood unless we appreciate the variety of meanings with which we are operating. The idealist thesis turns out to be a tautology that is not seen as such because of the ambiguity of the terms. The being spoken of here is essential being, and not even Spinoza saw this.[7] So the identity

---

4. Kierkegaard, *Postscript* 1, 302; S.V. 10, 9.

5. Wallace, ed., *Logic of Hegel*, 44 (cf. Wallace's characterization of Logic in ibid., cvii.).

6. Kierkegaard, *Postscript* 1, 302-3n; S.V. 10, 10n. cf. Kierkegaard, *Fragments* (Thulstrup edition), 92-93; S.V. 6, 69.

7. Kierkegaard, *Journals and Papers* 1057, *Papirer* X2 A 328. Kierkegaard would have echoed the following remark of Stirling but would have meant it critically: "No

claimed by idealism turns out to be something abstract and formal.[8] Kierkegaard is very confusing in his use of terms like "essential" and "abstract," but the point he wants to make seems to me to be that one must make a sharp distinction between being as real existence or actuality and being as essence or possibility.[9] The discussion of the traditional problem of being and becoming has the same purpose,[10] and it is this to which he turns in both *Concept of Anxiety*[11] and *Sickness unto Death*.[12]

PROBLEMATIC ASPECTS OF HEGELIAN PHILOSOPHY

There are several aspects of the Hegelian logic which Kierkegaard thinks show that this basic criticism of Hegel is valid. First, there is the question of "the dialectic of beginning."[13] The Hegelian system proposes to begin absolutely, and without any presupposition, with the immediate and the self-evident. But such a beginning can only be obtained by means of reflective thought, and such thought is infinitely continuous. In order to make a beginning possible then such thought has to be stopped. In that case, however, we decide to stop; but decisions have no place in logic. That is, the beginning of any system of thought is not created for us by the very process of thought itself.

Nor does Hegel succeed any better with his dialectic of doubt. For, even if we accept the assumption that all doubt rests on a substratum of abstract certitude, the latter cannot "for one moment be hypostatized so long as I doubt, because doubt consists precisely in departing from this certainty in order to doubt."[14] Hence one must say that "although the Hegelian philosophy may be free from all postulates yet it has reached this position by means of one crazy postulate, namely, the beginning of pure thought."[15]

---

man till Hegel ever explicitly saw the notion and no man, till Hegel, ever built a direct system on it." (Stirling, *Lectures on the Philosophy of Law*, iv.)

8. Kierkegaard, *Postscript* 1, 123, 320–22; S.V. 9, 105–6; 10, 25–27.
9. Kierkegaard, *Fragments*, 61; S. V. 6, 48.
10. Ibid. 90ff.; S.V. 6, 67ff.
11. Kierkegaard, *Concept of Anxiety*, 9ff., 11ff., 14; S.V. 6, 109ff., 111ff., 114–15.
12. Kierkegaard, *Sickness unto Death*, 55; S.V. 15, 117–18.
13. Kierkegaard, *Postscript* 1, 111ff.; S.V. 9, 94ff. Compare the dialogue in Kierkegaard, *Journals*, 552; Kierkegaard, *Papirer* VI A 145.
14. Kierkegaard, *Postscript* 1, 335; S.V. 10, 39n.; cf. *Papirer* IV B 21.
15. Kierkegaard, *Postscript* 1, 279; S.V. 9, 95 (my translation).

Kierkegaard and Philosophy (ii)

The second point that Kierkegaard criticizes concerning Hegelian dialectic is the concept of "mediation," which is the link intended to bind together two ideas and so keep the dialectic in motion. How, asks Kierkegaard, does this mediation arise? "Does it result from the fact that the two moments strive to unite? Is it contained in the *a priori*? Is it added to them as something new?"[16] On this matter Kierkegaard refers to Trendelenburg who shows that, although Hegel thought he was effecting movement through logic alone, he was actually presupposing it.[17]

EXCURSUS: THE INFLUENCE OF TRENDELENBURG

The influence of Trendelenburg's logic on Kierkegaard can hardly be overemphasized; but it would be quite wrong to say that he simply borrowed his logic from Trendelenburg. Though Kierkegaard himself had left us in no doubt about his indebtedness to Trendelenburg[18] no mention, I think, was made of this before Walter Lowrie drew attention to it.[19] It is strange that at that time when Kierkegaard was spoken of simply as a critic of Hegel nobody recalled the saying of Paul Hendel, "There can be no great philosophy on the European stage since the intriguer Trendelenburg murdered the hero Hegel." When Kierkegaard first read Trendelenburg is difficult to decide; but we are fairly safe in assuming that his interest in him was first roused by the latter's work on Aristotle. The first real reference to Trendelenburg, an undated entry in the *Journal* of 1842–43, in fact concerns Socrates' use of parable; the crucial reference is to Trendelenburg's work on Aristotelian logic: "Socrates is mentioned as using the parable—Aristotle Rhetoric II Chapter 20—The same passage is actually cited as an example of an incorrect analogical conclusion. See Trendelenburg, *Erlauterungen zu den Elementen der aristotelischen Logik*."[20] From the phrase "The same passage is actually cited" it is unclear whether Kierkegaard had in fact read the comment in Aristotle—at least perhaps as a quotation in Tennemann's history—before reading Trendelenburg. That is possible since his earliest references to Aristotle concern ethics and aesthetics; but our concern here is

---

16. Kierkegaard, *Repetition*, 33–34; S.V. 5, 130–31.
17. Kierkegaard, *Postscript* 1, 110; S.V. 9, 94.
18. See Kierkegaard, *Journals and Papers*, 5978; Kierkegaard, *Papirer* VIII1 A 18.
19. Lowrie, *Kierkegaard*, 7.
20. Kierkegaard, *Journals and Papers* 4252; Kierkegaard, *Papirer* IV A 205.

with what he owed to Trendelenburg's logic rather than what he learned about Aristotle generally from reading Trendelenburg. On 13 February 1843 he bought Trendelenburg's *Elementa Logices Aristotelicae* (2nd ed., Berlin, 1842) and *Erlauterungen zu den Elementen der aristotelischen Logik*,[21] then on 7 May *Die Logische Frage in Hegel System*, and finally, on 15 January 1844, the famous *Logische Untersuchungen*.

It would seem likely that this discovery of Trendelenburg lies behind the comment on Hegelian logic in *Concept of Anxiety*, which was published in 1844: "It is therefore a superstition when it is maintained in logic that through a continued quantification a new quality is brought forth. It is an unforgivable reticence when one makes no secret of the fact that things indeed do not happen quite that way in the world and yet conceals the consequences by permitting it to drift into logical movement as does Hegel."[22]

What Kierkegaard had learned from the Danish Hegelians and what he knew of Hegel had led him to regard this view of life as "unreal," but it was his study of Trendelenburg's interpretation of Aristotle's logic that helped him reach this kind of clarity. In 1844 he must have been reading Trendelenburg rather carefully since there are several undated entries in the *Journal* and the Papers of that year. The first of these is a rather puzzling discussion of the place of presupposition in philosophy, which is in fact reminiscent of Trendelenburg's *Logische Untersuchungen* I, pp. 24ff.: "The dialectic of beginning is quite commonplace; yet one side is forgotten—that the beginning must be a breaking off, and therefore it presupposed a whole line of thought in order to make a beginning; for if something else is not presupposed, the act whereby I abstract from everything is presupposed. But this I cannot do, I cannot get around to making a beginning since I am using all my powers in order to abstract from everything."[23]

Inference and the nature of demonstration were matters that Kierkegaard was considering in connection with the issue of ultimate proof. Here too he found some enlightenment in Trendelenburg. He notes: "Basic principles can be demonstrated only indirectly (negatively). The idea is frequently found and developed in Trendelenburg's

21. See the editor's note to Kierkegaard, *Papirer* IV A 40 referring to bills from the bookseller P. G. Philipsen.

22. Kierkegaard, *Concept of Anxiety*, 30; S.V. 6, 169.

23. Kierkegaard, *Journals and Papers*, 768; Kierkegaard, *Papirer* V A 70.

Logische Untersuchungen. It is significant to me for the leap and to show that the ultimate can be reached only as limit. (*In margin:* See Trendelenburg's *Elementa* p. 15n. and p. 16, and many passages in *Logische Untersuchungen*)."[24]

The same entry refers to Trendelenburg's *Erlauterungen* (p. 58) and then to the fact that analogical and inductive inference both involve a LEAP (a word that is put in capital letters), other inference being really tautologous. That comment displays a very clear understanding of the nature of inferential truth. However, what is significant with regard to Kierkegaard's view of logic and metaphysics is his final comment "Trendelenburg does not seem to be at all aware of the leap." The reason for this, he would think, was that Trendelenburg drew all his examples from mathematics and theoretical sciences and employed "almost no examples of the ethical in logic."[25]

KIERKEGAARD'S CRITIQUE OF HEGEL IN HISTORICAL CONTEXT

To return to the critique of Hegelian logic as a false claim to be a movement, this was Kierkegaard's clearly established view by 1844. In *Concept of Anxiety* he emphatically denied that movement can be a part of logic: "In logic, no movement must *come about*, for logic is, and whatever is logical only is. This impotence of the logical consists in the transition of logic into becoming, where existence (*Tilvaerelse*) and actuality come forth. So when logic becomes deeply absorbed in the concretion of the categories, that which was from the beginning is ever the same."[26] The contrast here is between logic with its unchanging necessity and the fluid changing world of movement. Therefore, when the notion of movement is introduced into logic the result is a contradiction in terms, as Kierkegaard puts it, at the point where movement begins logic sees merely an interruption of itself such as can only be overcome by a leap.[27] That is to say, there is no unbroken argument of which movement is a part.

---

24. Kierkegaard, *Journals and Papers*, 2341; Kierkegaard, *Papirer* V A 74.
25. Kierkegaard, *Journals and Papers*, 2352; Kierkegaard, *Papirer* V C 12.
26. Kierkegaard, *Concept of Anxiety*, 13; S.V. 6, 112.
27. Kierkegaard, *Postscript*, 109; S.V. 7, 93.

Thus far I have been concerned with the Hegelian notion of dialectic and Kierkegaard's criticism of it. It is worth pointing out that this has to be seen against the background of a debate concerning the foundation of logic which began in 1839 in Copenhagen and in which Mynster and Sibbern attacked the Hegelian position which was then defended by Heiberg and Martensen.[28] The controversy was, in a sense, sparked off by Martensen's dissertation, which evoked a response by J. A. Bornemann in *Tidsskrift for Litteratur og Kritik* in which he argued that the present age must go beyond the traditional postulation of irreconcilable opposites. Unity and coherence must be brought to life's diversity, a demand met by the Hegelian establishment of the subjective and the objective. Mynster too took up the cudgels against what he saw as a typical example of the Hegelian demolition of the fundamental principles of logic.[29] Mynster's point was that there was a clear dichotomy between rationalism's rejection of revelation and supranaturalism's adoption of revelation as a basis; and either this dichotomy is recognized or one abandons the principle of the excluded middle.[30] One can, he argues, mediate between contrasts (*modsaetning*) but not between contradictions (*modsigelser*).[31]

Inevitably there was a Hegelian response—papers by Heiberg and Martensen. Heiberg's was formal and haughty in tone as he opposed the "logical superstition" which used the principles of contradiction and exclusion as "bogeys although the very restricted understanding to which the said principles are reduced belong to the completely undisputed result of the new philosophy."[32] Martensen's paper in a sense sought to present an *ad hominem* argument against Mynster. Supranaturalism, he argued, is not one end of a disjunction. The essential doctrine of Christianity, the incarnation, cannot be fitted into an either-or but is a both-and. From this arises speculative theology with its presupposition

---

28. A detailed account of this debate and its significance for Kierkegaard's thought is given by Victor Kuhr in *Modsigelsens Grundsaetning*. Other references which yield some information about the course of this debate are: Arildsen, *Biskop Hans Lassen Martensen*, I, 142–50, and Martensen, *Af mit Levnet*, II, 70ff. In *Science of Logic* Hegel asserts that contradiction resolves itself and so dubs the law of contradiction one of the fundamental prejudices of logic (See Hegel's *Science of Logic*, 439ff).

29. Mynster, *Blandede Skrifter*, Vol. 2, 95f. See also Wange, *J. P. Mynster og de philosophiske Bevaegelse*, 130, and Schwanenflugel, *J. P. Mynster*, Vol. 1, 181 and 185f.

30. Mynster, *Blandede Skrifter*, 113.

31. Ibid., 114.

32. Heiberg, *Prosaiske Skrifter*, Vol. 2, 169, 170, 186.

of the identity of the objective and subjective. While the controversy was basically on issues of doctrine or, more precisely, on theological stance, there is no doubt that the logical problem was given a great airing.

Mynster returned to the debate three years later with another article in the same journal—"*Om de logiske principer*" ("Concerning Logical Principles"). He deplored the Hegelian tendency to abuse the correct meaning of terms like "principle of exclusion," "principle of contradiction," and "principle of identity." We must, he argued, be clear that "A is A, A is not not-A, and therefore A is either B or not-B."[33]

Kierkegaard does not seem to have taken much interest in the controversy—at least, to the best of my knowledge, nowhere in his *Journal* or *Papers* does he make any specific reference to it. The only *Journal* entry that could be so construed is that of 14 June 1839, asserting that absolute opposites cannot be mediated.[34] According to the editor's note in *Papirer* this is a reference to Mynster's article and Sibbern's review of Heiberg's *Perseus*. However, the reason for Kierkegaard's silence may simply be that even two years earlier he had already been thinking about the relation between logic and existence. Furthermore, a comment in *Concluding Unscientific Postscript* shows very clearly that he had noted it and had ever since counted Mynster on the side of the angels in regard to Hegelian logic. He says:

> As is well known, Hegelian philosophy has cancelled the principle of contradiction, and Hegel himself has more than once emphatically held judgment day on the kind of thinkers who ... have ... insisted that there is an either-or. Since that time it has become a popular game, so that as soon as someone hints at an *aut-aut* a Hegelian comes riding trip-trap-trap on a horse ... and wins a victory and rides home again. Among us too the Hegelians [Here the draft reads, "Messrs. Prof. Heiberg and Martensen"—*Papirer* VI B 54: 4; and the final draft reads, "Thus among us Prof. Martensen and Heiberg have ..."—*Papirer* VI B 98: 58] have several times been on the move especially against Bp. Mynster in order to win speculative thought's brilliant victory; and Bp. Mynster has more than once become a defeated standpoint, even though, for being a defeated standpoint he is holding up very well, and it is rather to be feared that the enor-

---

33. Mynster, *Blandede Skrifter*, Vol. 2, 134.
34. Kierkegaard, *Journals and Papers*, 1578; Kierkegaard, *Papirer* II A 454.

mous exertion of the victory has been too exhausting for the undefeated victors.[35]

What, of course, must be borne in mind is the fact that until his sojourn in Berlin Kierkegaard had only a scanty knowledge of Hegelian logic or indeed of any logic. Beyond reading Sibbern's 1835 book on logic during 1838 he had probably done nothing to acquire any knowledge of the development of logic. Even so, I would argue that he even then demonstrated his intuitive grasp of fundamental logic.

THE INFLUENCE OF ARISTOTLE'S PHILOSOPHY ON KIERKEGAARD

Though we are considering a period later than the controversy of 1839, it is worth mentioning that Kierkegaard's growing understanding of logic owes much to his close study of Aristotle, something probably first stimulated by his study of Tennemann's *Geschichte der Philosophie*.[36] In particular, he was fascinated by Aristotle's treatment of motion (κινησις) as the fulfillment of potential existence. He had noted the distinction that Leibniz made between quantity and quality[37] and had raised the question whether the passage from a quantitative conception to a qualitative one is possible without a leap, adding, "Does not the whole of life lie here?" This is, I think, indicative of the way in which Kierkegaard shared the nineteenth-century approach to ontology but was becoming very much aware that there were logical problems which were being glossed over by contemporary metaphysicians.

What concerns us at the moment is that this kind of logical investigation was very much in his mind during the 1840s. In 1842, A. P. Adler, whose name is more usually encountered in connection with the religious and especially the ecclesiological aspects of Kierkegaard's thought, had given a lecture in Copenhagen on Hegel's objective logic. The published version was bought by Kierkegaard (No. 383 of the auction catalogue of his library) and in 1844 he quotes p. 48 making reference to Hegel's *Science of Logic*.[38] Even more significant is the reference to Trendelenburg in the next entry because that is not a reference to

---

35. Kierkegaard, *Postscript* 1, 304–5; S.V. 7, 261.
36. See Kierkegaard, *Fragments*, 280ff.
37. Leibniz, *Théodicée*, 212–13. See Kierkegaard, *Papirer* IV B 37 and IV B 87.
38. Kierkegaard, *Papirer* V B 49.

the *Erlauterungen den Elementen der aristotelischen Logik*, which he had bought in February 1843, but to the two-volume *Die Logische Frage in Hegels System*. Not surprisingly he links the reference to his growing appreciation of Aristotle—Trendelenburg, he says, "is much interested in Greek philosophy and so does not accept nonsense for his money." It is quite clear, then, that during 1844 he worked hard on Trendelenburg's logic.

As was mentioned earlier, this absorbing interest in logic had begun with his reading of Tennemann's account of Aristotle. He had acquired the twelve volumes of the *Geschichte* and certainly from 1842 onwards had studied them carefully. Very early in his development he had been struck by what Kant has to say about existence[39] and it remained a point of departure for him in his thinking.[40] In his reading of Tennemann he had been similarly struck by Tennemann's translation of κινησις as "change," "The transition from possibility to actuality is a change—thus Tennemann translates κινησις; if this is correct this sentence is of the utmost importance. Κινησις is difficult to define because it belongs neither to possibility nor to actuality, is more than possibility and less than actuality."[41]

Arnold B. Come points out that the background to this is Aristotle's rejection of the Eleatic thesis that there is no distinction between potentiality and actuality.[42] He quotes W. & M. Kneale's comment that for Aristotle this "is equivalent in effect to a denial of motion or change of any kind ... To Aristotle it would appear to be a denial of the distinction between the possible and the actual."[43]

Typically what matters to Kierkegaard is not the technical issues in logic but its wider ramifications in ontology in regard to Hegel's notions of the possibility of movement and especially the notion of "mediation." It was not in fact until late 1842 that Kierkegaard had actually read Aristotle seriously, as he remarks in his undated *Journal* entry of 1844, "A year and a half ago I began a little essay *De omnibus dubitandum*, in which I made my first attempt at a little speculative development. The motivating concept I used was error. Aristotle does the same.

39. Cf. Kierkegaard, *Papirer* II A 47.
40. Cf. Kierkegaard, *Papirer* X2 A 328.
41. Kierkegaard, *Journals and Papers*, 258; Kierkegaard, *Papirer* IV 7.
42. Come, *Trendelenburg's Influence on Kierkegaard's Modal Categories*, 10.
43. Kneale and Kneale, *The Development of Logic*, 117.

At that time I had not read a bit of Aristotle but a good share of Plato."[44] It is interesting to note that in the same entry he exclaims "Praised be Trendelenburg"—which suggests that he was now guided in his reading of Aristotle by what he found in Trendelenburg. As Niels Thulstrup noted in his superb commentary on *Philosophical Fragments*, it is characteristic of Kierkegaard that, though his main concern in the work was to attack the speculative reconciliation of Christianity and Idealism, he goes back not only to Plato as the original Idealist but also to Aristotle, "the master of classical logic."[45] He owned the eleven-volume Aldin edition of Aristotle's works, Buhle's five-volume edition, and the two volumes then available of Bekker's Akademi edition as well as various translations. His comment that before 1842 he had not read Aristotle seems then something of an exaggeration; and, in any case, he would know Poul Møller's lectures on ancient philosophy as well as what mention would have been made of Aristotle in the lectures of speculative dogmatics which Martensen delivered during the winter semester of 1837–38 (*Prolegomena til den speculative Dogmatik*). Also, as was suggested above, he would have gained a quite substantial knowledge of Aristotle from his reading of Tennemann's *Geschichte*.[46]

The discussion in *Philosophical Fragments* of existence and the various logical formulations of statements about existence are extremely involved, if not indeed convoluted. They demand careful reading and unpicking of threads. This is due not so much to the difficulty of grasping the underlying philosophical purpose of the discussion as to the variety of the sources on which it draws. Yet one thing is clear enough: the reference on p. 92 to the "Aristotelian principle" would indicate that somehow Kierkegaard had been made aware of Aristotle's modal treatment of logical contradiction in *De Interpretatione*.[47] Whether he was sufficiently clear on the *metaphysical* issue here involved does not in any way minimize the importance of recognizing that knowledge of Aristotle lay behind his thinking at this time. That is evident from the other reference to Aristotle on the same page—again to *De Interpretatione*—when he speaks of "the two kinds of possibility in relation to the necessary."

44. Kierkegaard, *Journals and Papers*, 3300; Kierkegaard, *Papirer* V A 98.

45. Kierkegaard, *Philosophical Fragments*, 233.

46. See, for example, Kierkegaard, *Journals and Papers*, 5598; Kierkegaard, *Papirer* IV C 45.

47. Aristotle, *Works* I 216ff.

His own comment on "the Aristotelian doctrine" is rather trite—that Aristotle should have recognized that "possibility cannot be predicated of the necessary." The important point, as far as he was concerned, is the Kantian perception that in speaking of existence what matters is actuality. In working out this point he clearly reverts to his original interest in the Aristotelian understanding of change (κίνησις) and says, "The change involved in coming into existence is actuality; the transition takes place with freedom."[48] Thus he shows his typical interest in the relation of this logical question to ethics. What is equally typical is the way he glosses the remark with a further logical comment about coming into existence, "It was not necessary before the coming into existence, for then there could not have been the coming into existence, nor after the coming into existence, for then there would not have been the coming into existence." By the time he wrote *Philosophical Fragments* Kierkegaard had gained enough by way of logical competence to have a clear view on the issue of the 1839 debate and clearly rejected the Hegelian doctrine of the concept of identity. An undated passage in the *Journal* of that time shows this: "As long as I live in time, the principle of identity is only an abstraction. Therefore nothing is easier than to delude oneself and others into thinking the identity of all by abandoning diversity . . . As long as I live, I live in contradiction, for life is contradiction."[49]

AGAINST HEGEL'S SYSTEM OF EXISTENCE

What Kierkegaard does in *Philosophical Fragments* is to employ the logical apparatus he had acquired in order to engage with the Hegelian metaphysics that would explain both actuality and thought in terms of the absolute. The commentator has the difficult task of noting the *details* rather than the rhetoric of the "Interlude" in order to follow the main point that is being made by the plot of this drama. Before turning to what was and has remained a crucially important discussion of a fundamental problem in Christology, "The Apprehension of the Past,"[50] he refers in a note to "The Absolute Method, Hegel's discovery" as a "glittering tautology." The reference is to Hegel's *Philosophy of Religion*: "There can be but one method in all science, since the method is the self-

---

48. Kierkegaard, *Philosophical Fragments*, 93.
49. Kierkegaard, *Journals and Papers*, 708; Kierkegaard, *Papirer* V A 68.
50. Kierkegaard, *Philosophical Fragments*, 97ff.

governing Notion [*Begriff*] and nothing else, and this latter is only one."[51] Hegel's explanation of "the absolute method" is to be found in *Science of Logic*: "Accordingly, what must now be considered as method is no more than the movement of the Notion itself, whose nature has already been understood. This meaning, however, is now to be added, that the Notion is everything . . . Here the method must be recognized as universal . . . The method therefore is both soul and substance, and nothing is either conceived or known in its truth except insofar as it is completely subject to the method."[52]

Because his concern in *Philosophical Fragments* is in a sense more theological than philosophical, Kierkegaard leaves this issue of ontology to move on to the epistemological problem of what it is to know a historical fact. In the larger canvas of his oeuvre it is not forgotten and is something taken up again in *Concluding Unscientific Postscript*.

As a postscript, as this big work is ironically described, Kierkegaard could assume that the complex argument laid out in *Philosophical Fragments* would be presupposed. Now his main point regarding ontology is that because the Hegelian logic does not work, the notion of system—or more precisely that of a system of existence—cannot be defended. There may well be a system of existence that is situated only in the realm of possibility and does not attain to that of reality. Only by means of such subterfuges in his dialectic of the beginning and of movement can Hegel falsely present his system of being as a system of existence and transform his logic into an ontology. When he asserts then that in this system of pure thought the principle of contradiction is overcome by identity that is not surprising; for contradiction is the hallmark of the real and it is precisely the real which Hegel has abstracted: "Hegel is utterly and absolutely right in asserting that viewed eternally, *sub specie aeterni*, in the language of abstraction, in pure thought and pure being, there is no either-or. How in the world could there be, when abstract thought has taken away the contradiction . . ."[53] This passage echoes the note about the principle of identity to which reference was made above.[54]

One of the most important ideas for which Kierkegaard found confirmation in Trendelenburg was that proof moves *from*, rather than to,

51. Hegel, *Philosophy of Religion*, Vol. 1, 9.
52. Hegel, *Science of Logic*, 468.
53. Kierkegaard, *Postscript* 1, 305; S.V. 10, 12.
54. Kierkegaard, *Papirer* V A 68.

existence. This is an essential part of his criticism of the attempt to prove the existence of God.[55] It is, however, equally an essential part of his critique of the idea of an existential system.

On the first issue, what Kierkegaard has to say is well known. The ancient philosophers, he contends, were not as naïve as their modern successors. They did not pretend that they arrived at God's existence without starting from it. Whether this is an accurate account either of the ancient philosophers of Greece or of someone like Aquinas is really irrelevant to the validity of Kierkegaard's argument. Yet it is worth noting that on this there might very well be greater agreement between Aquinas and Kierkegaard than one would expect. It has not been sufficiently noted that St. Thomas's basic doctrine concerning God is that He is strictly unknowable, "*Hoc est ultimum cognitionis humanae de Deo, quod sciat se Deum nescire.*"[56] Also it seems to me unthinkable that St. Thomas should have been philosophically so obtuse as to have failed to see that the Five Ways are not capable of providing a rigid demonstration. The truth is that the identification of the maker referred to in the proofs with the God of the Bible represents, I think, what Kierkegaard calls "the leap."[57] What Kierkegaard saw so clearly was that arguments concerning the existence of God, though they clarify the concept of God, can never tell us anything about His real existence. If there is a conclusion it emerges by a leap.

Criticizing the metaphysical dream of a system of existence, Kierkegaard argued that all thought is abstract. The fundamental problem that Hegel does not face is the relation of the empirical subject of thought to the subject of pure thought. He asserts that the absolute is because I think it, and in order to make his position more secure he turns the statement round and says that my thinking of the absolute is the self-thinking of the absolute in me.[58] But pure thought is then described not only as absolute but also in terms of some subject which is absolute so that unless we are to go on talking of two subjects we are bound to assert the coincidence of the empirical and the absolute subject. The question, however, is whether there is any room for the empirical here.[59] How,

---

55. Kierkegaard, *Fragments*, 50; S.V. 6, 40–41.
56. Aquinas, *De Potentia*, 7, 5, 14.
57. Cf. White, *God the Unknown*, and Sillem, *Ways of Thinking about God*.
58. Cf. Kierkegaard, *Either-Or* II, 178; S.V. 3, 164.
59. Kierkegaard, *Postscript* 1, 301; S.V. 10, 9.

by what act, does this sometimes sad professorial figure transform itself into the fantastic subject of pure thought? This is Kierkegaard's ever-recurring question because he is primarily interested in the real existence of the thinker him- or herself, and this real existence is to be discovered by the thinker only in action. However, he says, one would look in vain for this interest in Hegel.[60] What was needed was a Greek or ethical dialectic, and to supply this was Kierkegaard's aim.

KINESIS

Before considering how such a dialectic is ethical we must consider the other Greek elements in Kierkegaard's dialectic. The decisive category on which all others depend, he says, is that of *kinesis*: "The category which I was anxious to make central . . . is that of movement [*kinesis*] which perhaps forms one of the most difficult problems in the whole of philosophy. In modern philosophy it has been expressed differently, *i.e.* as transition or mediation."[61] The transition from thinking to being is effected in the moment of *kinesis*.

Though he complains that "the moderns have given no definition of a category" and that Hegel thus always leaves the more difficult part of the job to the reader,[62] no more does Kierkegaard himself give one. He remarks that he would like someone to offer a critique of Hegel by taking up the question of category—or more especially the question "in what sense the categories constitute an abridgement of existence, whether logical thought is abstract after existence or abstract without any relation to existence."[63] The critique he himself effects is that the uniting of thought with being is achieved by *kinesis*, and here again there is indebtedness to Trendelenburg. Trendelenburg, Kierkegaard remarks, is much taken with the Greek philosophy and will not take nonsense for his money.[64] Once more, then, he sought to understand his distaste for

---

60. Ibid., 307–9; S.V. 10, 15–16.
61. See Kierkegaard, *Papirer* IV C 97.
62. Ibid., C 63.
63. Kierkegaard, *Postscript* 1, 111; S.V. 9, 95. cf. Kierkegaard, *Papirer* VI B 131 : "What is a category and what is it to say that being is a category? Is it an abbreviation as the history of the world is set aside?" Compare also the reference to Heiberg and to a lecture on Hegel's logic given by A. P. Adler in Copenhagen in 1842 (Kierkegaard, *Papirer* V B 495).
64. Kierkegaard, *Papirer* V B 496. This note refers to Trendelenburg's two-volumed work on the logical question in Hegel's philosophy.

Hegel in terms of the philosophical controversy in which Hegelianism was now involved.

What interested Kierkegaard was not so much the problem of categories in general, then, but the problem of transition—that of the transition from quantitative to qualitative, for instance, which Hegel accomplished with such ease. This was a problem that occupied his thoughts during 1842 and 1843. Reading Leibniz's *Théodicée* at this period he notes that Leibniz draws a distinction between quantity and quality.[65] Later he asks whether the transition from quantity to quality is possible without a leap.[66]

It was in *Fragments* and *Anxiety* that this criticism of Hegel's logic found expression. For example, he argues that it is "a superstition when in logic one will assert that from a continued progression of something quantitative there emerges a new quality; it is an intolerable subterfuge, when one does not make a secret of the fact that things are not entirely like this, but one does hide the consequences of this principle for the whole of logical immanence and asserts it within the logic of dialectic as Hegel does."[67]

The inference from quantity to quality can only be made by Hegel within the boundaries of logic because the being with which he is concerned is only a product of his immanentist thought and is not real being. The problem which confronted Kierkegaard here was how real being was presupposed in this process of supplying qualitative concepts to being; and it was here that Trendelenburg's exposition of Aristotle proved useful. In the series of notes dealing with the problem of being there is one that refers explicitly to Trendelenburg's work on Aristotle's logic.[68] Struggling with this logical problem in Hegel, Kierkegaard had read A. P. Adler, who had given a lecture in Copenhagen on Hegel's objective logic in 1842, and Rosenkrantz's book on Schelling,[69] as well as the notes he himself had made of Schelling's lectures in Berlin.[70] The subject of these lectures was the philosophy of reality, which is why they had filled

---

65. This is a reference to Leibniz's *Théodicée*, 212–13. Kierkegaard, *Papirer* IV C 37.
66. Kierkegaard, *Papirer* IV C 87.
67. Kierkegaard, *S.V.* VI, 125 (my translation); Kierkegaard, *Concept of Anxiety*, 30.
68. Kierkegaard, *Papirer* V C 10.
69. Kierkegaard, *Papirer* V C 5. He had bought this book on 30 April 1843—see IV A 185n.
70. Kierkegaard, *Papirer* V C 2.

Kierkegaard with such hope at first. It was, however, Trendelenburg and not Schelling from whom the real illumination came.[71]

As I have already indicated, Kierkegaard's concern was not purely logical. This becomes clear as he moves on to the further criticism that all thought is abstract so that the metaphysical dream of a system of reality is folly. Kierkegaard's point here is not only that thought lacks some of the detail of reality. This, for all that it will tell us about the open character of empirical language, is less important than Kierkegaard's characteristic point, which concerns the nature rather than the quantity of the detail. What he is attacking is the assumption that the philosopher is a spectator, an assumption which takes no account of the philosopher's own historical reality. And if the philosopher can delude himself that his historical situation does not make any difference then he may go on to say that his situation in real life is irrelevant to philosophy. We know that in life this is what is important.

So Kierkegaard contrasts existence with thought to show the difference between the necessity of logical relationships and the contingent connections of practical inference. If the philosopher pretends to make logic related to existence then his position is false precisely because what seems a necessity turns out to depend on some initial assumption. "In a logical system nothing may be incorporated that has relation to existence . . . The infinite advantage that the logical by being the objective possesses over all other thinking is in turn, subjectively viewed, restricted by its being a hypothesis, simply because it is indifferent to existence understood as actuality."[72]

In so far, then, as logical thought operates only in terms of one mode of being—ideal being—it cannot pose the problem of the relationship between two distinct modes of being. This was the argument of the *Fragments* to which reference has already been made; that everything that comes into being proves thereby that it is not necessary.[73]

What is very interesting as a clue to Kierkegaard's meaning here is the relevant portion of the draft, which is in fact not used in the book.[74] It contains a very sharp comment on Hegel's "absolute method," which Hegel claimed to be as applicable in historical science as it was in logic.

---

71. Kierkegaard, See *Papirer* VII C 1.
72. Kierkegaard, *Postscript* 1, 111; S.V. 9, 94.
73. Kierkegaard, *Fragments*, 90–91; S.V. 6, 67–68.
74. Kierkegaard, *Papirer* V B 14 and 41.

Certainly, it says, Hegel was a great logician, "but along with this he had a partiality for logical gimcrackery." Kierkegaard's reaction is to reject this "gimcrackery," and his studies in the history of philosophy confirmed him in this view.[75]

There is, of course, no doubt that his aim in all this work was to demolish the speculative idealism that had absorbed the Christian faith into itself, but my point is that he achieved this aim by expounding the nature of change. Both of these points can be appreciated if we consider the argument of *Fragments* on the change involved in coming into existence. "The change involved in coming into existence is actuality; the transition takes place with freedom. No coming into existence is necessary. It was not necessary before the coming into existence, for then there could not have been the coming into existence, nor after the coming into existence, for then there would not have been the coming into existence."[76]

What is most significant about this argument is the introduction of the concept of freedom, which brings us to the ethical dialectic of existence and its characteristic category of the leap.

THE ETHICAL DIALECTIC OF EXISTENCE AND THE LEAP

Though these concepts are most important for Kierkegaard's analysis of the nature of Christian faith and discipleship the notion of *leap* is, I think, also used by him to indicate the logical discontinuity generally.[77] Reading his papers of this period we can see that Kierkegaard was concerned with the philosophical problem posed by Hegel's alleged transition from essence to existence, and the fact that this is what is decisive in his later argument against the Hegelian synthesis of faith and

---

75. Kierkegaard had by this time read a great deal of the literature on Aristotle—histories such as Tennemann's *Geschichte der Philosophie* (see Kierkegaard, *Papirer* IV C 45) and especially studies such as Trendelenburg's *Elementa* and *Erlauterungen* (see ibid., A 40), and he had also read such Aristotelian texts as the *Nicomachean Ethics* (see ibid., IV A 209).

76. Kierkegaard, *Fragments*, 93; S.V. 6, 69.

77. For discussion of this aspect of Kierkegaard's thought see Thomte, *Kierkegaard's Philosophy of Religion*; Diem, *Kierkegaard's Dialectic of Existence*, and my own *Philosophy of Religion in Kierkegaard's Writings*. Examples of the use of "leap" with which I am here concerned are Kierkegaard, *Papirer* IV B 37 and 87 to which, reference has already been made; but the most significant is *Papirer* V C 1, which deals with the leap in the sphere of logic with reference to Hegel and not merely religion.

philosophy does not alter this in any way.[78] It is also worth pointing out that Kierkegaard's thought was obviously derived from the anti-Hegelian movement in philosophy. For instance, he was encouraged in his suspicion that this transition in the Hegelian philosophy was impossible by the criticism Schelling had made of Hegel.[79] For Schelling Hegel's philosophy was the most important example of what he called a "negative" approach to reality. Every philosophy must begin with a logical analysis; but this logical analysis is negative in the sense that it abstracts from real conditions. Hegel's mistake, thought Schelling, was to take negative philosophy as the exhaustive account of being. He himself, however, wanted logic to effect some limitation of its scope so that real existence could be treated by a positive philosophy. It is, I think, a mark of his greatness as a philosopher that Kierkegaard saw the issues more clearly and made his logical points more clearly than did Schelling and Von Baader, not confusing the issue by introducing mythology into metaphysics.

It is time now to show how Kierkegaard connects these logical points with the ethico-religious polemic that was his main concern. The first point that one needs to understand is that the problem of the relation of logic to existence is raised most acutely by the phenomenon of coming-into-being. This is why Kierkegaard argues so forcefully in *Fragments* and *Postscript* that "nothing comes into existence by virtue of a logical ground."[80] All other kinds of change quite clearly presuppose the existence of the thing that changes; but if I say that X comes into being I cannot presuppose the existence of X. Also Kierkegaard points out, in an argument that is reminiscent of Kant and his example of the Hundred Thalers, that the subject coming into existence remains unchanged during the change of coming into existence. If not, he says, "that which comes into existence is not this subject which comes into existence but something else."[81] Therefore, it cannot be the case that the transition from possibility to actuality is a change in essence. With Hegel

---

78. Kierkegaard, *Papirer* V C 2, 4 and 9 are ample evidence of this interest.

79. Cf. Kierkegaard, *Papirer* V C 2 where there is a reminiscence of a comment Schelling had made of Hegel's disapproval of "the plain intellectual intuition." On 30 April 1843 Kierkegaard bought Schelling's *Vorlesungen über des academischen studium* (ibid., IV A 185) and after the appearance of a discussion of *Repetition* in *Urania* he drafted a polemic (ibid., IV B 100–117) about Schelling's concept of movement and freedom in relation to Hegel's view.

80. Kierkegaard, *Fragments*, 93; S.V. 6, 69–70.

81. Ibid. 90; S.V. 6, 68.

the opposite was the case; for the only genuine possibility—indeed the only possibility—is a possibility that has been raised to necessity and coincides with the actual.[82]

It is interesting to see Kierkegaard referring here to Aristotle's discussion of negation of judgments of possibility,[83] but this is simply a gratuitous piece of logical refinement. His main point is that Hegel's kind of interpretation makes it impossible to view the transitions of existence as properly the products of freedom and therefore we do not take choice seriously.

It is this connection between metaphysics, morals, and logic which explains why Kierkegaard in his *Journal* expounded the point of *Either-Or* thus: "My particular concern with the whole of *Either-Or* is: that it should be quite clear that the metaphysical significance at the bottom of the whole work leads everything back to dilemma. The same thing is also at the bottom of the little philosophical essay: 'Tautology as the highest principle of thought.'"[84]

The relation of this essay to the controversy in Copenhagen about Hegel's logic has already been explained. What is important now is that we see that the significance Kierkegaard attached to this was the same as that which he attached to *Either-Or* as a whole. The very tools of the Hegelian dialectic are here used to make a fundamental criticism of it. The logical debate is in the interest of a religious purpose. Hegel wants us to be as gods, but our aim should be to produce a philosophy for human living. Though Kierkegaard often speaks as if Hegel had not written anything about human existence, what he meant was that all Hegel's treatment of human attitudes and outlooks was a reduction of choice to logic. From *The Concept of Irony* (1841) onwards he took characteristically Hegelian terminology and used it to make his great accusation against Hegel—that his philosophy made human existence a mere shadow play beside what is eternally decided from behind. In his delineation of the stages of life's way Kierkegaard insisted that the transition from one to the other was only effected by a leap. Thus his criticism of Hegel could be said to be that Hegel's phenomenology was not phenomenological enough. What Hegel had done in interpreting the various human out-

---

82. See Hegel, *Science of Logic*, 544, cf. Wallace, *The Logic of Hegel*, 264.

83. Kierkegaard, *Fragments*, 92; S.V. 6, 69, referring to Aristotle's *De Interpretatione* (Aristotle, *Works* I 21b ff.).

84. Kierkegaard, *Journals*, 405; Kierkegaard, *Papirer* III B 177.

looks was to foist a logical pattern of relations upon them. Instead of talking about the problem of choice we therefore talk of the progression of thesis through antithesis to synthesis.

As Paul Weiss remarks, Kierkegaard found Hegel's view of existence intolerable and in this he resembled Marx. Weiss, however, has other more dubious things to say:

> Hegel, in his logics, treated Existence as a category like any other; it was for him part of a single totality of categories or ideas through which the Spirit goes in the course of its relentless movement from mere being to the absolute idea. Kierkegaard, a Hegelian of the right, like Marx, a Hegelian of the left, found this view of Existence intolerable. Existence, for both of them was more than any idea or category or essence could ever be. Assuming with Hegel that he had written the Logic and *the* Philosophy, they had no other alternative but to abandon both logic and philosophy and try some other way of getting to Existence, as that which is forever and utterly beyond all understanding. They became activists, the one rushing headlong to his God, the other throwing himself into the violent currents of history.[85]

I have quoted Weiss at length to show how easy it is to misinterpret Kierkegaard. Also I want to comment on one aspect of Weiss's misinterpretation of the topic that we have been discussing. Kierkegaard is characterized as an activist who rushed headlong to his God. At the beginning of this chapter I suggested that it made very little difference here whether one accepted Kierkegaard's own understanding of his authorship as having from the beginning a religious purpose. If one does not accept it then one will not connect, say, *Either-Or* (with its metaphysical and logical theses) and the final "attack on Christendom"; but I have not concerned myself with this in trying to elucidate Kierkegaard's view of the relation of logic to existence. Further, though I have shown how this logical argument has an ethico-religious relevance it is also clear that Kierkegaard never abandoned either philosophy or logic. In conclusion I shall indicate how he makes further use of this logic in his philosophy of religion.

---

85. Weiss, *Modes of Being*, 193.

LOGIC AND THE EXISTENCE OF GOD

From the dissociation of logic and existence which Kierkegaard has advocated it follows that "I always reason from existence, not toward existence."[86] Applying this principle to the hoary problem of the possibility of proving God's existence, he is able to argue that proof is impossible on grounds other than that faith is inconsistent with proof or that God is transcendent. The point is simply that theistic proof can only succeed if the demonstrandum is presupposed in the proof. To prove that anything exists is a difficult matter because the proof invariably turns out to be something different from what it is assumed to be.[87]

Before moving on to the special case of God, Kierkegaard takes two other examples of proving the existence of something—proving that a stone exists and proving that Napoleon existed.[88] In both cases the demonstration turns out to be a demonstration that his existing thing is a stone or that the person who existed was Napoleon. The proof thus *presupposes* existence and does not establish it. It is little short of remarkable that in a philosophy the main object of which was to relate thinking to the ethical and religious character of life, the phenomenology of faith includes this very subtle logical attack on rationalist theology.

What I have attempted to do is to follow out the complexity of Kierkegaard's thinking on the problem of logic and existence and so show Kierkegaard as truly a philosophical reformer. What he wanted was not the end of philosophy but rather a renewed appreciation of the conjunction of thought and action by showing the fundamental *distinction* between thought and being. So he tried to keep the distinction between logic and existence clear in order to show that philosophy was a union of the intellectual and the ethical, the activity of existing man and not a disembodied or timeless mind. His understanding of Hegel led him to see him as a tragic figure who had failed—the Hegelian philosophy was neither pure logic nor existence. Kierkegaard's own achievement was the demonstration that the proper study of man is man.

---

86. Kierkegaard, *Fragments*, 50; S.V. 6, 40.
87. Kierkegaard, *Fragments*, 49; S.V. 6, 40. cf. *Papirer* V A 7.
88. Kierkegaard, *Fragments*, 50ff.; S.V. 6, 41ff.

6

Kierkegaard and Religion (i)

BACKGROUND TO KIERKEGAARD'S CRITIQUE OF THE DANISH CHURCH

Kierkegaard's Religious Upbringing

KIERKEGAARD DESCRIBED HIS UPBRINGING as "crazy" partly because his religious formation was so heavily imbued with melancholy and was so extremely unusual and severe. We recall that old Michael Kierkegaard had been close to the Moravians in Copenhagen and had supported them generously, providing money for building amongst other things. However, he was very solidly orthodox and a supporter of the established church. He had brought up his family as good Lutherans, having decided that they should attend the Church of the Holy Spirit because its minister, Pastor Bull, was in his view a sound and sincere Lutheran. After 1812, however, he had regularly taken the family to listen to the distinguished Mynster, who had recently come to Copenhagen and was to become the Bishop of Zealand. The great man's sermons and his conversations with old Michael during his regular visits to the Kierkegaard household were Søren's spiritual formation. So the background to his religious message is a Lutheranism that was very sophisticated for all that it was shot through with an ascetic piety of profound passion. However, if we are to understand it we must delineate the religious and social situation to which he addressed that message.

Social Changes in Kierkegaard's Denmark

It is difficult to recall that the Denmark of Kierkegaard's day had only just emerged from its feudal agrarian past into the modern world.[1] It was a rapid but peaceful transformation that had seen economic and social changes in all Danish society. Communal farming in small villages and on large estates disappeared as individual ownership of land grew and individuals practised farming as a business, as seems obvious from Kierkegaard's casual reference in his *Journal* during 1837 to battery chicken farming.[2] Within the cities too the economic change produced by the profit motive was obvious and with increasing competition the free enterprise system became the standard practice of industry. 1813, the year of Kierkegaard's birth, had seen a great economic crash, but with increasing investment in textiles, brewing, the new railways, and farming there was a dramatic improvement in Denmark's economic health.

The change in the economic and social situation was matched by the important developments in the political and generally cultural aspects of life. For the very first time there was an uninhibited exchange of political and cultural views thanks to the emergence of a free press. Criticism of the government became a commonplace and discussion of a variety of policies was possible. Consequently the power of the nobles and the clergy weakened as the power of the intelligentsia grew. The University of Copenhagen became a center of influence: its influence on the king in the period preceding the establishment of constitutional monarchy in 1848 was no less than its influence on the elected assembly, which became the constitutional organ of government. Nor was its more narrowly cultural influence insignificant. We have seen its importance for literature so that it is sufficient now to say that its encouragement of experimental science was such that when Darwin's *Origin of the Species* was published in 1859 the book was enthusiastically welcomed by Danish academics, who were already embracing an evolutionary view of life.

---

1. See Kirmmse, *Kierkegaard in Golden Age Denmark*.
2. Kierkegaard, *Papirer* II A 12.

KIERKEGAARD'S CHRISTIAN RESPONSE TO SOCIAL CHANGES IN DENMARK

Politically, Kierkegaard was a conservative and a snobbishly ardent royalist and it would be very easy to read his dissatisfaction with what he saw happening in society as the expression of mere prejudice and snobbery. Both faults are there, without doubt; but equally there is no denying that Kierkegaard's analysis of society shows his acumen as a sociologist of religion, as has been demonstrated by the distinguished sociologist Werner Stark.[3] In that analysis what he singles out for most serious comment is the growth of an egotism. As economic development became stronger so too there grew the prevalence of this egotism as an attitude that was part and parcel of the new social order. The very basis of society was then thought to be the priority of the individual and his inherent right to seek his own self-interest and this without reference to others. If, as Kierkegaard believed, human selfhood is "the relation of the self to the self" then this kind of attitude is the most dangerous policy inasmuch as it has the backing of anthropology.

However, what was worse, in Kierkegaard's view, was the fact that this social transformation was being given the backing of metaphysics and religion. As we have seen, Kierkegaard's criticism of the Hegelian philosophy was technical enough but its main motivation was a quite practical consideration. Like Luther's protest, it was born of a concern for what was happening to people. Men and women who had never read a page of Hegel were being supported in their error by the popular worldview engendered by philosophy. Unintentional it doubtless was, but the influence of religion in his society was, for Kierkegaard, equally harmful. It blessed this growth of self-interest. By being so much part of the social and cultural life of the nation, religion was in fact not inspiring it with an ideal but condoning something that was aspired by human greed and selfishness. His task was then nothing less than *to bring Christianity back into Christendom*. From 1846 onwards he was engaged in publication that was issued under his own name—part of his "direct communication" as distinct from the "indirect communication" he had espoused earlier—and the conclusion of that was the attack on Christendom. So this writing is an attempt at producing some kind of social change.

---

3. See Stark, "Kierkegaard on Capitalism."

As Kierkegaard saw it, his task was to remove three errors. The first was that of self-ignorance so that he had a Socratic task of calling people back to self-knowledge: the knowledge of one's self in one's eternal significance, which will make one choose the good and walk the way of righteousness, performing the works of love. The second was the illusion that everyone is a Christian and the third was the related assumption that Denmark was a Christian state. Society needed to learn that you could not talk of Christian faith as if you were discussing currency decimalization or a new breed of sheep that could be introduced. These can be introduced into a country *but* Christianity you cannot introduce.

CHRISTIAN FAITH AND SCIENCE: FAITH AND HISTORICAL KNOWLEDGE

What Kind of Faith Does Modern Denmark Need? Gruntvig vs. Clausen

When discussing Romanticism as the background to Kierkegaard I mentioned the great poet Gruntvig, who was destined to become not only an important religious figure in his own age but for many the very epitome of Danish culture. Gruntvig's great aim was to create in Denmark a synthesis of Nordic consciousness and Christian ethics that would receive its peculiarly Danish expression. Denmark had to recover its past if the Danish people were to be true to themselves. A nation for Gruntvig is not simply a people but the presence in them of a living and mysterious inner power that creates its history and fashions its life. If a human being is anything he is a nationally distinct being. "Not since mankind was divided into many 'peoples, races, and tongues' has there been any possibility whatsoever, humanly speaking, of a mere human being—for one finds only national human beings be they Hebrew, Greek, English, Danish."[4] Essentially Gruntvig was a nationalist first and last. Any appreciation of Christianity for him depended on a national consciousness by which he means something more vitally cultural than a geographical awareness. Participation of the whole people in the struggle and the ultimate establishment of a national identity—this is national consciousness; and it creates an awareness of the spiritual nature of life. Not that Gruntvig reduced Christianity to nationalism, for he denies that a nation

---

4. Quoted by Koch, *Gruntvig*, 126.

is self-sufficient: only Christ can restore it to real health. Christianity could, however, only re-enter Danish life through the folk-spirit. So for Gruntvig the wheel could come full circle, as he claims that it is impossible to be a good Dane without becoming a good Christian.

Far from being an advocate of mere civil religion Gruntvig was a very theologically concerned reformer and was to become very popular as one of the leaders of a revivalism. It is important to stress that, in a way, he wanted to bring Lutheranism back to its roots; Luther the vital reformer of individual and social religion. Just as much as Luther he wanted to ground the Danish church in its sacraments and make religion a matter of faith and grace. Lutheranism in his view had gone astray; and the error, he thought, was that it had made the Bible its central authority, something that had resulted in "exegetical popery." What he regarded as his "matchless discovery" was that the essence of Christianity is the congregation's life, a notion that very clearly echoes Luther's own thinking on *Communio Sanctorum*. Gruntvig's association with revivalism was tied in with his opposition to the liberalism that characterized Danish theology. Thus revivalism, which had been something of a schism, became, as a result of Gruntvig's influence, more and more part of the church. So ecclesiastical theology was in a sense a different if not separate element of theology from its academic counterpart.

In the academic world the leading figure was H. N. Clausen, who held the chair in the University of Copenhagen and lectured on dogmatics and on New Testament text and exegesis, illustrating the new science of biblical criticism. Though distinctly rationalist in outlook and tone Clausen's theology was very much centred on the Bible and, in that sense, quite obviously an orthodox version of Lutheranism. The task of theology for him was to combine the illumination of philology and that of philosophy and so remove what he saw as the vagueness of the Bible and the conflict between the way in which doctrines were expressed. Though this might be thought to reflect a Hegelian outlook, Thulstrup argues, the "young Kierkegaard's actual profit from Clausen's lectures ... was that he got a rather thorough, but not particularly original orientation in and knowledge of the areas of biblical theology, history of dogma, and systematic theology."[5] Gruntvig, however, saw this as a sinister threat to faith, displacing revelation and religious experience from their primary position, and he wrote a biting attack on Clausen, which

---

5. Thulstrup, *Kierkegaard's Relation to Hegel*, 42.

resulted in a libel suit and the silencing of Gruntvig for some twelve years.

The resolution of that debate was one of Martensen's contributions. The radical distinction between faith and knowledge and revelation and reason was, Martensen argued, ruled out by the very basis of Christian theology in the doctrine of incarnation. That this was a viable philosophical theology was implied by the Hegelian analysis of the dialectical relationship between historically different forms of self-consciousness. The contradiction between nationalism and orthodoxy could be overcome in a higher synthesis. This Hegelian style of theology became then the dominant fashion.

Kierkegaard on Academic Biblical Scholarship— Faith and Historical Knowledge

Kierkegaard's critique of Hegelian philosophy, as we have seen, was essentially that it confused thought and reality. Of Hegel's system he had said Hegel was like a man who builds a palace but lives in a hovel next door. The same point essentially lies at the root of his religious critique. As I have said, his main anxiety was to disabuse people of the notion that merely belonging to a nation or a society was enough to constitute Christian faith. But let us not rush on too quickly. The context of his upbringing and his youth was the combination of revivalism and orthodoxy, which had restored biblical study to some sort of pride of place. Kierkegaard was very critical of biblical scholarship, which he described as nothing more than a device to emasculate biblical faith. "Christian scholarship is the human race's prodigious invention to defend itself against the New Testament."[6] Addressing this kind of scholar he asks, "can you deny, do you dare to deny that this is very easy to understand, indescribably easy, that you do not need a dictionary or commentary or a single other person to understand" the New Testament command to despise this world.[7] What this kind of thing achieved, he contended, was an insidious reinterpretation of the very notion of understanding the Bible. So the Bible became something that, if we were to understand it, needed the kinds of tools which scientific investigation of history pro-

---

6. Kierkegaard, *Journals and Papers*, 2872; Kierkegaard, *Papirer* X3 A 34.
7. Kierkegaard, *Journals and Papers*, 2865; Kierkegaard, *Papirer* X1 A 221.

vided, *because* it was something antique. It had ceased to be an ethical challenge, a proclamation of guilt and forgiveness.

It is very easy to understand Kierkegaard's position here and make him some fundamentalist critic and opponent of biblical criticism. Were that the case, he would be guilty of a double hypocrisy. For not only would he, like every other reader of the Danish Bible, be dependent on the application of that method and on its results in the actual production of the Bible in translation, but his critique of the contemporary Christianity was equally so dependent. The first complete Danish Bible was published in 1550 and was the work of C. Pedersen and others in the faculty of theology at the University of Copenhagen. It seems to me that Kierkegaard's argument is at once sophisticated and simple. I am struck indeed by the similarity between his view and that of Bishop William Morgan, who translated the Bible into Welsh in the same period as Pedersen; the Welsh Bible was finally published in 1588. Morgan was a product of the Cambridge trilingual discipline, and a contemporary poet, Siôn Tudur, thanked him for turning every chapter of the Hebrew text of the Bible into the language of his "sad people." Another poet, Siôn Mawddwy, praises Morgan for bringing Welshmen, who were blind, from darkness to light. Yet another, Rhys Cain, puts it with elegant brevity:

> Rhoist bob gair mewn cywair call
> Rhodd Duw, mor hawdd ei deall.
> (You put every word in its proper place
> God's gift, so easy to understand.)

I mention these comments to illustrate how a scholarly task was recognized as a work of faith and love. In his Latin preface to the translation, Morgan set out what motivated him as translator. His main concern was to proclaim the truth to his fellow Welshmen. There were no Welsh preachers and people were unable to distinguish between the Scripture themselves and interpretations or commentaries on them. So he speaks of a hunger for the Word of God. It is the same Reformation emphasis on the Word that animates Kierkegaard's polemical and dialectical comments on the ambiguities that attended the popular reception of biblical criticism.

His point will be clearer if we appreciate the parallel between what he says here and his distinction in *Postscript* between the objective and subjective ways of handling the problem of truth of Christianity. There he had really been at pains to dissociate himself from an anti-intellectualist reflection of scientific historical investigation but had been arguing nevertheless that *the* problem of Christianity's truth was the one it posed for the individual's life. So here he says that everything depends on which question you are asking—the one about *knowledge* or the one about *the way of life*. If you are concerned with the document as an ancient text, a piece of ancient history, then history, philology, and all the other techniques of textual study are to the point. Again, if you are a Gruntvig interested in mythology, then literary analysis and history of literature are very relevant. But legitimate as these investigations are they are not treating the Bible as the word of God. This is objectivity. Hence his comment in the *Journal* that we should "collect all the New Testaments there are and bring them out to an open place or up on a mountain and then, while we kneel, let someone talk to God in this manner: Take this book back again. We human beings, such as we are, are not fit to involve ourselves with such a thing; it only makes us unhappy . . . This would be honest and human talk—something different from this nauseating preacher-prattle."[8]

I have argued, then, that Kierkegaard's attitude to the Bible is a development of the Reformation concept of the Word with reference to his characteristic notion of faith as subjectivity. Let me try to elucidate this further. The Bible, for Kierkegaard, is the expression of faith and thus something to be *understood in faith*. As I have argued elsewhere in more than one context, that leaves the issues of evidence and inferential knowledge untouched except insofar as it insists that faith is neither metaphysical nor historical inference but the presupposition of such theology. It seems to me that Kierkegaard was reminding his contemporaries of the danger of forgetting this when we look at that *depositum fidei* which is the starting-point of theology as it is often of individual faith.

What he wanted to clarify was this twofold role of the Bible and in this as in much else he saw his task to be that of holding different things apart in order to let people see the difference. His dialectical and indeed extravagant language has led to grave misunderstanding. Thus he is often accused of an unhistorical interpretation of Christianity; and in support of this view it is usually pointed out that, for instance, in

8. Kierkegaard, *Journals and Papers*, 216; Kierkegaard, Papirer X1 A 347.

Philosophical Fragments he maintained that we should have had more than enough basis for faith were we to have no more than the declaration of the contemporary generation's belief in Jesus Christ. It might therefore be argued that for Kierkegaard the object of belief is not the *fact* (historical or quasi-historical) of Jesus but the message that forms the basis of the New Testament account, and beyond which we cannot and perhaps should not try to go. It is easy to see how Bultmann's theology of the New Testament emerges. However, even though Kierkegaard had read Lessing and Strauss he can hardly be said to be inclined to share Strauss' scepticism, based as that was in the thoroughly Hegelian assessment of Christianity's truth as a religion. Indeed it is worth pointing out that, despite the fact that he takes issue with the followers of Strauss in chapter 2 of *Philosophical Fragments*, he hardly read Strauss' *Leben Jesu* and certainly did not possess a copy of it. The whole problem of the relevance of historical knowledge to theology is, for Kierkegaard, complicated and bedevilled by an epistemological problem about history. The discussion in *Fragments* to which I have referred is hardly clear and it cannot be denied that Kierkegaard in fact exploited the confusion latent in ordinary linguistic use of the word "belief."

It seems to me that he wanted to argue in two very different directions. On the one hand, he was concerned to point out how different historical certainty is from logical certainty. On the other, he wanted to say that *precisely because* history is in a way uncertain it is the appropriate basis for faith.

It is important to note this ambiguity latent in Kierkegaard's view of historical knowledge, which is at least one influence that has contributed to the skepticism of modern studies of the New Testament and of the life of Jesus. Proper weight must be given to those passages which belittle the importance of the historical; but it is abundantly clear that the reality of the presence of God and man in Christ is central not only to Kierkegaard's Christology but to his very understanding of the message of Christianity.[9]

The argument of *Practice in Christianity* is a demand for the identification of the Christian ideal with what is revealed and achieved in the person of Christ. The picture of what it means to expound the cross and

---

9. See Kierkegaard, *Fragments*, 127; S.V. 6, 92; Kierkegaard, *Practice in Christianity*, 106; S.V. 16, 107.

its meaning[10] makes it impossible for us to draw a distinction between what Kierkegaard has to say about the historical Jesus and what he regards as the kerygma. That Christian faith is faith in the *person* of Christ and not faith in some doctrine *about* the person is the main argument of the first chapter of *Philosophical Fragments*. In more than one place[11] Kierkegaard also emphasizes that this message is as much a message about Christ's life as it is one about his death.

Reverting to the issue of skepticism, it is also worth insisting that the message was really communicated according to Kierkegaard; and the theme of Christ's incognito does not commit him to the radical skepticism of some New Testament scholars on this score either. Wisely, Kierkegaard insists on both Christ's recognizability and His incognito. This is the paradox that he expresses in *Point of View* when he says "The whole life of Christ on earth would have been a mere play if He had been incognito to such a degree that He went through life totally unnoticed—and yet in a true sense He was incognito."[12] Thus the miracles Jesus performed are ambiguous witnesses that do not constitute an irresistible proof but force one to a decision about the miracle worker.[13]

It is thus clear that for Kierkegaard "the historical is the essential point" about Christianity.[14] What is also relevant here is his treatment of the explicit claim of Jesus to be God. In *Practice in Christianity* he raises the question whether Jesus' verbal claim to be God does not destroy the indirectness of His communication, only to answer his question in the negative because the assertion is contradicted by the fact that the speaker is a human individual.[15] Further, as is argued in both *Concluding Unscientific Postscript*[16] and *Practice in Christianity*[17] it is impossible to avoid the challenge to faith contained in this message of the *Deus absconditus* by some argument from history about the *Deus revelatus*. The

---

10. Kierkegaard, *Practice in Christianity*, 170–71; S.V. 16, 169–70.

11. E.g., Kierkegaard, *Christian Discourses*, 78–79, 266–67; S.V. 13, 76, 246–47; Kierkegaard, *Practice*, 238–42; S.V. 16, 221–25, 164–65, 222–25; Kierkegaard, *Papirer* I A 27, 28; III C 6; IX A 57, 207.

12. Kierkegaard, *Point of View*, 16; S.V. 13, 560.

13. Kierkegaard, *Practice in Christianity*, 96–97; S.V. 16, 99.

14. Cf. Kierkegaard, *Papirer* IV C 35.

15. Kierkegaard, *Practice in Christianity*, 131–32; S.V. 16, 130–31.

16. Kierkegaard, *Postscript*, 25ff.; S.V. 9, 25ff.

17. *Practice in Christianity*, 24ff.; S.V. 16, 35ff.

revelation in history is a message that can well be described in Victor Hugo's words as "an obscure text and a mysterious language."

What more can be said about the content of this message? First, it is argued in *Philosophical Fragments*, *Concluding Unscientific Postscript*, and *Practice in Christianity* that the message is that the absolute paradox has appeared and that here is the difference between the gospel message and speculative idealism. God has appeared in the form of a servant—His true form, and thus He has demonstrated the omnipotence of His love.[18] The distinctive contribution of *Practice in Christianity* is the stress upon physical pain and suffering,[19] though *Concluding Unscientific Postscript* also says that the "paradox is that the Christ has come into the world in order to suffer."[20] The second point is that the life of Christ is a life of suffering on my behalf.[21] Thirdly, His life is the pattern. Christ's message is that humans should receive the God who loves them; but the acceptance of this means that they are called to an *imitatio Christi*.[22] Finally, "Christ's death is the atonement, is the making of satisfaction." Both the promise of Christ's message about Himself and the message of Christianity about His death is that the strongest assurance is given to anyone who doubts whether his sins are forgiven, that Christ laid down His life for the forgiveness of our sins.[23]

In expounding the significance of what Kierkegaard had to say about religion I have been very mindful of there being two levels or contexts for such discussion; the theoretical and the existential. I deliberately use the latter term, though it is perhaps rather ambiguous or misleading, precisely because it is less misleading a contrast with the former than the term "practical." The words of St. Thomas Aquinas that theology transcends the distinction between *theoria* and *praxis* have always seemed to me extremely wise as well as true. The point I have in mind about the two contexts is that anyone who reads Kierkegaard honestly and carefully will be aware of a great deal of technical achievement

---

18. See Kierkegaard, *Philosophical Fragments*, 39; S.V. 6, 331.
19. Kierkegaard, *Practice in Christianity*, 32–36, 69; S.V. 16, 40–43, 71–72.
20. Kierkegaard, *Concluding Unscientific Postscript*, 529; S.V. 10, 261.
21. Kierkegaard, *Practice in Christianity*, 49–50, 175–76; S.V. 16, 51, 169–70.
22. Kierkegaard, *Papirer* X 4 A 366; Kierkegaard, *Christian Discourses*, 44; S.V. 13, 44.
23. Kierkegaard, *Practice in Christianity*, 235–36; S.V. 16, 219–20.

in those areas of thought which, since the Middle Ages particularly, have constituted the discipline of theology.

SOME THEOLOGICAL THEMES IN KIERKEGAARD'S WORK

As was said earlier, the young Kierkegaard made good use of the academic opportunity he had as a student in Copenhagen and gained a thorough knowledge of the basic disciplines within theology and real skill as a theologian. Therefore his work is a useful quarry for theologians. I have not indicated all the areas that can be usefully quarried. Neither do I intend to do so as I now sketch some of those themes.

Christology

To begin with the Christology, there are three ways in which I see Kierkegaard to have raised fundamental questions in novel and fruitful ways. First of all, he saw more clearly than anyone in the nineteenth century the nature and the impact of Lessing's "ugly ditch." After *Fragments* and *Postscript* any easy appeal to a historical argument for the truth of Christology was impossible and it has probably become a truism to say that much of twentieth-century Christology owes its historical skepticism to Kierkegaard's analysis of the relation between historical statements and the assertion of faith in Christ. Whether one looks at the thought of Tillich or Barth or Bultmann what needs to be emphasized is that the very obvious debt reflects aspects of that analysis rather than the subtlety of the analysis as a whole.

It seems to me that much can be achieved in Christology by an examination of the logical and epistemological issues discussed by Kierkegaard as he protested equally against the easy assumption that historical truth could amount to the truth of faith and against the reduction of faith to a non-historical metaphysics. Secondly, Kierkegaard's Christology was remarkably orthodox or indeed traditional since, as has been pointed out by many commentators, he was not really interested in offering any revision of Christology but rather in the new issue of what Christology means. It is safe to say that his Christology was deliberately Athanasian and that he was in that sense a defender of that tradition. That he should have met the challenge of Hegel's metaphysical Christology with such a clearly metaphysical Christology is worthy of note; but what is even more remarkable is that he was able to articulate that (though obviously he never developed it fully) without recourse to outmoded and misleading language about natures. The crucial issue of Christology for him was the relation of Christ, the historical figure of humiliation triumphant, to God the Father in that action of costly love. The theme of paradox is the clearest expression of Kierkegaard's keen appreciation that the relation of Godhead to manhood in Christ is an internal and not an external one, while being the vehicle of a polemic against the tendency of Hegelian and much orthodox Christology to reduce or smooth out the contradiction to which the insistence on the historicity leads the theologian.

The mystery of the incarnation in theology is what brings into focus the fundamental problem of Christian theology, the ontological relation of time to eternity. By insisting in *Fragments* on the contemporaneity of Christ and in *Practice* on the unity of the God-man, Kierkegaard has mapped out the desiderata of a post-Hegelian Christology.

Finally on this point of the usefulness of his Christology, Kierkegaard makes a good guide in the theologian's progress through the logical and linguistic maze of what can only be called the self-employing of the Son. That he was aware of both the historical background to such Christology and the way in which the theologian's metaphysical task brings him here to the point where the consciousness of faith's living communion is central to his task only makes his achievement the greater. It is this which perhaps Forsyth had in mind when, in his celebrated phrase, he called Kierkegaard "the great and melancholy Dane in whom Hamlet was mastered by Christ."[24] Without concerning himself about historical examples of the limitations of knowledge and so on, which were important for later kenoticists, Kierkegaard grasped the point that kenoticism is a clear emphasis on the mystery of salvation achieved under the conditions of our human existence.

In passing, one can briefly mention that herein too lies the other aspect of Kierkegaard's greatness as a theologian. He saw very clearly that Christology is a matter of allowing the incarnation to shed light on what we say about the nature of God and his relation to the world. Perhaps when one reflects on Dante's description of love as "Lord of terrible aspect" it is not surprising that of all theological doctrines God's nature as love is one which theologians consistently tend to neglect. In a variety of ways, and especially in the soteriologically motivated kenotic

---

24. Forsyth, *Work of Christ*, xxxii.

Christology, Kierkegaard tried to spell out the complex notion of God's love. What cash value he saw this to have is best revealed in the profound and poignant passage in the *Journal* of 1852 in which he comments, "In Christianity being loved of God is suffering."[25] Little wonder that this theme is the undercurrent in Kierkegaard's theology to the constant assertions of transcendence—God's unchangeableness, God's unknowability, God's majesty.

Aspects of the Christian Life

To read what Kierkegaard says about these matters in his *Journal* is to discover how essentially devotional and practical his thinking was. So I conclude this very abridged summary by looking at some aspects of what he has to say about the Christian life. We are familiar enough with Kierkegaard's elucidation of the difference between morality and hedonism, on the one hand, and that between Christian morality and any human notion of virtue, on the other. The themes of choice, leap, despair, and especially the teleological suspension of the ethical have become part of what one might call the popular knowledge of Kierkegaard's thought. One of the things I am most anxious to emphasize is the error of presenting Kierkegaard's view of the Christian life as some extreme asceticism. As he says, he had to introduce severity "precisely for the sake of giving impetus towards the leniency of Christianity."[26] True, his picture of the Christian life is one of radical obedience, a following of the way that has been shown, the *imitatio Christi*. Yet, if we think of these demands as impossible there are two things that should give us pause before we dismiss the picture as extreme asceticism. One is that behind most of Kierkegaard's thought is Luther's more rounded theology and here what comes to mind is Luther's insistence that the Christian life is a promise fulfilled by grace. The second is the way in which Kierkegaard's thought is so firmly grounded in anthropology and thus he emphasizes the fact that the command to love others is based on our duty to love ourselves. It would be utter folly on my part to suggest that in his portrait of the Christian life Kierkegaard is any the less prone to error than elsewhere. For instance, a rather misogynist attitude and a very distinct tendency to identify sexuality and sin are very obvious defects. Even so,

---

25. Kierkegaard, *Journals and Papers*, 1433; Kierkegaard, Papirer X5 A 39.
26. Kierkegaard, *Journals* 1072 X2 A 525.

one can learn from this very waywardness the earnestness of what he sees to be involved in becoming a Christian.

In conclusion, I would mention only two things. Let no one suggest that Kierkegaard's Christian ethic is an ethic of individualism. His view of the ecclesial character of that ethic is precisely what lies at the root of his polemic against Christendom; for, in his view, the church's proclamation is a mode of existence. Similarly let no one believe that his ethic is merely a grand external gesture, whether negative or positive. The reality of Christian living for him is prayer: and prayer is that talking to God that finally discovers that the whole point of such language is that we should listen.

Sin

Mention has been made of *Either-Or* where the Judge refers to the fact that as against God we are always in the wrong. It was this sense and its appreciation of the infinite qualitative difference between God and man that Kierkegaard found to be lacking in the Danish Christianity of his day. We could rephrase the remark of Forsyth that Kierkegaard had rediscovered the concept of grace and say that he had rediscovered the sense of sin. The context of his view is clearly the notion of stages; but it is important to note that he regarded sin as a specifically *Christian* concept rather than a merely religious one.

All this makes his understanding of sin radically different from Hegel's. Sin for Hegel is indeed unintelligible but it is a meaningful negativity, a *necessary* movement in the dialectical evolution of mind. By contrast, for Kierkegaard sin is personal and as such a matter of becoming and potentiality and not necessity. His view of life's three "stages" meant that only the religious person "exists." Without that choice of himself "in his eternal significance" a man has not begun on the process of becoming spirit. This double reference to choice and becoming shows the distance between Hegel's and Kierkegaard's views of sin. Moreover, the concept of paradox that we have already noticed is decisive here because it is this that disrupts the religion of immanence, which he called Religion A as distinct from Religion B, Christianity. Typically, then, Kierkegaard's emphasis is on sin as a free, personal decision: I take a stand against God. Thus in *Sickness unto Death* he sees this voluntary character of sin as a distinction between Christianity and the Socratic attitude: "What determinant is it that Socrates lacks in determining what sin is? It is will, defiant will."[27] This is, he says, how Christianity has distinguished itself "qualitatively and most decisively from paganism." In contrasting the Christian concept of sin with the Socratic determination of sin as ignorance Kierkegaard meant that Christianity begins with the doctrine that sin presupposes itself. Therein lies for him the beauty of the Christian notion of sin, that it addresses what is the very problem of the Socratic definition. The Socratic view "lacks a dialectical determinant for the transition from having understood something to the doing of it." Here again one can hear the echo of Kant's insistence that nothing is good except the good will; but what clinches the issue for Kierkegaard is the Christian dogma of original sin. What is clear from *Concept of Anxiety* is that he did not regard this as a historical matter or some biological inheritance. However, just as the first cause proof of God's existence stops the causal sequence, so he thinks that the nature of sin is that no biographical event explains the fact of my proclivity to sin. This is why it is wrong, I think, to argue, as some critics have done, that Kierkegaard's description of sin as a state contradicts his insistence that it is an act of will. What is perhaps most significant about his discussion of sin in *Sickness unto Death* is that it sees the consciousness of sin to be dependant on a prior revelation: "there must be a revelation from God to make manifest what sin is."[28]

At several points Kierkegaard's "doctrine" of the stages has been seen to be relevant to what was being discussed and here again this is the case. He begins his treatment of despair as sin by pointing out the emphasis on the fact that the conception of God is involved. Though he declares that in the second part of *Sickness unto Death* psychological description is not his concern he does speak of gradations in the consciousness of self; but this is to be "viewed in a new way."

> The point is this. The gradations in the consciousness of the self with which we have hitherto been employed are within the definition of the human self, or the self whose measure is man. But this self acquires a new quality or qualification in the fact that it is the self directly in the sight of God. This self is no longer the merely human self but is what I would call, hoping not to be

---

27. Kierkegaard, *Sickness unto Death*, 90; S.V. 15, 142.

28. Ibid., 96; S.V. 15, 142. Compare the *Journal* entry of 1840 (Kierkegaard, *Journals and Papers*, 1100; Kierkegaard, *Papirer* III A 39) where he speaks of sin and the assurance of the forgiveness of sins as a free act.

misunderstood, the theological self, the self directly in the sight of God. And what an infinite reality this self acquires by being before God.[29]

The phenomenological character of this account is most impressive. Though the language is not specifically first-order language—the language of confession and prayer—it is much closer to the language of devotion than to any typical theological analysis. This is indeed the background to the prolix argument that "sin is not a negation but a position."[30] The point being that he wants to remove sin from the context of discourse about understanding and locate it in a particular kind of discourse about ethical behavior, indicating in a very clear way the trans-ethical character of sin.

It is little wonder that this massive emphasis on sin gave rise to the description "melancholy Dane"; but the other half of Forsyth's phrase shows the true legacy Kierkegaard left in this emphasis: he saw so clearly that the unique role of the Mediator was to convict of sin *and also* to be the means of sin's forgiveness. As sin was for him the rock on which ethics foundered it was also the indication of the fulfillment of ethics. That is, the ethical ideal was nothing less than the model afforded by the Deity in time. It is this revelation that teaches man what sin is; but the essence of Christianity, for Kierkegaard, lay in the fact that as the model the Christ is also the one who forgives sin: "it is so profound that Christ also bore the sin of the world—alone—not merely because no one would or could understand him, but also because he had to take upon himself all the guilt as only man bears it."[31]

I have moved back and fore from theory to practice and constantly I have done no more than offer a tantalizing glimpse. This is because I want to insist that Kierkegaard is simple; not easy, not trivial, but single-minded. He himself summed up his religious message as quite simply: "neither severity nor softness but honesty." However, ever since the *Corsair* episode he had come to feel more and more the all-consuming power of the religious demand.

---

29. Kierkegaard, *Sickness unto Death*, 126–27; S.V. 15, 133.
30. Ibid., 156ff.; S.V. 15, 148ff.
31. Kierkegaard, *Journals and Papers*, 1971; Kierkegaard, *Papirer* IIa 187.

A SKETCH OF THE DEVELOPMENT OF KIERKEGAARD'S RELIGIOUS MESSAGE

There is, I have always maintained, a remarkable consistency in Kierkegaard and a beautiful coherence in his thought. Let me illustrate this by offering a sketch of what I see as the development of his religious message. The notion of subjectivity—which was his development of the Lutheran view of faith as involving the *pro me*—is, in my view, one of the fundamental themes in his thinking about philosophy and faith. So his early quest had been for the idea for which, as he says, "I can live and die." His first work *Either-Or* ends up with the suggestion of Judge William's friend, the Jutland priest, that there is infinite *edification* in the thought that as against God *I* am always in the wrong. He works out the problem of defining Christianity as something that cannot be reduced to quantifiable assertions. *Philosophical Fragments* introduces the notions of paradox and contemporaneity and the *Postscript* makes very clear that this is indeed a new way of looking at faith, as he notes in his *Journal*. What he says there is that nobody had noticed what he had done and what was, he felt, his novel contribution to religious "thinking"—to define faith as a *how* rather than the *what*. *Fear and Trembling* had already spelt out the way in which faith involves a risk and now these accounts are brought together to highlight the way one must talk of faith. The problem is how "I Johannes Climacus can *become* a Christian." It is a problem of existence.

There are hosts of questions about the indirect communication through the pseudonyms and the development of an asceticism, which I am deliberately not raising. My contention is that it is all too easy in dealing with such a complex character as Kierkegaard to lose sight of the wood for the trees. Admitting all these problems, I argue that these concepts carry one on to what scholars now call the "second literature," the writings after 1846.

Let me resume my sketch. We are talking of the *Postscript*. Here already an Erasmian satire on contemporary Christianity is visible in his depiction of the priest in the confessional. After hearing the confession he says, "Your sins are forgiven" and then, "That will be ten dollars please." "You must remember," he says to the penitent, "that I have a wife and family to keep and keeping up my station in society is a costly business. I can't be here forgiving sins day in day out for nothing, you know." If Christianity is a subjective truth believed in passion and so a matter of existence then it follows that as its object is a paradox so its practice is a matter of passionate existence. The themes of *Practice in Christianity*—the paradox and the offense, the humble contemporaneity with the Pattern of faith and love—are all consistent and even implied by what has been said.

So what emerges as the constant in Kierkegaard's view of religion is the polarity of New Testament Christianity as the genuine form of Christianity, the claim that the revelation in Christianity is the truth, a truth that judges and redeems and the individuality of every man is challenged to believe. Sacrifice and suffering, the motifs of *Fear and Trembling* and *The Gospel of Suffering*, are the refinements of this definition of what it is to be the single individual, *den enkelte*. As he pondered more and more in his last years what it meant to "be in the world" he became more and more convinced of the hypocrisy that was the life of bourgeois Christian society. That last attack which rejected the established church was all of a piece.

KIERKEGAARD'S ATTACK ON CHRISTENDOM

But what about the final attack? Specifically it was an attack on Christendom, Protestant Danish Christianity. Several years ago it was suggested by more than one scholar but especially by my friend Cornelio Fabrio, the Italian translator and distinguished exponent of Kierkegaard, that if he had lived he would have become a Roman Catholic. This seems to me a misunderstanding for at least two reasons. One is that what Kierkegaard was attacking was not a particular polity. That much was made very clear when he rejected the interpretation of his critique by a Dr. Rudelbach, who was an advocate of disestablishment. He says quite explicitly that he is not interested in these secondary issues of what kind of institution the church will be but only in the primary assertion of whether there will be a church, a community of individuals.[32] In the second place, it seems to me that you cannot take at face value all the comments on the cloister, celibacy, the betrayal of Luther's vision by his Lutheranism, and so on, with which the *Journal* of the last year abounds. There is only one way in which Kierkegaard can be read and that is dialectically. What he wanted to be was a corrective and so there

---

32. Kierkegaard, "Open Letter."

is absolutely no justification for thinking that his final words are simple statements.

Neither am I entirely persuaded by what Ronald Gregor Smith makes of the Kierkegaard of the last year when he says that "we face here a challenge to all the traditional forms of 'Christianity' Protestant and Catholic and even sectarian . . . Protestants in the face of Kierkegaard's challenge must be ready to say that the old Reformation is over. We face now an unprecedented situation in Christendom."[33] I am sure he is right in his contention that we delude ourselves if we say that, of course, this is a criticism of nineteenth-century bourgeois hypocrisy just as English society is so prone to delude itself that hypocrisy died with the Victorian era. Yet I cannot agree with the reading that makes the direction of thought "clearly away from every kind of objective certainty, of objectified metaphysics either of the spirit or of culture," and the rather empty rhetoric of the claim that "Kierkegaard himself, in his faith, is his only foothold, his Archimedean point."[34] This is to romanticize Kierkegaard and make a shibboleth, as he never did, of subjectivity.

The "attack on Christendom" was born of Kierkegaard's increasing dissatisfaction with the established church, his growing conviction that it presented a false picture of Christianity. It failed to recognize that it was not the Christianity of the New Testament. This is what is evident in *Practice*, which is concerned with the illusion of a church triumphant and is a far harsher critique of contemporary Christianity than anything that preceded it. It is evident, too, from Kierkegaard's history; for we know that Mynster's reaction to *Practice* was, as it were, the last straw. His respect for Mynster as a person and pastor was such that he felt Mynster's dismissive attitude to the challenge to be little less than a betrayal. Interestingly the method of communication was still the indirectness of the pseudonym, Anticlimacus. He is extraordinary by contrast with Kierkegaard's view of himself as just a simple Christian. That contrast was a deliberate decision not to confuse the issue despite the fact that, as he says, *Practice in Christianity* had great personal significance for him.

The picture of Christianity in *Practice* is, then, a dialectical ideal: indeed Kierkegaard himself refers to it as "idealism." To forget the dialectics would be completely to misunderstand Kierkegaard's views

33. Smith, *The Last Years*, 15.
34. Ibid. 17.

of Christianity and of the church as it existed in the Denmark of his day. Talking of his authorship, he himself said that he did not wish to advocate "a pietistic severity." The ideal is neither a simple aspiration nor something unrealistic: it is quite simply the life of Christ, which is the paradigm for the disciple's action. In an undated *Journal* entry of 1851 he shows his understanding of both the ethical nature of Christian spirituality as action and the factual or realistic nature of its ethical ideal. "Christ's story," he says, "always is ideality and not like history, which usually is not pure ideality, and therefore the poet can add ideality to it. But here the ideality is the historical."[35] As mentioned above, the publication of *Practice* was for him a test of Mynster's understanding of the situation and the honesty of his response to it. One does not need unduly to elevate the concept of "governance" (*styrelse*) to see that in Kierkegaard's eyes the enormity of Mynster's dismissive attitude to the work was that he should have seen the demands of Providence upon him. Equally it is all too easy to view him as some arrogant fanatic when the truth of the matter is that he expected Mynster to show more insight than he himself commanded.

Without entering on a discussion of Kierkegaard's view on the nature of church, a word must be said concerning his attitude to the establishment of the church. It is well known that, on his death bed, he refused Communion from a priest, saying to his boyhood friend, Emil Boesen, the only priest allowed to visit him, that he would wish to have Communion but not from a state hireling, a royal functionary. Also, the protest made at the funeral by his half-nephew, Henrik Lund, would have confirmed the impression widely held and indeed repeated to some extent by the press reports of the funeral.[36] This was that Kierkegaard rejected the concept of establishment. That was an impression that had been, to a large extent, created by the approving comments which A. G. Rudelbach made in his book published in 1851. That moved Kierkegaard to publish an article in *Faedrelandet* (The Fatherland) on 31 January where, with his usual ironic modesty, he disclaims any competence to deal with affairs of church and state but makes clear that he was not interested in the question of establishment. What he wrote in his *Journal* makes that very plain. In 1849 he had noted the danger of relating church, which represented "becoming" (*vorden*), and state, "the

---

35. Kierkegaard, *Journals and Papers*, 1645; Kierkegaard, *Papirer* X, part 4, A 208.
36. See Croxall, *Glimpses and Impressions of Kierkegaard*, 91ff.

established" (*betsaaen*), and elsewhere dismissed the idea of a "Christian state" as "a self-contradiction, humbug."[37]

A proper understanding of Kierkegaard's "attack on Christendom" requires doing justice to each strand of his great complex of attitudes. One can see how easy it is to make the Kierkegaard of 1854–55 a Catholic;[38] but it is much safer to regard the whole of what he has to say as his dialectical contribution to the crisis of faith that he discerned in the Denmark of his day and indeed the emerging modern world. He agonized over his own situation and claim to faith and for that reason felt that so many issues that were thought to be expressions of Christian faith were a case of "fiddling while Rome is burning." He saw himself as a corrective, which was a decisive existential category for him.[39] Neither, then, a sectarian nor a disestablisher, he wanted *reality* in liturgy, church, and the worshipper's life.

THE LEGACY OF KIERKEGAARD'S RELIGIOUS MESSAGE

It hardly needs to be said that the legacy of Kierkegaard's message on religion is an extremely subtle evaluation of what being a Christian means. I have tried to show something of the theological and the practical value of his thought and so let me end by further emphasizing the ecclesial character of his views. Many of those comments that are the basis of a Wittgensteinian reading of Kierkegaard are in fact concerned with the nature of the Christian church as the Body of Christ. Thus in *Postscript*[40] he remarks that the Christian proves the existence of God by his obedience. As his Christology had raised the question of what we mean by the notion not simply of God *per se* but also of God acting in the world, so here the ecclesiology raised the question of what is meant by the concept of Christ both intrinsically and practically. The beauty of *Practice in Christianity* is that it shows these two issues in a very deliberate exegesis of Christ's invitation "Come unto me." The basis for a Christian reply to that invitation in the content of the message that I have spelt out briefly; but as the basis of the Christian response of faith is the contemporary

---

37. Kierkegaard, *Journals and Papers*, 4168; Kierkegaard, *Papirer* X2 A 240.

38. Perhaps the best and certainly the most judicious discussion of this issue is given by Louis Dupré in *Kierkegaard as Theologian*, 213ff.

39. Cf. Kierkegaard, *Papirer* X4 A 598.

40. Kierkegaard, *Postscript*, 546; S.V. 10, 216.

reality of Christ so the nature of that response is the work of love, which is his commandment.

It is very important, I feel, to resist that romanticizing of Kierkegaard's view of the Christian life, which I find in Gregor Smith, because this deprives us not only of the concreteness of his thinking but also of its properly eschatological optimism. It seems to me that in his understanding of Christian discipleship Kierkegaard was not offering some vacuous account of an unrelated and individualist ethic. When he speaks of God as our measure and goal, of the challenge of Christ and the invitation to imitate him, Kierkegaard means exactly that. Human existence in the world is something that should reflect the life of God as its measure in the way that Christ's life did and that life of love in and for a community is to be the goal of a Christian's existence. I am far from ignoring the extent to which Kierkegaard's thought is a critique of any notion of the church, yet I do want to insist and shall argue in the next chapter that, for all its insistence on individual responsibility and the constant tendency for community to be lost in the crowd, Kierkegaard's theology does contain an ecclesiology. His view of the self is social both in its insistence on God's creativity as the source of that relation which is the self and also in the description of a person as related to others. Consistent with this anthropology then is the view of Christian discipleship as an ecclesial existence. The strains and stresses of his thought are evident enough in what he has to say about the life of faith in relation to the world and in particular all those anti-ecclesiastic remarks in the *Attack*. Yet surely what motivates all this is the very notion that Christians should be the church, that community which in some *absolute* sense communicates the revelation of love as perfect redemption and judgment. As early as 1840 there is a note that protests against "flirtation" with the metaphor of the Bride and Bridegroom as the description for the relationship of the "congregation to Christ."[41] But more important perhaps is the absence from the *Papers* of 1849 onwards of any suggestion that the church is an impossibility or again that it is anything other than the Lutheran notion of *sanctorum communio* (*menighed*). What he rejects is any compromise with this that would make the "doctrine" right but the reality a communion of indifferent existences (*existentser*), which he rightly calls paganism.[42]

41. Kierkegaard, *Journals and Papers*, 1587, Papirer III C 15.
42. Kierkegaard, *Journals and Papers*, 1600; Kierkegaard, *Papirer* X4 A 246.

In fine, the legacy of Kierkegaard's writing and life in regard to religion is, as he said, simply a plea for honesty. And if anybody thinks that is a small thing then he need only reflect on the glorious ambiguity of Shakespeare's words for Polonius in *Hamlet*—"To thine own self be true."

7

Kierkegaard and Religion (ii)

A Non-Ecclesial Religion?

THE QUESTION: DID KIERKEGAARD SEE ANY PLACE FOR CHRISTIAN COMMUNITY?

ALREADY OUR REVIEW OF Kierkegaard's interpretation of religion has presented an extremely radical picture, that of a faith that is not only so inward but seemingly so individualist that it is in no way an *ecclesial* practice. In a very important sense this goes beyond the issues with which we were concerned at the end of the previous chapter. Catholic or Protestant, whichever Kierkegaard was at the end of his life, there is a real problem to be addressed when we ask whether, in his understanding of faith, he had any place for *the church*.

Perhaps our best starting-point is the contemporary view of his protest and its impact. It was Martensen's opinion that Kierkegaard not only attracted an audience of those who were opposed to the church but also encouraged opposition to the established church in Denmark and indeed to Christianity itself.[1] However, nobody could claim that this was Kierkegaard's *intention*, no matter how much doubt one might cast on his own interpretation of his career as an author. Even so, if, as I do, one takes that interpretation as, in essence, sound and accurate so that the authorship from the beginning is regarded as being entirely a religious

---

1. Martensen, "Af mit Levnet," III, 14. In Part III of *Glimpses and Impressions of Kierkegaard* (84–100), T. H. Croxall collected some of the public and private expressions of the impact made by Kierkegaard's final polemics and also his death and burial.

undertaking, one still has the difficult task of establishing the precise significance of the "attack on Christendom."

Basically, these articles by Kierkegaard are either seen as an extravagant gesture—the shriek of a tortured and increasingly psychotic soul—or viewed as the inevitable development of a theological position that would allow no easy doctrine of the church. Typical of the great Lowrie's intuitive grasp of what Kierkegaard was and did was his view of the pieces: "There is nothing in the *Attack* which cannot be matched by many entries in the *Journals* which were written after 1850. It has often been said that Søren Kierkegaard during these last years accumulated in his *Journals* the material for the open attack. This is true in a sense. He stored up ten times as much material as he needed to use—but, strangely enough, he did not use it except in very few cases."[2]

On the content of the attack Lowrie has this to say: "Outrageous as Søren Kierkegaard's criticism often is, I am sure that where it wounds most deeply the effect is most salutary. To me it has proved to be a wholesome diet and most wholesome when I might be expected to be allergic to such food—for I too am a 'priest.' Apart from the profit one may derive from criticism, that is, from the negative factors in the *Instant*, one surely will not fail to notice how much there is that is positive and edifying."[3] This, however, is to be concerned with what might be called the *application* of Kierkegaard's attack rather than its contextualization, and the latter is my first concern. I want to begin by trying to see where the attack stands in the development of his thought or, thinking of it in his own terms, its place in the plan of his work.

KIERKEGAARD'S ATTACK IN THE CONTEXT OF HIS WORK

The period 1848-51 was significant in the authorship as the period when indirect communication gave way to a direct one. This means that we can consider the two pseudonymous works *Sickness* and *Practice* as belonging to a direct communication. Yet it is important to note exactly what Kierkegaard himself wrote in his *Journal*: "The pseudonym is Johannes Anticlimacus in contrast to Climacus who said he was not a Christian. Anticlimacus is the opposite: a Christian on an extraordinary

---

2. Lowrie, "Introduction by the Translator," xiii.
3. Ibid., xv.

level—but I myself manage to be only a very simple Christian."[4] The works belong to the period of direct communication, then, in the sense that they belong to what the Hongs call "the germination period for the direct critique culminating in the articles in *The Fatherland* and the pamphlets under the common title *The Moment* in the very last months of Kierkegaard's life in 1854–55."[5] This is also the sense in which one can speak of there being in Kierkegaard's history a "transition to Christian authorship." Reading the *Journal*, however, one cannot avoid feeling that the transition is more a matter of what was publicly visible than one of authorial attitude and intention. How should one characterize the mood of this period?

It is well known that Kierkegaard was profoundly influenced by two circumstances of the 1840s: the struggle with *The Corsair* and his concern with the case of Adolf Peter Adler, a parish priest on the island of Bornholm. We know that the greatest sadness to him with regard to *The Corsair* campaign of ridicule was not that he should be destroyed by journalists. That was indeed bad enough—"it does not interest me that I fall at the hands of the journalists." Yet the *essential* sadness was that this journalistic attack had seduced the general populace into an attitude of scorn towards him. "In this respect there is something that filled my soul with sadness. What is called the ordinary class, the common man, has rarely had and in Copenhagen has rarely had anyone who has Christianly loved him more disinterestedly than I have. On the other hand, here as everywhere we have plenty of those, who in the capacity of journalists, want to make money on him—in exchange for false ideas that can only make him unhappy and make the relation between class and class more bitter."[6]

While, as far as he could, he continued his usual conversations with the public, the easy-going walks through the streets became more difficult as the urchins would shout after him, "Socks! Drainpipes!" More and more he withdrew from the kind of social life he had enjoyed and had clearly seen as a Christian life, one that exemplified the kind of unity of church and people that was a feature of Luther's ecclesiology. He withdrew into his shell and was alone with his sense of a religious destiny.

---

4. Kierkegaard, *Journals and Papers*, 6431; Kierkegaard, *Papirer* X1 a 510.

5. Hong and Hong, *Armed Neutrality*, 25.

6. Kierkegaard, *Journals and Papers*, 6354; Kierkegaard, *Papirer* X1 A 181.

His consciousness of a vocation that he had not fulfilled was heightened by his reflection on the Adler affair, which had taken place in 1844–45. Adler had published a collection of sermons, the preface recounting a revelation of Christ who had commanded him to write certain words and to burn some books of Hegel, keeping in future to the Bible. Adler had been suspended and pensioned off from the priesthood of the established church. The affair raised in a very dramatic way several problems that had occupied Kierkegaard greatly—the relationship between the individual and the universal, the distinction between a genius and an apostle, and finally, the irony of a Christian priest being dismissed by the church because he had obeyed a call from Christ. The last is what he describes in the section "Magister Adler as an Epigram upon the Christianity of Today." There he says:

> Mag. Adler was born, brought up, confirmed in and belonged to, Christendom in the geographical sense of that term. Therefore he was a Christian (in the sense that all are Christian). He took a theological degree—and was a Christian (in the sense that all are Christians). He became a Christian priest, and only then did the strange thing happen to him, that out of life's experience he came into serious contact with the decisive business of becoming a Christian. And precisely when, by being religiously shaken, he undeniably came nearer to becoming a Christian than any time before (though all the time he had been a Christian)—just then he was dismissed. And this dismissal was quite in order, because the state church only then got its chance to know how it stood with regard to his Christianity. But the fact nevertheless is, put epigrammatically, that as a heathen he became a Christian priest, and that when he came somewhat nearer to becoming a Christian he was dismissed.[7]

Ever since 1830 he had regarded the concept of the church as one of the great problems of contemporary Christianity and he had reflected more than once on the difference between introducing into a country something like a breed of sheep and introducing Christianity. But now the problem of an objective public Christian existence became a burning issue for him. And since he had quite early on grasped that Christianity is direct communication, the polemic against the Danish church was an inevitable consequence of this growing worry. What shows this so clearly is the reluctance to publish *The Book about Adler* and his rejec-

---

7. Watkin, *Nutidens Religieuse Forvirring*, 219–20.

tion of the various pseudonyms he considered, such as Peter Minor, Thomas Minor, and Vincentius Minor or M.M., etc..

It is strange to reflect that what characterized the years 1842 to 1855 in Kierkegaard's thinking about the church—as it was in particular in Protestantism and most especially in Denmark—was a very obvious reluctance or at least hesitation in mounting an attack. There are, I think, two aspects of this that need to be noted. The first is his relation to Mynster. Obviously Mynster was someone he venerated: he was his father's friend and priest, his own favorite preacher, and a considerable thinker who had shown himself capable of withstanding the tide of intellectual fashion. In many ways Mynster must have seemed to Kierkegaard on the side of the angels in both his views on philosophical issues, such as the value of personality, and the necessity of a principle of contradiction, and again in his general attitude towards internalizing religion. This, coupled with the psychological background mentioned, would surely have made Mynster into something of a father figure for Kierkegaard as a thinker and indeed a touchstone of his views on religious faith and practice. We know from the *Journal* how he visited Mynster regularly and how after 1848 he became more and more impatient with Mynster. Already in 1847 after being, as he thought, rebuffed by Mynster after the publication of *Works of Love* he wrote, "this has given me a serenity I have not had before. I have always winced at writing anything I knew might offend him . . . it would have made me indescribably happy to have him agree with me."[8]

By 1849 things were very different; and for all that Mynster, for his part, protested friendship and Kierkegaard, for his part, scrupulously showed respect, there was now a clarity in Kierkegaard's view of church that did not fit into Mynster's thought and position. An undated *Journal* entry of the period refers to the eulogy on Mynster which is contained in *The Book about Adler*: "This eulogy is given on the presupposition that the 'state church' and 'established Christendom' are valid concepts. That from a Christian standpoint this must be denied is an entirely different matter."[9]

In September 1850 *Practice in Christianity* was published and, as was his wont, Kierkegaard took Mynster a copy. A *Journal* entry of that year records his "conversation with Mynster October 22 1850 after he

---

8. Kierkegaard, *Journals and Papers*, 6071; Kierkegaard, *Papirer* VIII1 A 390.
9. Kierkegaard, *Journals and Papers*, 6441; Kierkegaard, *Papirer* X1 A 535.

had read *Practice in Christianity*." The main points as far as we are concerned are the following. Mynster's reply to Kierkegaard's request that Mynster should tell him if he had "distressed him in any way by publishing such a book" was, "Well, I do not believe it will prove useful," though he had said at the outset of the conversation, "Yes, half the book is an attack on Martensen and the other half on me." Secondly, Kierkegaard evidently thought that the established church might take action against him but nothing had happened and all were silent. Kierkegaard records that he was left with the suspicion that "a little nip may well come out in a sermon."[10]

Kierkegaard's suspicion was correct enough though the "nip" came out not in a sermon but in Mynster's response to the book *On Civil Marriage*, published by the theologian Andras Gottlob Rudelbach in 1851. There Rudelbach had quoted Kierkegaard in support of his contention that the church should be emancipated from the state—"from what one can rightly call customary or state Christianity." "This is the same point," he said, "which one of our most prominent modern writers, Søren Kierkegaard, seeks to imprint, impress and, as Luther says, drive home upon all who will hear."[11] In March 1851, Mynster published a work with the title "Further Suggestions as to How the Affairs of the Church in Denmark Should Be Handled" in which he linked a reference to Goldschmidt (editor of the *Corsair*) to a mention of Kierkegaard, describing the former as "one of our most talented authors" while Kierkegaard is simply called "the gifted author." It is easy, all too easy, to dismiss the reaction on Kierkegaard's part as mere hurt pride. The truth is much more complex; and what may well have been no intentional slight in Mynster's words became, as the various interviews and conversations went on, a revelation of Mynster as the target of Kierkegaard's protest, the good man who is, even so, a "hollow man."

Having spent so long on Mynster I need to explain my second point more fully. Essentially it is that Kierkegaard put off an open attack on the church for as long as he could because he was not sure that he had the right to launch such an attack. In the little treatise of 1849—*Has a Man the Right to Let Himself Be Slain for the Truth?*—he had given a negative answer to his question. Such an action could be undertaken only by Christ because only his death was not merely a death but an atonement

---

10. Kierkegaard, *Journals and Papers*, 6691; Kierkegaard, *Papirer* X3 A 563.
11. Rudelbach, *Om det borgerlige Aegteskab*, 70.

for the sins of men. That is, the evil consequences of such an action were overcome in advance. Also, he could see that people could, in fact, very easily misconstrue his position as something *less* than a plea for an absolute Christianity. This was what happened with Rudelbach and it elicited from Kierkegaard's pen the article, "An Open Letter," in *The Fatherland* of January 31 1851. The letter has many interesting features but two are of singular importance here. First, Kierkegaard emphasizes how his concern had been to encourage "the inward deepening of Christianity." Christianity is "inwardness, inward deepening."[12] This has nothing to do with external changes. It is in that sense that he willingly accepts the description of himself as a hater of habitual Christianity, fearing only that this would become a literary cliché. Secondly, with some of his old ironic modesty he describes himself as a "poor bungler, a Christian fool . . . so Christian-dumb am I who, incidentally, have had nothing to do with 'church' and 'state'—this is much too immense for me."[13] There is probably some element of his political conservatism in his suspicion of "the free institutions" Rudelbach had mentioned; it was a suspicion of politically achieved free institutions, "especially of their saving and renewing power." No democrat, he clearly had no faith in the essential virtue and wisdom of the general populace. However, more significant, I think, is his customary precision even in extravagance: "their saving, renewing power" is the telling phrase and that is his point. What he is saying is that *such a political arrangement cannot be the means of encouraging a real Christianity*. With regard to himself what he emphasizes is that at no time was he interested in the reform of the established church.

Here, as in the wider field of doctrine, we misunderstand Kierkegaard if we take his argument to be an attempt at the revision of theory. For instance, in *Practice in Chrisitanity*, which must be regarded as one of the most significant contributions to Christology in the nineteenth century, he made no comment whatever on the Chalcedonian Definition or the slightest reference to the "degree" Christology of Schleiermacher, almost suggesting a radical separation between such theory and the practice with which he was concerned. Just so here, in regard to an issue of practical theology he leaves aside the question of possible ecclesiastical change.

12. Kierkegaard, *Armed Neutrality*, 49.
13. Ibid., 50.

WHAT KIND OF CHURCH DID KIERKEGAARD WANT?

This leads us to the first of our concluding two or three questions. What kind of church did Kierkegaard want? We must begin by returning to the issue of Catholicism. Was he advocating or, if not actually advocating, was he tending towards a Catholicism? The great Jesuit theologian Erich Przywara was one of the most important scholars, if not indeed the first, to take this view.[14] As Heinrich Roos shows in his book *Kierkegaard and Catholicism*, it is a view that has been widely canvassed; and the revered Italian translator and scholar Cornelio Fabro was more or less persuaded by Przywara.[15]

However, it seems to me that there is no possibility of our being able to give a simple answer to this question; and certainly we need to read the polemics with care and sensitivity in order to attempt an answer. For instance, it would be wrong to pick out only the increasingly strident tone of the critical references to Luther in the *Journal* of the last years because, in many ways, Luther's Reformation was still Kierkegaard's norm. Commenting on Protestantism in 1849, he contrasted the way in which Luther had urged the claims of *faith* with the declension of Protestantism into "sheer paganism and Epicureanism."[16] The *Journal* of the following year has several entries on Luther, in fact twenty-two of the hundred items in the Luther section of *Journals and Papers*. It is significant that the twenty that antedate 1849 occupy only six of the forty-three pages of this section. The contrast just mentioned, referring to Protestantism, is echoed in the contrast that he makes between Luther himself and Luthera*nism*. Recognizing that the rapid "lumping together of secularity and religiousness" is to be deplored, yet he thinks that Luther is the "place where we need to begin again."[17] Capable of observing Luther's greater use of Paul than the Gospels[18] he yet professes "the deepest respect for Luther."[19] Even clearer is his comment that Luther could in fact be used as a direct attack on the establishment: "If the established order wants to have a direct attack, well, here it is—In order not to say too much and in

---

14. Przywara, *Das Geheimnis Kierkegaards*, 82 and passim.
15. Fabro, *Diario*, I, Introduction, lxxx–lxxxiv.
16. Kierkegaard, *Journals and Papers*, 2484; Kierkegaard, *Papirer* X1 A 213.
17. Kierkegaard, *Journals and Papers*, 2518; Kierkegaard, *Papirer* X3 A 153.
18. Kierkegaard, *Journals and Papers*, 2517; Kierkegaard, *Papirer* X2 A 244.
19. Kierkegaard, *Journals and Papers*, 2513; Kierkegaard, *Papirer* X2 A 559.

order not to leap to quickly to the highest things, the established order has taken Luther in vain. The guilt of the established order is that it has nullified Luther's positive contribution. Luther rescued 'discipleship, the imitation of Christ' from a fantastic misunderstanding—but the present age has completely secularized Luther, as if this were what Luther meant."[20]

The tone becomes more and more critical so that in 1854 Luther is declared to have the "enormous responsibility" of having toppled the pope and put "the public upon the throne" and he is further accused of having "altered the New Testament concept of 'the martyr' and taught men to win by numbers."[21]

The single entry of the final year entitled "Luther—the Reformation" is even more cryptic: "Luther is the very opposite of 'the apostle.' 'The apostle' expresses Christianity in God's interest, comes with authority from God and in his interest. Luther expresses Christianity in man's interest, is essentially the human reaction to Christianity in God's interest. Thus Luther's formula: 'I cannot do otherwise,' which is not at all the apostle's formula. What confusion just at this point when Luther has been made an apostle!"[22]

It might be thought that this increasingly critical attitude to Luther and the Lutheran Church is a progressively Catholic attitude regarding the authority of the church. One is reminded of what Newman says concerning his writing of *Development of Doctrine*, that while he had begun by talking of the "Roman Catholic Church" he had come finally to speak simply of "the Catholic Church." The comment on authority in the final entry quoted would then be seen as a piece of Catholic ecclesiological apologetics. If so, one could construe the comments to presuppose a theory of apostolic succession. However, if we go back to the distinction made in *Of the Difference between a Genius and an Apostle* between the concept "with authority" and that of "without authority" we can see that such interpretation can hardly be allowed. Kierkegaard contrasts the relative insignificance of the *content* of Christ's word with the infinite authority that the word has because it is his. The authority of the apostolic doctrine likewise comes from elsewhere than its content. Authority on this view has nothing to do with doctrinal definition or

---

20. Kierkegaard, *Journals and Papers*, 2528; Kierkegaard, *Papirer* X3 A 510.
21. Kierkegaard, *Journals and Papers*, 2548; Kierkegaard, *Papirer* XI1 A 108.
22. Kierkegaard, *Journals and Papers*, 2548; Kierkegaard, *Papirer* XI1 A 108.

institutional structure. The comic dialogue "Pick up tha musket, Sam" may seem an inappropriately trivial analogy; but it is only when the Duke of Wellington tells him that Sam agrees, saying, "Well, because it's thee, Duke . . ." To use a favorite opposition of Luther himself, it seems to me that for Kierkegaard *authority was a matter of spirit and not structure*. In a *Journal* entry of 1849 he relates the authority in Christianity to its nature as an "existence-communication"[23] and in another of 1852 he contrasts the authority of Christ's preaching with that of the present-day clergyman who has in reserve "the police and the house of correction."[24] During these years, then, he pondered on the notion of apostolic authority, presenting the Socratic and the apostolic as the ends of a spectrum between which "lie the half-measures and finally the nonsense,"[25] concluding in 1854 that "only a person who is bitten by men becomes an apostle."[26] This view of authority has more similarity with the Puritan notion of obedience to the guidance of the Holy Spirit and the *presence* of the Holy Spirit among the faithful than it has to any Catholic doctrine of church and authority. It will be recalled that this was a far cry from any Adler-like appeal to inspiration.

The one thing that is perfectly clear is that Kierkegaard consistently rejected any notion of Christianity as some external historic tradition and in that way he definitely rejected the key element of Catholic ecclesiology. James Collins' verdict is typically judicious and sound: "Catholicism was not treated by him as one of the serious alternatives of our time, but only as having taught us valuable historical lessons, which will be useful in determining the future course of Christianity."[27] Though Kierkegaard might have answered the question whether he was a Protestant with a typically ironic comment about his inadequacy for such a task, his *attitude* or stance is, I contend, firmly Protestant.

DID KIERKEGAARD HAVE ANY NOTION OF CHURCH?

But did Kierkegaard have any notion of a church? The question was negatively answered by Martensen in a newspaper article as early as 1854:

---

23. Kierkegaard, *Journals and Papers*, 187; Kierkegaard, *Papirer* X2 A 119.
24. Kierkegaard, *Journals and Papers*, 190; Kierkegaard, *Papirer* X4 A 644.
25. Kierkegaard, *Journals and Papers*, 109; Kierkegaard, *Papirer* X4 A 388.
26. Kierkegaard, *Journals and Papers*, 111; Kierkegaard, *Papirer* XI1 A 173.
27. Collins, *The Mind of Kierkegaard*, 126.

"Dr. Kierkegaard's Christianity," he said, "is without church and without history."[28] I shall not try to outline the history of such a view, which, as already mentioned, stretches down to the twentieth century but simply address the issue. The basic mistake of such a view, I contend, is that it reads the polemics undialectically. It will not do to argue that there is an essential difference between the authorship prior to the article and pamphlet "War" because these polemics go back further than the compositions of the final months. I agree that there *is* a sense in which the notion is an idealized one; but that is a very different matter. That is the perfectly normal situation where we say such things as, "But what I really call X is . . ." This, then, is to me an example of Kierkegaard's philosophical perspicacity in that he sees how "church" belongs to that group of words which have inbuilt into them some kind of ideal reference. To take an example, nobody can deny that the word "wise" is used perfectly clearly when we describe the actions of a president or prime minister as "wise" and yet in the face of instant criticism recognize that these thinking politicians can hardly be taken as paradigms of the wise person. We may not be able to say what exactly constitutes true wisdom but we do know what "wisdom" means and how it points to that perfection which is a divine attribute. However, it seems to me an extremely strange theology that would protest against the propriety of using *ideal* notions or language when talking of the instantiations of faith. It is surely the case that if theology has any validity it is based on the conviction that there is, as the poet says, a ladder pitched between heaven and Charing Cross.

That Kierkegaard did not show the realism of a Reinhold Niebuhr or the recognition of ambiguities characteristic of a Paul Tillich goes without saying. Yet what I am conceding in saying this is no more than that he did not *show* this: to have done so would have meant producing an entirely different authorship. I am not convinced that he was not capable of these virtues. His position is a dialectical emphasis on the pole of solidarity, inward faith without which, it must be recognized, a *doctrine* of the church is impossible. A remarkable feature of Tillich's ecclesiology is the characterization of church in terms of spiritual presence while insisting that the church as a fact participates in the ambiguities of life in general. Kierkegaard was all too ready to recognize that in such a simple matter as one's own upbringing one is indissolubly linked with the tradition of faith, its being handed on faithfully from one age

---

28. Martensen, *Berlingske Tidende*, December 28, 1854.

to the next by those who express faith and so evoke it. His protest, as was early pointed out in the controversy aroused by the "attack," was itself impossible if there was no possible recourse to the church as the mother of faith. Indeed he himself acknowledged that a dialectical attack on Christianity is ultimately a defense of it. The relevant *Journal* entry is a long one with a characteristic refrain, "Christendom has betrayed Christianity." Referring to *Postscript* he says, "Dialectically Johannes Climacus is in fact so radical a defense of Christianity that to man it may seem like an attack . . . It is easy to see that dialectically Johannes Climacus's defense of Christianity is as radical as it can be, for dialectically the defense and the attack are within a single hair of being one."[29] From this and other such dispassionate references, if I may so term them, it must be concluded that the "real" Kierkegaard's view of the church is a positive one, however much it may be qualified by anxiety and doubt about the church in its historicity.

It does not need any great spirituality or even spiritual acumen to see how Kierkegaard is so often doing nothing more than spelling out the difficulties of *Christian* existence. I emphasize the adjective not out of bias, presumption, or even provincialism but simply from a phenomenological interest; for the problem of Christianity as a religion is that it cannot be lived in isolation any more than it came into existence in isolation or bereft of a historical background that was *ethnic*. So having grasped that religion is indeed (to borrow a phrase from a much later philosopher) what a man does with his solitariness, Kierkegaard saw how difficult it is to establish a church that is by definition not only a community but a community *of believers*.

Anyone who thinks that Kierkegaard's philosophy is so essentially individualistic that community is for him an impossibility or an infernal encumbrance of life has not paid attention to *Works of Love*. There he recognizes the categorical imperative of social existence as something that is the Christian transformation or elevation of essential personal existence. The picture is not one of roses all the way and the prospect is that of crucifixion; but for all that it is how he paints what victory over the world means.

It is in *Works of Love* too that we find the answer to the second aspect of the problem of the church, that it is a community of *believers*. A careful study of Kierkegaard's language here and especially in the *Papers*

29. Kierkegaard, *Journals and Papers*, 6523; Kierkegaard, *Papirer* X2 A 163.

shows how the Lutheran idea of a human solidarity is acknowledged side by side with the emphasis on *my* responsibility for faith as an individual *before God*. That solidarity has nothing to do with "the public," he says, precisely because it is characterized by this awareness. The "individual" is the "middle term" (and here I wonder what weight of recollection of formal logic, if not indeed medieval logic, gave that remark the force it held for him).

Love, the good fruit of the good tree of faith, to use Luther's own language, is for Kierkegaard *essentially social* and builds up the other. In a word, I think that Kierkegaard's view of the church is a positive one that is, in the main, based on Luther's ecclesiology. What makes it new and difficult to clarify is that his Lutheran perspective was deepened and sharpened by his own prophetic vision of spirituality in the modern world. Called to "introduce Christianity into Christendom" he was prophetically aware of the modern trend towards an anonymous existence and peculiarly perceptive regarding the political problem of church and state. However, in the end I think he must be said to have seriously tried to support organized Christianity.

8

Kierkegaard on Revelation, Knowledge, and Proof

KIERKEGAARD'S (SUPPOSED) NONMETAPHYSICAL CHRISTIANITY

KIERKEGAARD IS SO OFTEN quoted as an example of a nonmetaphysical Christianity that it is instructive to look again at *Fragments* to see what light it throws on this view. Though a related theme, this description of Kierkegaard is different from the surprisingly long-living myth that Kierkegaard is an irrationalist. While there have been numerous attempts to lay that ghost, what has not been attempted is a clarification of the issue by locating Kierkegaard's endeavor in the history of nineteenth-century philosophy of religion. If it is appreciated that the nature of nineteenth-century philosophy of religion was determined by the double legacy of Kant's rationalism and his pietism, one can instantly grasp how there can be a very close relation between Kierkegaard and Kant. One form of expression that could be given such appreciation is the argument that what Kierkegaard did was to push Kant's *rational* (that is, logical) critique of speculative theology to the point of destroying any possibility of a metaphysical understanding of Christianity. This is very suggestive and a very attractive view, but it seems to me that such an argument is a classic example of wrong conclusions being drawn from correct premises. What I want to argue here is that in *Fragments* Kierkegaard was calling philosophy of religion back to Kant in order to build upon the critical philosophy a much *better metaphysic* than that which historically had followed, namely, Hegelianism.

To see how this is a useful and illuminating way of reading *Fragments* we need to treat two kinds of issues, philosophical and thought-historical. There was a time when Kierkegaard was read as if the history of philosophy was the account of a meeting of the Aristotelian Society at which Hegel read the first paper and Kierkegaard was the critical reply. Now we are very much aware of the complexity of nineteenth-century idealism and the equally complex relation between Kierkegaard and the various European philosophers of whom he had heard. The more research that is done on his background the clearer it becomes that *his perception of the starting point of philosophical theology is Kant's critique of metaphysics and rational theology.*

This is not a simple matter. The crucial problem for the interpreter of Kierkegaard's thought is, first, to clarify Kierkegaard's problems so that the relation between them and Kant's is identified and, second, to demonstrate the way he uses the Kantian legacy both to clarify the problems of idealist theology and to offer his *correction* of it.

HISTORICAL-PHILOSOPHICAL BACKGROUND TO FRAGMENTS

Beginning with the historical analysis of *Fragments*, we can take it as incontestable that the intention and the theme of the work are clear. As Billeskov Jansen pointed out, Kierkegaard's general method was to propose a single main problem for each of his works, matching form to content with a remarkable skill.[1] The form of *Fragments* has been aptly described by the late Niels Thulstrup as "at once like a classical drama in five acts, with an interlude interpolated between the last two acts ... suggestive of the 'passage of time' ... and a Platonic dialogue which has as its purpose the internal clarification of concepts and categories and their distinction from others."[2] We know too, as Thulstrup has shown, that both the title page and the preface were originally cast in first-person language so that it is proper to infer that the issues were of decisively personal import.[3] That is, of course, significant when we want to map Kierkegaard's development; but it is also important for an

1. See Billeskov Jansen, *Studier i Søren Kierkegaards litteraere Kunst.*
2. Kierkegaard, *Philosophical Fragments*, lxvii–lxviii.
3. Ibid. 145–51 and 152–54. It is worth noting that the classical introduction by Swenson and the very important scholarly commentary of Niels Thulstrup are not to be found in the 1985 Hong edition.

analysis of his relation to the development of philosophical debate on these issues. The problem is Lessing's "ugly ditch" and it was brought to Kierkegaard's attention by his reading of Brøchner's translation of Strauss's *Die Christliche Glaubenslehre*.

In his *Fragments* commentary, Thulstrup points out that the conflict of references (Kierkegaard following Strauss's reference to volume six of Lessing's work when the relevant passage in the edition he owned is found in volume five) suggests that it was only after reading Strauss that Kierkegaard purchased Lessing's work and made the close study that is evident in *Postscript*. This seems to me of more than trivial significance in that it could be argued that the problem of *Fragments* is precisely that—a problem. Kierkegaard is not here continuing some polemic against Hegelianism, as one tends to think of the progression of the *oeuvre*. He is in a very real sense working from within that tradition to face what he sees to be *the* problem. Exactly as Kant had not set out to criticize or repudiate rationalism in *The Critique of Pure Reason* but worked out the problems of rationalism until he "found" that he "had to make room for faith," so Kierkegaard here works out the idealist problems. My contention has to do with *Fragments*, not with the position Kierkegaard held in 1844. To confuse these two would be to forget the indirect communication exemplified in it, a work by Johannes Climacus for which Kierkegaard himself takes only the responsibility of publication. The argument that I have tried to develop seems to be confirmed by the language of the original preface: "My intention in that undertaking is not at all polemical, to defend something or to attack something."[4]

Once again I would emphasize that this in no way alters the nature or the effect of the argument in *Fragments*, which is the clear demonstration of the contradiction between Christianity and idealism. If, then, it is important to remember that Strauss is the context of the problem as formulated, it will be useful to look at the features of that context. Strauss's two-volume dogmatics was the companion work to the *Life of Jesus*, which strangely enough Kierkegaard seems not to have possessed and to which he makes no reference. The work represented Strauss's rejection of any biblically based theology. It is indeed a dogmatics that "attacked theism from every side" and openly used pantheistic language.[5] Influenced

---

4. Heiberg and Kuhr, *Søren Kierkegaards Papirer* V, B 24.

5. Letter to Adolf Rapp of 27 February 1840 in Strauss's *Ausgewählte Briefe*, 90, as quoted in Harris, *David Friedrich Strauss and His Theology*, 134.

though it is by Schleiermacher, it is essentially Strauss's attempt to revivify Daub's Hegelian dogmatics.[6] Strauss begins his apologetic section by contrasting "two classes of human society as the intellectual and the people, that is, the non-philosophically minded of the higher as well as the lower classes." This is an unbridgeable gulf in his view, and has the peculiar consequence of an intolerant attitude towards the intellectual.[7]

There is no need to concern ourselves with the details of the doctrine expounded beyond saying that since God is not conceived as personal or even as universal personality, the Christology is essentially metaphysical. The person of Jesus is irrelevant to the truth of the doctrine that has to do with the applicability of divine predicates to humanity. Discussing Strauss's achievement and influence, Horton Harris describes him as an antitheologian and neatly characterizes his dogmatics as "simply a negative criticism of the Christian doctrine, the work of a critical philosopher" and says that he began not with "the supernatural presupposition of orthodoxy" but with "those of Hegelian philosophy" where a personal God was replaced by an impersonal "Idee."[8]

It might be thought that this historical investigation has either come to a dead end or that it was an unnecessary task. Either it yields nothing about the background of *Fragments* or it points us merely to the Hegelian background that we knew well enough anyway. However, my reason for pointing out the historical effect of that quotation from Lessing is simply to indicate the significance of the adjective "eternal" when it is used to modify "consciousness" and "happiness." Any of these expressions, but especially the phrase "necessary truths of reason" quoted by Strauss from Lessing, brings us into the domain of metaphysical theology. And so I wonder whether there is an echo here of Fichte's insistence that only the metaphysical saves; for it should not be forgotten that Fichte had sought to elaborate the first distinctively postcritical theology, one founded squarely on the next stage of Kant's metaphysical theology, but one which at the same time corrects Kant. Certainly what Kierkegaard is doing with Strauss and the Christology of the left-wing Hegelians is bringing them back to the issue of Christology as that emerges in Fichte.

It is important to remember that while the very idea of special divine revelation presented difficulty for the skeptical rationalism of the

---

6. See Harris, *David Friedrich Strauss*, 135.
7. Strauss, *Glaubenslehre*, 1:355; cited by Harris, *David Friedrich Strauss*, 137.
8. Harris, *David Friedrich Strauss*, 276–77.

eighteenth century, the effect of Kant's philosophy of religion was to shift the understanding of revelation beyond the traditional notion of the provision of transcendent truths. Kierkegaard's contention is thus that these modern theologians on whom he comments have elaborated a theory that has distorted the very function of the theory. Instead of offering an answer to the question "Who or what is Jesus Christ?" it substitutes itself for that very historical anchoring of faith in the person. This will be clearer if a brief sketch of Fichte's development of Kant is attempted.

Fichte had set out as a disciple and the heir of Kant and his *Critique of All Revelation* is a deliberate spelling out of the consequences of the notion of Kant's view of religion as essentially morality. "God," for Fichte, "is to be thought of in accordance with the postulates of reason, as that being who determines nature in conformity with the moral law. The entire world is for us a supernatural effect of God."[9] The concept of God is thus not something that is derived *a posteriori*, but something that *precedes* religion.

There are two features of Fichte's argument that are relevant to the historical development I am mapping: his distinction between religion and revelation, and his acceptance of Kant's emphasis on radical evil.

Fichte did not view religion as some abstract scheme of ideas but understood that the theological idea only becomes religion when we make those critical postulates the policies of our behavior. In a very Kantian fashion Fichte sees the notion of right as God's commandment to be that extra dimension that transforms morality into religion, "religion in its *most proper* meaning."[10] Such an understanding of religion yields, Fichte argues, the twofold classification of religion as natural and revealed. The latter presupposes "a fact in the world of sense, whose causality we would posit *forthwith* . . . in a supernatural being."[11] If such a revelation is a rational possibility, Fichte agrees with Kant that there is a radical tendency in man towards sin. The concept of revelation presupposes this "empirical datum," he says, that "there could be moral beings in which the moral law loses its causality *for ever*, or only *in certain cases*." This he establishes.[12]

9. Fichte, *Attempt at a Critique of all Revelation*, 119–20.
10. Ibid., 76.
11. Ibid., 79.
12. Ibid., 100–102; paragraph eight is entitled "The Possibility of the Empirical Datum Presupposed."

It is true that just as Fichte was less emphatic than Kant on the radical evil in man, so too his view of revelation is that it is really necessary only for sensuous beings rather than human beings in general.[13] One concludes one's reading of Fichte's *Critique* with a sense of confusion as well as disappointment. It is disappointing to find something so crucial to our understanding of morality and religion as the fact of evil being treated as if in the end it is not a disease but a peculiar and rather limited aberration. And if revelation is, after all, not a matter of *general* importance but merely the strong medicine that is needed by these few, or many, but certainly a limited number of cases, then the assertion of its meaningfulness and rationality must be said to be confusing.

I have deliberately avoided complicating the matter further, but I am well aware that there is a missing actor in my account of the drama of nineteenth-century philosophy, namely, Schelling. The reason I do not mention him here is that it seems to me that he did not contribute to the peculiar force that Lessing's affirmation of his "ugly ditch" had for Kierkegaard as he read those words in Strauss. Still, it may well be that Schelling was important for some of the metaphysical discussion in Kierkegaard's argument in the "Interlude." The obvious influence of Trendelenburg and Aristotle should not blind us to the relevance of Schelling's discussions of potentiality and reality. Yet Kierkegaard's more epistemological discussion of revelation is surely pitched in a very clearly Kantian key. As Kant and Fichte had said, revelation does need a fact in the sensible world and it presupposes an empirical datum of radical evil. That idealism was prepared to make such an admission did not, however, alter what seemed to Kierkegaard to be its hollow optimism. It ends up by offering a travesty of a logical analysis of the basic concepts of Christian faith. Providing such an analysis and sketching its proper epistemology constitute the basic critical concern of *Fragments*. What critical philosophy had made clear about revelation was the relation to the two very different concerns of public history and the human moral need.

Interestingly enough, Fichte's *Critique* represents a step from critical philosophy to idealism because it abandoned the Kantian dualism of the phenomenon and the noumenon and made that very move the key to our solution of the problem of relating the theoretical and the practical. *Fragments*, I contend, should be seen as taking up that issue,

13. See ibid., 144.

especially as it relates to the problem of the presupposition of revelation. It does so moreover *as* a problem of idealism because that is what the critical philosophy of religion has become. Furthermore, it does this very much in Kant's manner, not least because it poses the problem as one that is raised by the implication of idealism. Perhaps Kierkegaard was reminded of his dissertation and its treatment of Socrates, which bears the imprint of his reading of Hegel. However, it seems to me that he had understood both that the vital thought in idealism had been grasped by Plato and that the great contribution of Christianity to the history of philosophy was that it stood Platonism on its head. Hence, Kierkegaard neatly begins his book with Socrates because this point of departure will raise those two problems of history and human need. In the remainder of this chapter I want to discuss the significance of the book's argument for the elucidation of the concepts of revelation and transcendence in the epistemological and metaphysical discussion of the complex notion we call Christian faith.

KIERKEGAARD, REVELATION, TRANSCENDENCE, AND FAITH

What has been said of *Fragments* already, quite apart from its pseudonymous authorship, makes it impossible for me to suggest any simple connection between it and the Kantian philosophy of religion. However, it will also be clear that in Fichte's estimate of the significance of revelation we have reached a point not very far from Hegel's. Moreover, even the ethical emphasis in Kant does not remove religion from the sphere of the rational. My suggestion about *Fragments* is that in the analysis of what is meant by "learning the truth," which opens the work, we are not far removed from that double legacy of the Kantian philosophy of religion that we have just uncovered. That there should have been a moment of concrete revelation was a matter of indifference to both Kant and Fichte. However, the other "empirical datum" was of greater significance, especially to Kant. This is surely the point on which Kierkegaard insists as the first feature of what is implied by our making the moment in time of decisive significance, that the learner is in error.[14] That is, the achievement of Kierkegaard is that he was able to restore the problem of revelation to the kind of context it had in the philosophical discussion of the

---

14. Kierkegaard, *Philosophical Fragments*, 13–16.

Fathers. Modern philosophy had separated the issue of historicity from that of salvation, which was the answer to the question about the "why" of a historical revelation. But by linking the two sides of Kant's legacy Kierkegaard had shown the complexity of the Christian language. For the next step is to illustrate what is involved in such an ethico-religious development—that it is a matter of the teacher giving the condition of learning as well as the truth, and secondly, that there must be a change, a conversion, a departure by the disciple from his former state. This is what *Fragments* asserts in the opening chapter, and this is meant to show that the kind of theory that idealism was offering could be shown to be false from within its own tradition.

There is almost a reactionary quality in the argument in the sense that Kierkegaard seems to be saying that the Hegelians should turn the clock back. "You would not talk the nonsense you do," he might say, "if you realized how the Kantian legacy has been distorted. Get back to the honest appreciation of the tragic element in human history." Chapters 3 and 4 again take up distinctly Kantian motifs. Though there is not the slightest evidence to suggest that Kant's antinomies were the inspiration of the theme of the absolute paradox yet there are two ways in which the whole discussion is undeniably Kantian. First, the problem is described as a "metaphysical crotchet" and, second, it is seen by the author as a *sine qua non* of a real philosophy. Undeniably, Kantian themes prevail in the basic problem of chapter 4 with its distinction between faith and any form of knowledge,[15] which is perhaps the clearest indication of the importance of the fundamental epistemological problem of the first *Critique*. The necessity of making room for faith in any account of knowledge is thus an obvious concern that Kant and Kierkegaard had in common.

Finally, what is so forcibly reminiscent of Kant's *Critique of Pure Reason* is the way Kierkegaard inserts into his discussion of the Absolute Paradox the little excursus on theistic proof.[16] Just as Kant need not have offered any specific argument to demonstrate the invalidity of the traditional proofs, so too Kierkegaard has made it abundantly clear here that the unknown cannot be a matter of deductive or inductive inference. Yet out of the same conviction that he has something worthwhile to say he gives the subtle argument about the proofs and the nature of proof. This

15. Ibid., 59.
16. Ibid., 38–44.

is more than the kind of outright rejection of speculative theology that had characterized Lutheran pietism. It must be said that this section of *Fragments* is extremely difficult to interpret, more so indeed than the analogous section of *Critique of Pure Reason*.[17] This is partly because the argument is so cryptically brief and partly because it relates to logical discussions in particular that are more fully conducted elsewhere.

Even so, these comments on the philosophical problem of theistic proof are haunting suggestions of a metaphysic and not merely powerful negative criticism. In much the same way, Kant's thoroughgoing demolition of the proofs can end up by saying not only that rejection of the notion of a "first cause" brings us to an abyss, but also that the teleological argument is the oldest and best suited to reason. In his *Kant and the Transcendental Object*, J. N. Findlay argued that Kant was a latter-day Platonist who agreed with Plato both that human life is lived in a realm of phenomena and that there is a better, "noumenal" world outside it.[18] The difference between these worlds is simply one of the connection between them or rather the epistemological manifestation of the transcendent. For on this view the transcendent is not a mere notion but an evident fact. Seen in that light, Jacobi's well-known criticism and apophthegm is perhaps an apt description of Kierkegaard's view of Kant's account of the transcendent: "without the thing-in-itself, no entry into the *Critique of Pure Reason*; with the thing-in-itself no staying in it." Though Kierkegaard did not want to stay in it he did think that there was no way forward except through the *Critique*.

That said, we tend to forget that with regard to his sharp distinction between theoretical and practical reason Kant took the view that it is the latter that has "primacy." This is what motivates Kierkegaard's understanding of how the situation of the learner must be viewed as he contrasts the two presentations of it in *Fragments*. On the one hand, the Socratic position has an entirely noetic approach to the truth while, on the other hand, for the Christian position the whole process of learning has to be seen as the effort of a moral agent who is "in the wrong." It is not fanciful to find an echo of that "edifying" thought here. Viewed in

---

17. Kant, *Critique of Pure Reason*, 500–531.

18. Findlay, *Kant and the Transcendental Object*. Cf. the claim made by Alain Boyer, in *Hors du Temps, un essai sur Kant*, that we cannot understand Kant's philosophy properly if we disregard its religious aspects. Time is only one of the forms of human intuition and not a condition of the existence of all being. The basis of being is "outside time" (*hors du temps*).

this way the distance between Kierkegaard's position in *Fragments* and Kant's in his *Critique of Pure Reason* is perhaps less than we might think.

Let us, for a moment, reflect on that essential starting point of philosophy that is indicated in the early pages of *Fragments*—a knowledge of what the human person is. For both Kierkegaard and Kant, persons are not just inquirers but *moral agents*. As Kant had often spoken as if the whole of ethics consisted in our being honest to ourselves, so Kierkegaard here suggests that the entire weakness of contemporary philosophy was that it lacked the honesty of Socrates. Instead of recognizing that the discussion could not begin unless we knew what a man was, the philosopher pretended that we could begin our metaphysical investigation without any presuppositions. The moral nature of the human person as a free will gives rise to the conception of what Kant called the "kingdom of ends"; but how free action is possible remained for him a mystery. As Cassirer puts it, "A sphere of the 'in itself' is indeed pointed to and defined by freedom in contrast to the world of appearances, the objective reality of which is manifested in the moral law 'just as through a fact' but we can approach it only in action; we grasp it only in the form of a goal and a task, not in the form of a 'thing.'"[19] What this amounts to is that, for Kant, humanity's moral nature and its moral life lead us to a larger view of life than a scientific rationalism but it adds nothing to our knowledge.

Cassirer argues that in the *Critique of Judgment* the discussion of aesthetic judgment shows that the gulf between freedom and nature can be bridged, imagination and understanding being harmonized: "Here, in the free play of the powers of the mind, nature appears to us as if it were a work of freedom, as if it were shaped in accordance with an indwelling finality and were formed from the inside out—while on the other hand the free erection, the work of artistic genius, delights us as . . . a creation of nature."[20] This might be thought more reminiscent of Schelling than of Kant; but that will serve as a reminder of the way *Fragments* is raising the Kantian question from *within* its idealist expression. For what is so thoroughly Kantian is the awareness that the transcendent is not visible in the world, not something we can read in the face of nature. Here is, in fact, one reason for saying that there is no echo of the Antinomies in the

---

19. Cassirer, *Kant's Life and Thought*, 256.
20. Ibid., 333.

Absolute Paradox. Another is that this Kantian theme seems to me to play a more fundamental role in Kierkegaard's epistemology here.

FRAGMENTS

It is time to illustrate my thesis by an analysis of *Fragments* itself, and in so doing I want to try to avoid useless discussion of misleading debates regarding this "exercise of thought." In his introduction to his commentary on *Fragments*, Thulstrup gives "a summary sketch" of the various arguments by Drachmann, Bohlin, Hirsch, and Holm in support of the view that Kierkegaard's view of Christianity is a flawed version of faith because it reflects the influence of the very idealism it opposed.[21] Now, Thulstrup is right enough in his clear rejection of this view,[22] but it is also true that historical analysis does not really tackle the central problem of interpretation. That is a matter of classifying a philosophical attitude, and my view of the matter is that Kierkegaard's philosophical method anticipates logical analysis. If that is the case then we should approach the discussion in *Fragments* as less an attempt at doctrinal definition than an exercise in grammar.

The particular problem is the logical grammar of the notion of revelation, asking the question of its use in relation to the relationship between revealer and believer; how far the Platonic model of learning the truth which idealism adopted could accommodate both the transcendent reference of "an eternal consciousness" and the concern for "an eternal happiness" and the historical anchoring of anything that could be called revelation. This explains why Kierkegaard describes his task as a "project of thought" and "an essay of the imagination": it is not a description or analysis of defined faith but a more formal undertaking that only serves to give greater force to the conclusion of the book's argument that idealism is inconsistent with Christianity.

It is thus beside the point to complain that the notion of paradox is a philosophical conception. It is like complaining that when we purchase a pound of apples arguing about the number of apples or their weight is too mathematical and not sufficiently dietary or whatever. It is perhaps relevant to recall just what "eternal happiness" means. The

---

21. Thulstrup, *Philosophical Fragments*, lxxxixff.
22. See Heywood Thomas, *Philosophy of Religion in Kierkegaard's Writings*, 103–15.

phrase is an example of what I. T. Ramsey called the model-qualifier[23] structure of religious and theological language, with "eternal" reminding us of the way in which the "story" about "happiness" needs to be developed so that the proper illumination dawns. In his study of this concept Abrahim H. Khan offers the following summary:

> Kierkegaard understands *Salighed* as an ethicoreligious good. It is ethical because of its bearing on human behavior and character. It is religious because it nurtures the kind of human character that will make a person become sensitive to his spiritual needs, to his inner stirrings, or to the yearning of his soul. However, *Salighed* is never acquired completely in this life, for it is a reality that is essentially in the future and is of the spirit rather than of the flesh and senses. This does not mean that it has no significance for an earthly human existence. In fact, for Kierkegaard, the means through which life constitutes and reveals itself as properly developed and genuine is through the wish for, the concern for, the expectation of *Salighed* as a good and a future reality. But *Salighed* provides meaning for a life only through an individual's inner striving rather than through his abstract thinking.[24]

This makes clear both the way in which *en evig Salighed* (an eternal happiness) is indeed reminiscent of Kant's "summum bonum" *and* the way in which it cannot be contained within such a conception; for it is clearly a much more multifarious concept—concern for salvation, hope for an ideal existence, and a striving for perfection.

As I have said, it seems to me important to appreciate that Kierkegaard's discussion in *Fragments* is of a "problem." Thulstrup reminded us of Clausen's revulsion against the excessive domination of the student mind by Martensen. He wrote of "Hegel's terrorizing the spiritual life and of the fanaticism of his followers."[25] The viewpoint Kierkegaard himself described as "a positional philosophy,"[26] and this very choice of words throws into higher relief the different mood and character of his own work as a "fragment of philosophy." Nevertheless the point of departure is Hegel's own formulation of Socratic or Platonic epistemology.

23. Ramsey, *Religious Language*.
24. Khan, *Salighed as Happiness?* 38–39.
25. Thulstrup, *Philosophical Fragments*, 157–58. The reference is to Clausen's memoirs, *Optegnelser om mit Levneds og min Tids Historie*, 210ff.
26. Kierkegaard, *Papirer* X 2 A 155, 117.

The emphasis is not only on the interiority of knowledge but on the spiritual nature of the inward. Knowledge only seems to be received but is in reality nothing but recollection. "The spirit of man contains reality in itself and in order to learn what is divine he must develop it out of himself."[27] This is why I register a slight dissatisfaction with the way Thulstrup expounds the nature of *Fragments*'s problems. He reminds us of the formulation in the first draft,[28] where its reference to Lessing is a further explanation of the formulation. This seems to me to limit what is indeed Thulstrup's own proper perception of the real nature of the argument, namely, that it examines the adequacy of *any* idealist analysis of revealed religion.

This insistence that the argument of *Fragments* works from within idealism enables one to make better sense of what Kierkegaard says about Plato in his journal entry of 10 July 1840:

> It is a thought just as beautiful as profound and sound which Plato expresses when he says that all knowledge is a recollection, for how sad it would be if that which should bring peace to a human being, that in which he can really find rest, were external to him and would always be eternal to him, and if the only means of consecration were, through the busy, clamorous noise of that external science (*sit senia verbo*), to drown out the inward need, which would never be satisfied. This point of view reminds one of that which in modern philosophy has found expression in the observation that all philosophizing is a self-reflection of what already is given in consciousness, only that his view is more speculative and Plato's view more pious and therefore even a little mystical.[29]

What the *Journal* entries of 1840 show is that Kierkegaard was far from having abandoned the world of idealism and yet was aware of the problem that Christianity posed for such an epistemology. Thus he says, "All this big talk about having experience in contrast to the *a priori* is all very well" but it can lead to ludicrous nonsense.[30] And then, presumably

27. Hegel, *Lectures on the History of Philosophy* 2:32; quoted by Thulstrup, *Philosophical Fragments*, 168. Thulstrup discusses Kierkegaard's knowledge and understanding of Plato at some length in ibid., 164–71. He points out that Kierkegaard's critique is not simply of Hegelianism but of every possible form of idealistic philosophy (ibid., 170).

28. Kierkegaard, *Journals and Papers*, 2370; Kierkegaard, *Papirer* V B1 2.

29. Kierkegaard, *Journals and Papers*, 2274; Kierkegaard, *Papirer* III A 5.

30. Kierkegaard, *Journals and Papers*, 2275; Kierkegaard, *Papirer* III A 9.

later in the same year, he defined his own philosophical, indeed speculative, position under the heading of the Pauline declaration "Everything is new in Christ": "This will be my position for a speculative Christian epistemology. (New not merely in so far as it is different but also as the relationship of the renewed, the rejuvenated, to the obsolescent, the obsolete.) This position will be simultaneously polemical and ironical. It will also show that Christianity is not a construction around a particular object, around a particular normal disposition."[31]

This latter entry is a lengthy one and goes on to contrast "the idea of mediation, the watchword of modern philosophy" with the Christian position. His conclusion is that it is necessary both to deny that Christianity arises in any person's thought and to affirm its naturalness because it is something that God creates. There seems to me little doubt that the Kantian philosophy of religion is a motive force here. Kierkegaard's quest is for a new speculative Christian epistemology. His stance is the paradoxical insistence on the transcendence necessitated by the human situation and the kind of immanence implied by the Kantian conviction that knowledge is a transcendental possibility.

The philosophical problem of *Fragments*, then, is precisely that of revelation, which had been first queried and then ignored by Kant but re-examined by Fichte. Kierkegaard seems then to take up the latter's analysis that shows how a knowledge of the truth is in fact achieved.

Earlier I compared the total undertaking with Kant's in *Critique of Pure Reason* where, despite the fact that the general thesis makes certain discussions such as that of theistic proof unnecessary, nevertheless these are pursued. So far is *Fragments* from coming up with "no results at all," as Louis Mackey says,[32] that these are the extra results over and above the basic thrust forward from the understanding of revelation to which Kant had been brought in idealism. There is a very fundamental sense in which *Fragments* is an appeal to idealism to go back to Kant and that is the distinctly ethical tone.

As I said earlier, Kant had often spoken as if the whole of ethics consisted in being honest to ourselves: Kierkegaard similarly suggests that the entire weakness of contemporary idealism was its lack of Socratic

---

31. Kierkegaard, *Journals and Papers*, 2277; Kierkegaard, *Papirer* III A 21.

32. Mackey, *Kierkegaard: A Kind of Poet*, 68. Climacus, he says, makes light of everything in *Fragments* and "reneges the conclusions he implies and comes up with no results at all."

honesty. Instead of recognizing our fundamental ignorance and agnostic situation, the idealist philosopher pretended that we could undertake the task of metaphysical inquiry without any presupposition, confident of the presence of knowledge within us already.

It cannot be emphasized too often that what Kierkegaard was actually doing in this work was *not rejecting metaphysics but seeking an alternative metaphysical theology*. Too often his polemic against idealist theology is taken literally and indeed is even overstated. Thus Josiah Thompson would have us view any philosophical exposition of a work such as *Fragments* as misguided and "missing the point" about all the pseudonymous works, "that ultimately they seek to show the vacuity of all philosophy and metaphysics."[33] It was precisely because the traditional theistic proofs illustrated this that a discussion of the issue was included in *Fragments*.

A very interesting feature of this discussion is that it follows Kierkegaard's very clear contention that in knowing its limit reason is aware of something. That is, *there is a revelation in the very awareness of the limits of reason*. It is not the passive nature of knowledge that is of importance for the moment but the simple fact of *some kind of knowledge*. And however un-Kantian he was in identifying a something that is transcendent, Kierkegaard is now very Kantian in his anxiety to distinguish between such knowledge and a logical proof. As is often the case, Kierkegaard's argument is very convoluted and one sometimes feels he is being just a little too clever. First, he makes the point that calling the unknown something "the God" is no more than assigning a name to it;[34] and what exactly he means by this is not at all clear. Probably he wants to call attention to the discontinuity between any such logical construct and the Revealer. If so, then it is quite the opposite of how Barth thinks of the Name of God in his account of the ontological proof.[35]

The next step is a quite different point—that a proof of God's existence is irrational. "For if the God does not exist it would of course be impossible to prove it; and if he does exist it would be folly to attempt it." The first alternative is clear enough, since if X is not the case then no proof that it is the case can be valid. However, why is it "folly" to try to prove that something that exists does exist? One's first reaction is that

---

33. Thompson, *Kierkegaard*, 146.
34. Kierkegaard, *Philosophical Fragments*, 41–42.
35. Barth, *Anselm*, 73–89.

if this were so then no detective story could be written. In a murder case that seems an accident, the solution that concludes the story is the manoeuvring of the puzzle that established the fact that there is a murderer, and in all the best detective stories he or she is there all along. Two things seem to be in play in Kierkegaard's argument: the ever-lively fascination of theistic proof (and especially the ontological argument) and the Kantian appreciation of the synthetic nature of existential assertions. Thulstrup calls attention to Kierkegaard's notes of Martensen's lecture given in 1837 (*Prolegomena til den Speculative Dogmatik*) where he comments: "It is remarkable that the above proofs [cosmological and theological] were known in the ancient world; whereas this one [ontological] first appeared in the Christian world . . . This was later advanced by Leibnitz . . . and by Wolff . . . *cuius essentia existentia*."[36] Thusltrup refers to Kierkegaard's minimal knowledge of Spinoza, and though he relates the argument of this passage to the thought of Kant, Hegel, and Schelling, he sees little of note in this discussion.

Once again, though I applaud and agree with Thulstrup's scholarly account, I feel he does not go far enough. He is quite right to reject any sort of connection between Kierkegaard's argument here and the argument of Schelling that God's existence cannot be proved. To imagine that similarity of position implies a historical connection is the easiest and the most disastrous of mistakes in the history of philosophy. Thulstrup does not seem to appreciate either the full significance of the ontological argument in the development of the *Fragments* or the logical problems with existential claims. Kierkegaard puts to good use the lessons he learned from Trendelenburg about the logical weakness of the Hegelian system; and it is also important that the use to which he puts Trendelenburg's insights is a religious one. Kant's subtle critique of speculative theology and his declared aim of limiting knowledge to make room for faith are the same kind of exercise. There are one or two things that Thulstrup thus misses.

In the first place, there is a very revealing mistake in Kierkegaard's formulation of Anselm's ontological argument. He sees clearly enough that it is no simple argument from thought to being and regards the ontological argument as indicating the necessity of thinking God because "the thought of God is in me." This is much more like Bonaventura

---

36. Kierkegaard, *Papirer* II C 22 336; as quoted by Thulstrup, *Philosophical Fragments*, 213.

than Anselm; but what is perhaps more significant is the recognition that thinking God is a very different matter from thinking other things. Is Kierkegaard not here pointing out that anyone who seeks to prove the existence of God will be faced with the difficulty of laying hold of this idea? The reference to the contrast between the proofs known to the ancient world and the one that emerged only in the context of Christian thought is surely more than an idle observation of history. Both the ancient proofs were *a posteriori* proofs, and this is what makes the connection of this argument of Kierkegaard's with Schelling's critique of the ontological argument quite unlikely. It seems to me that what Kierkegaard is saying is that if our purpose is to outline the grammar of Christian talk of God's existence then we must grasp the way in which that has a very distinctly *a priori* character. That the thought of God is in oneself is the Augustinian recognition that God is to be conceived as Revealer. If so, then the story of our discovery is the very opposite of the detective story mentioned above. This is why it is nonsense to talk of "proof" here. Moreover, the other half of the argument is a logical point that shows that the only kind of proof that can be offered of an existential statement is *a posteriori* so that an *a priori* proof is indeed nonsense. It is worth returning to the issue of Schelling's influence the better to grasp this point about the nature of God's existence.

The significance of Schelling is primarily that in his positive philosophy he was attempting to express the religious attitude of a return to the living God. Thus Tilliette in his definitive study of Schelling points out more than once that the connection between Kierkegaard and Schelling, though studied by several scholars, has not been exhaustively treated. He also speaks of the way in which, though they form a common front against Hegel's panlogism, the allusive language of *Fragments* shows that Schelling does not escape Kierkegaard's criticism.[37] Even so, Tilliette says, in *Fragments* Kierkegaard has selected what he wanted to retain of the "Bore" of Berlin.[38] From his ambivalent relation toward Schelling one sees most clearly what I have described as the difficulty of interpreting Kierkegaard's purpose and attitude toward idealism in *Fragments*. It is clear that Hirsch was wrong to see it as continuing some kind of idealism but it is equally clear that Schelling occupies a special place in his struggle with idealism. The point I have tried to argue is that

---

37. Tilliette, *Schelling une philosophie en devenir*, 2:238 n. 18.
38. Ibid. 2:336, 86 n. 18, 466.

the theological problem posed by post-Kantian idealism constitutes the framework of the argument of *Fragments*. For all the echoes of Schelling in the talk about time and eternity, the irony of nature, subjectivity, and existence, the form of the servant and the importance of freedom, all these are in fact involved in the issue of the possibility of salvation and revelation. That is to say, it is the problem that is important and once again the particular idiom is that of Kant, which was so faithfully and effectively echoed by Fichte.

That Kierkegaard is elaborating the Kantian perception that the idea of God is both unique and elusive seems to me to gain credibility from the next stage of the argument. The point about existential statements being synthetic is obvious enough; but more significant, I feel, is the Kantian tone of the argument about "developing the content of a conception" and the passion of reason to which I called attention elsewhere.[39] Not only do I remain very convinced of this, but I see the same perception of the gap between faith and empirical knowledge in Kierkegaard as that displayed by Kant. This development of a concept is a nice example of what Kierkegaard sees as the interplay of transcendence and immanence.

As we have seen, one thing is quite clear to Kierkegaard as a matter of logic: proofs cannot yield existential statements. Yet in that same spirit of thoroughness Kierkegaard, like Kant, wants to look at what *kind* of knowledge we seek from these theistic proofs. So he considers the analogical case of proving Napoleon's existence from his works. We face, he says, the problem that these works could be someone else's, unless we have "already understood the word 'his' so as thereby to have assumed his existence."[40] There is a weakness in the causal-type argument for Napoleon's existence that the theistic proof lacks. There is "no absolute relationship between him and his deeds." God's works, by contrast, are his and his alone. Then comes his *coup de grace*: "Just so, but where then are the works of God?" Kierkegaard conflates here the cosmological and teleological proofs; and that makes clear the lesson he had learned well from Kant. In his seminal paper on Kant's philosophy of religion, Donald M. MacKinnon reminds us of the impact that the Lisbon earthquake of 1755 made on the intellectual world to which Kant belonged.

---

39. See Heywood Thomas, "Paradox," 203.
40. Kierkegaard, *Philosophical Fragments*, 40.

It was not only the crude metaphysics of those who argued this to be the "best of all possible worlds" that receives a heavy blow from this disaster. The circumstances in which men and women met their deaths reminded such a philosopher as Kant that if indeed "ought implies can," he must reckon with the seeming total indifference of the environment in which men and women lived towards the sort of moral self-discipline, the sort of strenuous struggling after honesty, on which he laid such emphasis. Questions were raised concerning the relation of the "realm of nature" to the "realm of ends" to which theoretical answers were already ruled out as inconceivable.[41]

Kierkegaard's rhetorical question indicates his own intellectual struggle with the question of natural teleology. The starting point of this discussion was the assertion that Kierkegaard's use of his Kantian legacy was a more subtle philosophical development than a simple rejection of metaphysics: that too is its conclusion.

This has been an attempt to contextualize this critique in the tradition of the metaphysical discussion of Christianity. More than once Kierkegaard's position has been characterized as Kantian. That description is something more than a historical or chronological point. It is not simply that one cannot ignore the way in which Kant's critique of metaphysics and speculative theology was already part of the history of thought. Rather what is significant is that Kierkegaard recognized and approved of what Kant had done—especially Kant's attitude. It is telling that in 1847, in an undated journal entry, the adjective Kierkegaard applies to Kant is "honest."[42] Even more significant is a comment recorded two years earlier on the inadequacy of immanence being made clear by the relation between Kant and Hegel on radical evil.[43] Several times in the *Papers* Kierkegaard makes clear his dissatisfaction with Kant; and what seems to me most significant is his impatience with Kant's view of the *ding an sich* as a limit of thought that excludes this entire sphere from human consciousness.[44] The contradiction of Kant's philosophy is that it recognizes a sphere of the ethical as essentially real and yet wants to make the *ding an sich* a limit. In short, Kierkegaard feels that Kant did

41. MacKinnon, *Themes in Theology*, 26.
42. Kierkegaard, *Journals and Papers* 2236; 3558; Kierkegaard, *Papirer* VIII1 A 358; X1 A 666.
43. Kierkegaard, *Journals and Papers* 3089; Kierkegaard, *Papirer* VIII1 A 11.
44. Kierkegaard, *Journals and Papers* 2252; Kierkegaard, *Papirer* II C 48.

not press far enough ahead with his own recognition that the error of rationalism was its failure to recognize that reason too had its *interests*. Consequently, though he praises him for not pretending that his notion of radical evil was "a speculative comprehension of the Christian problem,"[45] Kierkegaard takes Kant to task for not establishing that this "inexplicable is a category."[46]

This longstanding dissatisfaction with a solution to what Kierkegaard regards as the real problem of a philosophical treatment of Christianity is, I have argued, the background to the way the discussion proceeds in *Fragments*. Kierkegaard was considering the latest solution that was in fact more unsatisfactory than had been Kant's own, and this precisely because idealism had failed to appreciate the very clarification of the problem that had been achieved in the idealist tradition by Fichte. I have specifically *not* claimed that Kierkegaard is in any way dependent on Fichte but simply asserted that his question and mode of attack are formed by the same Kantian outlook of a transcendental idealism. If this argument is right, then *Fragments* must be seen as continuing the critique of a transcendent metaphysics while also effecting a critique of the critical limitation of the range of meaningful discourse.

Kierkegaard's great achievement was to show how Kant's argument is essentially a metaphysical one, and that it is a paradoxical recognition of the dimension of reality of which we have no knowledge but still attempt to grasp by mere thought. Looking at such an argument and not merely the random reflections of the *Papers* that relate to this argument of *Fragments*, I am constantly struck by the way cleverness and confusion seem often to go together in Kierkegaard's thinking. Thus it seems clear that there is in *Fragments* a very strong sense of the critical outlook in philosophy that is developed in the final section into a radical scepticism with regard to historical knowledge.

The same mood had characterized both the discussion of what I called the "grammar" of the words "God" and "revelation" and is indeed most obvious in the very concern with what is said about proof. Yet it is the same Kantian concern with the conditions of knowing the transcendent and with a recognition of the fact of sin that animates Kierkegaard's rejection of both the critical philosophy and idealism. As Kant failed to articulate the way in which the transcendent impinges

---

45. Kierkegaard, *Journals and Papers* 3093; Kierkegaard, *Papirer* X2 A 501.
46. Kierkegaard, *Journals and Papers* 3089; Kierkegaard, *Papirer* VIII1 A 11.

on our experience and forces upon thought the facts we neglect, so Hegel had reduced the notion of the transcendent to a mere immanence, emptying Christianity at once of the very presence that brings joy and of the objectivity of that joy.

It would be foolish to suggest that *Fragments* has delineated that new speculative epistemology that was mentioned earlier; but if anything is established by this examination of its argument and the context of its composition it is that this epistemological purpose is the nerve of its argument. This means then that it will not do simply to lump Kierkegaard with Kant and see his enterprise as some accessory to Kant's alleged "murder" of metaphysics. What Kierkegaard sought to do was, in a sense, something more profound than the composition of a piece of philosophy. One of the illuminating features of Thulstrup's comparison with classical drama is precisely that reading *Fragments* is like reading John's Gospel or a Greek or Shakespearean tragedy. Here is a philosopher who has, like the poet, plumbed the depths of the human psyche and seen man's sinfulness illumined by the presence of God. His thesis is that we can only understand the grammar of "God" and "revelation" when we resist the temptation to apply the wrong models of knowledge and proof and pay attention to that radical evil that Kant and Fichte had indeed recognized as part and parcel of the talk of "revelation."

9

Kierkegaard's Alternative Metaphysical Theology

THERE IS OFTEN MUCH to be said for saying at the outset what it is that one is seeking to say though one is all too keenly aware that one cannot say it clearly and adequately. So let me say that what I want to say is that *Kierkegaard's achievement in criticizing metaphysical theology was but a prelude to the development of an alternative metaphysical theology.*

KIERKEGAARD'S DESIRE TO BE A METAPHYSICIAN

Kierkegaard's "Crazy" Upbringing

Kierkegaard was born in 1813—the year in which, he said, so many wild banknotes were circulating. Two things only about Kierkegaard's life and character need to be mentioned. The one is the well-known fact of what he calls his "crazy" upbringing by his father, who had retired from business to live the life of an amateur philosopher and theologian and patron of church activity, and the other is his paradoxical or ambivalent attitude to his nationality.

Notwithstanding Kierkegaard's formal training, his real education was received from his father. Biographers generally make much of the way in which his father withdrew from the real world of immediate social contact, for example the "walks" in the study on the many occasions of bad weather when the father would imaginatively recount the scenes around town which they would encounter on their walks. Though I have argued against the tendency to make too much of this in biographies like Thompson's, where a psychological estimate turns out to be trivial,

Kierkegaard's Alternative Metaphysical Theology 163

it is undoubtedly important.[1] Without this kind of training Kierkegaard probably would hardly have developed his capacity for literary portraiture—not so much of real or historical figures as of imaginary types. This was of fundamental significance to his development as a thinker because his philosophical reflection begins in the elaboration of these basic types or figures—Don Juan, the Wandering Jew, Faust—as in *Either-Or* where the empiricist tendency of Kierkegaard's epistemology is already evident. What is of even greater importance is that we can see here the deliberate quest for an adequate philosophy of nature.[2] Moreover, without this not only would the mode of the Kierkegaardian attack on Hegel be different but so would be the very basis of that attack.

Essential to Kierkegaard's argument is that what is wrong about the Hegelian metaphysics is that it forgets what is to be *this, that*, or *the other*.[3] From the vantage point of later history and with the benefit of the development of philosophy after and because of him we can see this as a failure of Hegel's phenomenology to be really and radically phenomenological. However, that is precisely why I do not want people to be blinded by the very dramatic significance of the indoor walks taken by Kierkegaard, father and son; for it seems to me that they cultivated a very keen awareness of the difference between fact and fantasy. If people doubt this let them look at the subtle distinction between various functions of imagination as picturing and fantasizing that Kierkegaard makes. There are two terms translated as "imagination" which were distinguished by Kierkegaard—"*indbildingskraft*" and "*phantasi*." The former is what relates to fantasy and most of his comments on imagination made in the *Journals* are concerned with such illusions.[4] By contrast "*phantasi*" was associated with the Romantic imagination, which, for Kierkegaard, had the great merit of presenting an infinite goal.[5]

A more significant part of the upbringing, for my present purpose, was the early and prolonged exposure to dialectical debate. J. P. Mynster,

---

1. Heywood Thomas, Review of Josiah Thompson, *Kierkegaard*.

2. Cf. Kierkegaard, *Either-Or* I, 70–74; S.V. 2, 70–73.

3. Cf. Kierkegaard, *Journals and Papers*, 1567 (I A 317), 1582 (II A 808), 1593 (II C 33), 1598 (IV C 66), and frequently in Kierkegaard, *Concluding Unscientific Postscript*; S.V. 9.

4. See Kierkegaard, *Journals and Papers*, Vol. 2, 311–14.

5. Cf. Kierkegaard, *Concept of Anxiety*, 40; S.V. 6, 134; Kierkegaard, *Stages on Life's Way*, 42; S.V. 6, 29.

later Bishop and primate of Denmark, was a close personal friend as well as M. P. Kierkegaard's priest. Generally known only as a shadowy figure in Kierkegaard's biography as the person who, by his refusal to act, launched Kierkegaard on his final polemic against the established church and the person at whose funeral Martensen, his successor as Primate, preached the eulogy of him as "witness for the truth," Mynster, as we have seen, made quite significant contributions to the development of Danish theology and philosophy. We know him best from Kierkegaard's caricature of him as the easy-going preacher of a bourgeois Christianity: but, if we appreciate that we are looking at a caricature, we shall grasp how effective and relevant a preacher Mynster was. Again, we do know from the contemporary journals and from O. Waage's book that he played an important part in the debate about Hegelian philosophy and logic. In the light of Ammundsen's and also Thulstrup's more recent research it is impossible to see in Mynster either an early anti-Hegelian influence or a source of Kierkegaard's early knowledge of Hegel.[6] What I am making at the moment is the weaker claim that in the debates that the young boy witnessed between Mynster and Kierkegaard senior there is to be found an important inspiration to philosophical reflection.

Kierkegaard's Ambiguity about Denmark

The second point can be put more briefly. Kierkegaard felt very keenly the remoteness and smallness of Denmark as a rather insignificant part of the continent of Europe. This "harbor of merchandise" was a suffocating context in which his genius had to develop and flower. The great range of his own literary knowledge contrasted all too predictably with the narrowness of his fellow countrymen's. In particular he deplored the overestimation, as he felt it was, of German culture. Denmark was just beginning to emerge from its feudal past into the modern world and part of that was the development of what was indeed a golden age of Danish literature. To mention just one example, Oehlenschlager, the poet, was an instance of what was for Kierkegaard cause for real national pride. There is a sense in which the great difference between Kierkegaard and Grundtvig is illustrated by the style of the national pride which each exemplified; but to follow that theme would be to wander from our topic.

---

6. See Ammundsen, *Søren Kierkegaard's Ungdom*, 13, and Thulstrup, *Kierkegaard's Relation to Hegel*, 39–40.

The point is that as Kierkegaard rejoiced in the creation of a truly *Danish* literature which would bear comparison with German literature so, I think, he wanted to see a *Danish* philosophy that was not simply some German metaphysics put in the Danish tongue.

WHAT WAS THE SITUATION IN METAPHYSICS AND THEOLOGY?

The Dominance of Hegel

Danish Hegelianism

Having established a genuine desire in Kierkegaard to be a metaphysician I pose the next question: What, then, was the situation in metaphysics and theology? Though it is true to say that there were opponents whose voices were heard in Denmark yet the dominant voice was that of Hegel. That is to say, we know (again mainly from Thulstrup's research) just how much Kierkegaard had been exposed to the non-Hegelian philosophy of Sibbern and Møller and the equally non-Hegelian theology of Clausen. Of the theological faculty in Copenhagen Thulstrup concludes: "it must be taken as doubtful that Kierkegaard got any overall impression of Hegelian thought from them, or any impression of attempts to employ Hegelian thought outside of philosophy alone."[7] Nevertheless, I have not seen anything by way of evidence which contradicts the position I took in my earliest studies of Kierkegaard and which I have just repeated above. Clear illustration of the way in which Danish philosophy and theology were dominated by Hegelianism—just as much as British philosophy and theology were to become by the end of the century—is the work of J. L. Heiberg and H. L. Martensen.

Fortunately we are not left in doubt of Heiberg's Hegelianism because he relates how he was converted to this position in the summer of 1824 (and for good measure we can see Kierkegaard's satirical comment on this[8]). Heiberg bought a copy of the *Encyclopedia*, he tells us, and in between some desultory conversation with the driver of the stagecoach managed to complete his reading of it by the time the coach arrived in

---

7. Thulstrup, *Kierkegaard's Relation to Hegel*, 42; cf. Thulstrup's commentary on *Concluding Unscientific Postscript*, 70ff.

8. Kierkegaard, *Concluding Unscientific Postscript*, 1, 200–202; S.V. 9, 153–54.

Berlin. He met Hegel himself and returned to Kiel in some confusion of thought, stopping off in Hamburg:

> I constantly brooded over what was still obscure to me. It happened that one day while I was sitting in my room in the "König von England" with Hegel on my table and Hegel in my thoughts, and at the same time listening to some beautiful hymns which almost constantly sounded from the choir of St. Peter's Church, suddenly, in a way which I have never before or since experienced, I was gripped by a moment of inner vision, like a flash of lightning which suddenly illuminated the whole region for me. From that moment on, the system in its longer outlines was clear to me . . . I can truly say that this wonderful moment was the most important in my life, for it gave me a peace, a security which I had never before known.[9]

The first fruits of the conversion were Heiberg's contributions to the debate about determinism, which raged in Copenhagen in 1824. In his treatise on human freedom, published that December, Heiberg argues that the opposing positions taken up in the debate are moments in the dialectical progression towards the Olympus of speculation represented by Hegel. He closes his treatise by saying that all speculation is a leap out of the world of time into the world of ideas. The mood and the method are thus essentially Hegelian and there is abundant evidence in the work of a determination to follow Hegel's lead. The sketch I gave of Heiberg in my earliest comment on the matter still seems to me a brief and accurate enough outline:

> Just as for Hegel so for Heiberg, Philosophy and Religion have the same content and only the form is different. The absolute (God) appears in the latter in the form of a representation, that is imaginatively, whereas in the case of the former it appears as a concept. One reaches Paradise by two ways—either by becoming absorbed in the historical form of Christ or by having speculatively apprehended God. Only the latter is a satisfactory way and to it we must return again and again, if Religion is to have validity.[10]

In a letter Heiberg indeed speaks of Hegel as the supreme achievement in philosophy—"everything is found in his system without the

---

9. Heiberg, *Prosaiske Skrifter*, XI, 499.
10. Heywood Thomas, *Philosophy of Religion in Kierkegaard's Writings*, 43.

least lack."[11] It is interesting to reflect that Hegel's abandonment of the Cartesian interest of epistemology to concentrate on ontology is seen by Heiberg in this light and is indeed a view endorsed by Hegel himself.[12] Reviewing the development of Heiberg's Hegelianism from the treatise on freedom to the prospectus for lectures on philosophy, Thulstrup says that it is "a certainly close, yet ultimately inadequate understanding and development of Hegel's philosophy" but adds that his view of religion in general and of Christianity in particular correspond by and large to Hegel's.[13]

Turning to Martensen one can again rejoice in finding an autobiographical statement of the evidence we seek. Clearly Martensen had, as a student, been much taken by Schleiermacher and had felt that what he could not find in Schleiermacher he would find in Hegel. The great ideal of his youth, he tells us was: "There must be a view of life and the world in which everything that has meaning in existence (*Dasein*)—nature and spirit, nature and history, poetry and art and philosophy harmoniously unite to form a temple of the spirit in which Christianity is the all-governing and all-explaining centre."[14] This objective worldview would express all the orthodox dogmas in "a new and fresh form" and reveal their objective validity.

Rather like Heiberg, Martensen was struck by the way in which the Hegelian philosophy enabled one to understand everything against the background of the Trinity and Christ as the centre of creation. Arildsen says of Martensen's prize essay and its relation to positive theology that Martensen "has allied himself with Hegel and with speculative theology. He has to a certain degree adopted Hegel's speculative method, of which he has made abundant use in his resolution of the problem, as well as in his view of the relation between faith and knowledge—the idea of God can be elevated from the form of faith to the form of knowledge, and human knowledge is not only subjective but objective idealism—and on history, the development of which is understood logically."[15]

Martensen is a very strange theologian—not least because he was once so popular in Britain that all his main works were translated into

11. Heiberg, Letter to Orsted, No.126, in Borup, *Breve*.
12. Hegel, *History of Philosophy*, III, 545ff.
13. Thulstrup, *Kierkegaard's Relation to Hegel*, 32–33.
14. Martensen, *Af mit Livnet*, 23.
15. Arildsen, *Biskop Hans Lassen Martensen*, I, 69.

English, and yet he has for so many years been a completely forgotten figure. What is particularly odd about him is the way in which one's first impression is that Kierkegaard must have made a mistake in attacking him. Sensitive to mysticism (especially Eckhardt and Boehme) and Anselmian in his quest for faith's own understanding he seems the very model of an orthodox theologian. Yet there is, in everything he wrote, the clear refrain of a Hegelian reconciliation of oppositions in a speculative unity. He is indeed "the real Danish Hegelian."[16]

Hegel's Own Thought

So far I've spoken of Danish Hegelianism and to make clear that it was, despite its variation and difference from Hegel's own writings, an authentic enough expression of his metaphysical theology let me risk repetition very briefly and quickly sketch Hegel's position. It is, I think, fair to say that Hegel's intention was to produce a Christian philosophy and he did this by "translating" the theological doctrine of the Trinity into an abstract logical principle which he then applied as the explanation of nature.[17] Nature is a system of stages in the development of the immanent idea, the slumbering form of the spirit that is more adequately expressed in the unfolding of human history. The history of the world, then, both as nature and as human history is the actual realization of the infinite, eternal, and objective mind. Hegel emphasizes the internal nature of evolution—all development is a stage in the history of the idea. We need not concern ourselves with his views on the relation of the individual to the state beyond saying that for him the true worth and significance of the individual is revealed only in his participation in society in the life of the state. His aim as a philosopher was not indeed to bring people to religion but he was convinced that a philosophical understanding of religion can only serve to strengthen and deepen religious conviction. As Bernard Reardon says: "we have to acknowledge that unlike many of the leaders of the Enlightenment thinking he definitely considered himself not only a Christian but a good Lutheran Protestant, anxious moreover to leave no doubt of the fact in the minds of others. Further, he maintained that his own system comprised a metaphysical restatement

---

16. Heywood Thomas, *Philosophy of Religion in Kierkegaard's Writings*, 45.
17. Cf. Bruaire, *Logique et religion chrétienne dans la philosophie de Hegel.*

of Christianity of a kind to enable it to give a finally satisfactory, because at last wholly intelligible, account of itself."[18]

Anyone who has read his *Early Theological Writings* will know of his development from Romanticism and Kantian ethical rationalism to an individual position. He saw orthodoxy as fighting a pointless battle to defend a false literalness in religion and rationalism as an anthropomorphic form of theism. So his view of philosophy's task is the liberalization of people's minds by the translation of the content of religion into the form of thought. What religion grasped intuitively philosophy must state abstractly. His philosophy is indeed theistic; but its views of man, history, and God make it finally a *pan*theism.

Two concepts need a brief final clarification—God and incarnation. For Hegel God is not a person. God is the Absolute and as such identical with all that really exists. In the perfect religion it is "the notion itself that is its own object." Again, Hegel often suggests that he maintains a doctrine of Incarnation; but this too turns out to be something rather different from what we would normally mean. God is not incarnate in one person only—Jesus of Nazareth—but in all people and in everything final. So the story of Jesus is true as a means for us to grasp what otherwise eludes our understanding, the pure notion of incarnation as the essential unity of divine and human natures.

KIERKEGAARD'S REJECTION OF HEGELIANISM AS AN ALTERNATIVE METAPHYSIC

It may seem as if I am never going to discuss Kierkegaard's metaphysics; but the point I am anxious to emphasize is that *Kierkegaard's well-known rejection of this metaphysical theology was itself the development of an alternative*. There is an important sense in which his aim was the much more practical and prophetic one. On 1 September 1855 he writes in *The Instant*: "The only analogy I have for myself is Socrates; my task is a Socratic task, to reach the concept of what it is to be a Christian."[19] So he says that he does not call himself a Christian—to leave the "ideal free." Disagree as they will about the details of Kierkegaard's Christianity—a disestablished church, a return to Catholicism, or some individualistic non-religious attitude—scholars are ready enough to acknowledge its

---

18. Reardon, *Hegel's Philosophy of Religion*, xvi.
19. S.V. 19, 319.

ideal character: what presents the great difficulty is his determination in the last years to see that something was *done*. My problem at the moment is that of defining not the nature of this ideal but the relation to it of Kierkegaard's obvious concern with metaphysics. My contention is that if his task was in that sense a *religious* one (and this is what makes sense of his claim in *The Point of View* about the purpose of his whole literary production) he achieved it by means of a *metaphysical* clarification of the error of bourgeois orthodoxy and the real nature of Christianity. I should like to give a very rough outline of these two complementary sketches.

The Error of Bourgeois Orthodoxy: A Sketch

We have seen that the main positions of the metaphysical theology that was the vogue were the following theses:

(i) It is possible to construct an objective system of truth.

(ii) There is an integral relation of harmony between religion and philosophy as two forms of experience.

(iii) An illustration of the harmony is the proof of God's existence.

(iv) Likewise there is an indubitability about the truth of the incarnation.

(v) Sin, salvation, and faith are all concepts that reveal the unity of logic and reality.

To give an outline of Kierkegaard's critique of these need not lead us into any difficulties about either the dating of his first real knowledge of Hegel or the use of pseudonymous authors or indeed about the coherence of Kierkegaard's total work. We know that in the early work *Either-Or* he argues for the discontinuity between ethics and any form of life that neglects the choice of an ideal self and the discontinuity between ethics and religion. I tried to show years ago how *Either-Or* was also a very subtle argument against the notion of a philosophical system.[20] The development of this kind of thinking through *Fear and Trembling*, *Philosophical Fragments*, and *Concluding Unscientific Postscript* is familiar to everyone.

---

20. See Heywood Thomas, *Philosophy of Religion in Kierkegaard's Writings*, 12–14.

The Real Nature of Christianity: A Sketch

Likewise it is easily enough appreciated how the development of an interpretation of Christianity as the religion of transcendence and paradox in *Postscript* leads on to the emphasis on offense in *Practice in Christianity* and to the final onslaught on the Danish established church. What, then, are its features?

(i) First, the assertion that essential and objective truth is a myth and that truth lies in subjectivity.

(ii) Second, the harmony of religion, especially Christianity, and philosophy is a misunderstanding of the nature of Christianity.

(iii) Proof of God is impossible.

(iv) Logic and existence are separate.

(v) The incarnation is an event not an idea.

(vi) Sin shows the mystery of time as an idea elucidated by the fact of salvation.

Perhaps I should add a seventh assertion that is, at any rate, implicit in what has been said:

(vii) Christianity is the only system of thought that can do justice to the human situation both as an analysis of it and as holding out the possibility of its great quest, namely eternal blessedness.

Kierkegaard as Metaphysician

I am well aware of the difficulty of trying to see Kierkegaard as a whole. Equally, ever since hearing the distinguished philosopher and logician J. Jørgensen reduce Kierkegaard's philosophy to the advocacy of honesty I have realized how easy it is to be satisfied with and misled by partial truths. What I am insisting is that *there is in Kierkegaard genuine and significant philosophy*. He understood himself as having, we remember, only one analogy: Socrates. If so, then as a latter-day Socrates he was anxious to recall people to a self-knowledge, to a philosophical modesty, and to the appreciation of the *indirect* nature of the communication of truth.

He was in many ways a strange and difficult man—and Regine would have agreed with the comment as readily as Mynster; but he was never troubled by any false modesty. He knew his prodigious gifts—his enormous talent as a short story writer and his genius as a philosopher. In one of his late *Journal* entries he remarks on his "by no means insignificant legacy" of intellectual achievement.[21] His distinction, he knew, was to have marked out a new way of *doing* philosophy and with that goes metaphysical theology. Time and again in the *Postscript* he comes back to what he had thus claimed in his *Journal* about the novelty of his view of Christianity and I need not repeat my interpretation of what he understood to be a subjective view of philosophy.[22] The imaginative understanding of what Wittgenstein called "forms of life" is part of this but so too is what he called the resolving of functions of philosophy as it releases us from the bondage of linguistic conventions and habits. Is the question of God's existence like that of the existence of a man in the moon or like that of numbers? Or is it not more like the existence of what I can speak of as my destiny? There is a Welsh hymn that speaks of the ways of the wilderness being plain to my sight when I view them from the heavenly Jerusalem's hills. If that is so it is not a matter of some peculiar geometry of an eternal perspective but, as Shakespeare put it, "a destiny that shapes one's ends." That is, we are making ontological claims and therefore revealing certain onlooks.

KIERKEGAARD'S ALTERNATIVE METAPHYSIC

In conclusion, then, let me amplify my seven points—or, rather, the essential six.

Truth

First, the problem of truth is a perennial issue of philosophy and it still concerns metaphysicians as well as logicians. Despite the contention of Frank Ramsey in his 1927 paper on "Faith and Propositions" that there is no problem but only "a linguistic muddle,"[23] the problem remains. The nature of a truth claim is that it says how things are so that however much we want to insist on the fact that "truth" relates to what is said, it is in the end an *ontological* rather than a logical or semantic one.

---

21. Kierkegaard, *Papirer* X4 A 628, 443.

22. See Heywood Thomas, *Philosophy of Religion in Kierkegaard's Writings*, 66ff. and the discussion in chapters 4 and 5 above.

23. Ramsey, "Faith and Proposition," 157–59.

The importance of Kierkegaard's discussion of truth has never, I think, been properly recognized.[24] It is perhaps one of the best illustrations of the difficulty of interpreting him because, as one grasps a certain aspect in all its subtle technicality, there is some other feature that attracts one's attention and its very obvious non-theoretical concern tempts me to see Kierkegaard as the prophet of a new inwardness with a Wittgensteinian view of language. This is why I was so anxious to begin with his historical context and to understand the problems as they confronted him. It seems to be essential that we understand how his constant interest in the problem of truth springs from the necessary interplay of *theoria* and *praxis*. So we must see that just as he was himself not bewitched he wanted others not to be bewitched by the constancy of the relation between a true proposition and what makes it true. Even if, like the great idealists, we want to say that coherence is the criterion of truth rather than correspondence with fact, there is some temptation to see truth as something that is factual and therefore unrelated to me. By calling attention to the necessary relation of truth—when we speak of moral and religious truth—to persons Kierkegaard was raising a metaphysical problem and not merely one about the self-involving nature of this language.

True, when I say "This is good" or "God is the creator" I am committing myself to certain kinds of action. However, this is because these statements show how or what things *are*—the nature of *reality*. The failure to see this is what has led so many critics to speak of Kierkegaard's theory of truth as a subjectivity. On the contrary, what he says is that the importance of the issue of truth is that it is my means of expressing my assessment of any assertion about how things are and that it is complicated and varied.

The Failure of Idealism to Harmonize Christianity and Philosophy

The second point concerns Christianity and philosophy directly. It is well enough known that Kierkegaard's early work—particularly *Fragments* and *Postscript*—had argued that a philosophy which is idealist in style cannot give a proper account of the relation between Christianity and

---

24. A notable exception is C. Stephen Evans' discussion in *Kierkegaard's Fragments and Postscript*, lvii. Evans makes the very important point that Climacus' whole discussion of truth and subjectivity is a commentary on John 14:6: "I am the . . . truth."

philosophy. Thus the former had discussed the matter formally and the latter had shown how irrelevant for the would-be Christian an idealist philosophy is. What is worth noting, I feel, is that as the second work deliberately recognized the validity of metaphysical theology as an enterprise so it also occasionally picked up what different metaphysical theology had in fact been attempted in the first.

My point is that there are several philosophical concerns in these works and Kierkekgaard is not simply saying that idealism is false because it gives us a wrong map of the way in which I come to know God in Christ. He understood more clearly than most how idealism is the insidiously constant *temptation* for the theologian. We can hail him as a sociological philosopher because his critique of idealism is as radical as that of Marx. His emphasis on the practical character of Christian faith—and Christian theology too—anticipates the contemporary appreciation of the ideological nature of Christianity.[25] The epistemology of faith had been misconstrued he argued, and the phenomenology of *becoming* a Christian was ignored.

Yet there was, I think, something else argued too—the erroneousness of the account given of the human situation. Here the Christian motivation to Kierkegaard's philosophizing is as important as is the Kantian-critical nature of its outlook. It seems very clear to me that Kierkegaard belongs with the development of philosophy from Kant through idealism to the emergence of an anti-idealist stance but that place is strictly in the nexus of critical and idealist trends. Indebted to Trendelenburg, he is also very close to Schelling and is as radical as Marx would later be. Like Kant, he was anxious to define the *limits* of coherent thinking and just as scrupulously as Calvin he was not prepared to pretend that the knowledge of what transcended those limits could yield speculative information.

His practical interest meant that he refused to follow Kant in the latter's strict separation of pure and practical reason and was able to relate metaphysics to the practical life by insisting on the importance of our knowing ourselves. This is well illustrated by his contention that in idealism the phenomenology of becoming a Christian is ignored. That is, this kind of philosophy treats the issue of Christianity as if it were not a matter of *becoming* and in so doing makes a false assumption about the nature of human beings.

25. Cf. Lash, "Theory, Theology and Ideology."

The basic assumption is the Socratic one that the truth is already in us and knowledge is its recollection. Christianity's claim, however, is that the *condition* for knowledge is absent and must be given.[26] *Fragments* contends that the change from error to truth is like a change from non-being to being. The movement from one to the other is not like the idealist translation of imagination into thought, alternative experiences like looking through plain glasses or looking through dark ones. It is an ontological change.

Theistic Proofs

The introduction of the notion of becoming must not lead us to the issue of logic and existence before we look at the problem of theistic proof. One of the most interesting features of Kierkegaard's work is his critique of this stock piece of metaphysical theology and it is not always appreciated how complex his argument is in *Fragments* and *Postscript*. There is the well-known satire on the theologian who has so nearly proved that he no longer needs to believe. There is also the related point about the benefit of proof: do you need it? But by far the most interesting arguments are those in *Fragments* about the tautological nature of the ontological argument as an elaboration of the *concept* of God and the failure of the cosmological argument as a causal proof with no reference.

There are moments here when Kierkegaard sounds like Hume or, even more, Kant: we prove Napoleon's existence, he says, from his works; but where are the works of *God*? Two very different points are asserted which make for the impossibility of theistic proof—(1) any argument moves away from and not towards existence and (2) there is a distinction between the factual nature of God—it is true that God exists—and the necessary character of God's being. On the first it might seem that he is really doing little more than repeating Kant's point about the Hundred Thalers. However, that would be an oversimplification of what he did; for he explicitly refers to this and remarks that even this was not a sufficient clarification of the way in which existence is outside thought and logic.[27] The second point is clearly very much an Anselmian mode of thinking; that the nature of God's existence is necessary, a necessity like

---

26. Cf. Kierkegaard, *Philosophical Fragments*, 13; S.V. 6, 16.
27. Kierkegaard, *Journals and Papers*, 1057; Kierkegaard, *Papirer* X2 A 328.

that which cannot be thought not to be. God, says Kierkegaard, does not *exist*: He *is*. He exists only in Christ.

Logic and Existence are Separate

We can now take up the fourth and more general point about logic, essence, and existence. Herein lies one of Kierkegaard's ontological innovations. Ever since his student days he had been interested in Aristotle and his earliest papers are littered with references to categories. Whether, like Aristotle, he was motivated by a desire to get away from the Platonic metaphysics of the Ideas I cannot say; but certainly Kierkegaard would have noted Aristotle's point that *ousia* is that which is neither in a subject nor said of a subject such as an individual human being.[28] His interest was not so much in categories in general but in the question, "In what sense do categories constitute an abridgement of existence?"[29] His claim was that *existence precedes essence*. This analysis of ontological categories led him to his sustained attack on Hegel but also to a view of metaphysics that is at once modest and excitingly ambitious inasmuch as the philosopher is not playing God. In particular the fullness of the Christian assertions about Christ and God and faith becomes possible as metaphysical theology.[30]

Incarnation as Event

Fifthly, in his scattered comments on Christology or rather on the Person of Christ, particularly in *Practice in Christianity*, Kierkegaard showed the fundamental flaw in Hegelian theology: its transformation of Christology into some abstract principle. By contrast, he recalls us to an awareness of the *event-character* of the doctrine's central statement.

Several others come together here; but let me make the bald brief claim that Kierkegaard's appreciation of the irredeemability of this paradox is a discovery of the essential pardoxicality of metaphysical theology.

---

28. Cf. Aristotle, *Categories*, 2a 11.

29. Kierkegaard, *Concluding Unscientific Postscript* 1, 121–22; S.V. 9, 95.

30. I have sketched some of these lines of thought in chapter 5, "Kierkegaard and Philosophy (ii): Kierkegaard on Ontology"; cf. Thulstrup's commentary on *Concluding Unscientific Postscript*, 98ff.

A Christian Anthropology

Finally there is a sense in which Kierkegaard is not only a polemical author but an apologist. The whole doctrine of the stages is a kind of *reductio ad absurdum*—the aesthetic life crumbles before the challenge of ethics and ethics becomes absorbed in the religious. Religion A, that of immanence, is inadequate and man proceeds through sin to the religion of transcendence, Christianity. Here is elaborated, then, an anthropology which makes sense of the Christian notion of salvation. Man is not just a self but a spirit. He is temporal being seeking the balance of past, present, and future. If we progress through the stages we come the more to appreciate the importance of time. Only at the Christian level is the equilibrium achieved and the importance fully acknowledged.[31]

I have tried to show what was on offer for Kierkegaard in metaphysical theology and what its classical source was. His rejection of that led us to this view of metaphysical theology as basically concerned with human existence but classical too in the concern with issues of ontology. Finally there thus appears a real theology that confidently but modestly takes up the metaphysical issues of existence, time, paradox, and the relation of truth and untruth.

---

31. As I have tried to show in chapter 11, the view of time is elaborated on the basis of Christology and justified by phenomenological analysis.

10

A Mature Rationalism

Kierkegaard's Reaction to Reason

KIERKEGAARD'S DELIMITATION OF REASON

THE MOST COMMON INTERPRETATION of Kierkegaard's thought is that it advocates and exemplifies an irrationalism. In an earlier paper I have shown the error of such an interpretation.[1] Similarly, I have argued in chapter 9 that it is wrong to see Kierkegaard's aim as the elimination of metaphysics in theology. What I now wish to do is to give a precise account of this outlook that I have thus characterized and of the task thus defined, an account that is precise because it shows the *reaction to reason*.

Kierkegaard's Delimitation of Reason is Rational

I emphasize the phrase "reaction to reason" for two reasons. First, I think that the contextualization of Kierkegaard's work given in my description of where he stood in relation to metaphysics is less than complete. While it is indisputable and indeed obvious that Kierkegaard's work is very largely a polemic against Hegel and the Hegelians, it does not mean that the reaction to reason is merely a rejection of Hegelianism. Moreover, to say that it is a rejection of Hegel's view of reason does not specify what it is: for, as Russell said long ago, negations are incomplete statements—S is not P (but Q). Without, then, disagreeing with the usual account of Kierkegaard as an anti-Hegelian, I have come to link him more closely

1. Heywood Thomas, "Lukác's Critique of Kierkegaard."

with Kant, if only because the reaction to reason is the same kind of *delimitation* of reason's range.

The Hegelian stimulus to Kierkegaard's development of his philosophy and theology is clear. The very purpose of *Philosophical Fragments* is to show the impossibility of the Hegelian theology which thinkers like Martensen were developing. That purpose was in line with the intention of each of his earlier works, starting with the M.A. dissertation, *The Concept of Irony*. It is not possible to argue the matter here; but the view of this I set out in my book has become the standard interpretation of the work.[2] It is an ironic examination of Hegelian aesthetics. It uses Hegel's theory to attack Romanticism; and yet in Hegelian-sounding language and by a seemingly Hegelian methodology it destroys the Hegelian synthesis.

To continue, *Either-Or* is a work that would have struck any Hegelian thinker as disordered, trivial even, and certainly more literary than philosophical. However, there is deep irony here too; for the whole intention of that work, according to Kierkegaard, was the study of tautology. This is rather obscure because this amazingly clever pastiche of Romanticism seems to have little to do with logic. The point simply put is that one of Kierkegaard's major concerns here was the debate about the foundations of logic that had occupied Copenhagen at the time (see chapter 5). The point at issue was whether the Law of Contradiction was, as Hegel insisted, not the ground or basis of logic. Thus, Kierkegaard contends, the whole argument of *Either-Or* is summed up in the theme of one of the essays in the *Diapsalmata*—tautology as the highest principle of thought. The thesis is that nothing can remove the either-or of the Law of Contradiction.

Fear and Trembling comes next and this develops a theme of *Either-Or* where an anthropology had begun to emerge. Life is a choice between attitudes—either the hedonism of the young aesthete or the morality of his friend, the judge. The indication of a third "stage" with which *Either-Or* ended is developed in the account given in *Fear and Trembling* of the religious faith typified by the story of Abraham. Already the attack

---

2. Heywood Thomas, *Philosophy of Religion in Kierkegaard's Writings*, 11ff. In *Kierkegaard's Critique of Religion and Society*, Merold Westphal argues that the alleged irrationalism is really the unmasking of society's attempt to legitimize itself by calling its historically contingent first principle "reason." Alastair Hannay's account of Lukac's progression from idolatry to critique is both interesting and instructive (see Hannay, *Kierkegaard: A Biography*, 428–36).

on Hegelianism had, in *Either-Or*, been extended into logic and philosophy. Now the attack clarifies the rejection of this view of life in its basics, showing that religious faith makes the particular higher than the universal. Hegelianism is wrong because its account of faith and ethics completely distorts what a phenomenology of morality and religion shows to be the case.

The complexity of this argument that Kierkegaard thus develops can be understood only if we see him continuing the development of Kant's critical philosophy. We have seen good historical grounds for linking his work with the whole idealist movement from Fichte onwards. What is more important for our purpose here is that his intention is that of Kant in the *Critique of Pure Reason*—to limit knowledge (i.e., reason) to make room for faith—and likewise that of Fichte in his *Critique of Revelation*, to ask what were the transcendental conditions of a revelation. If Kierkegaard's inspiration is thus Kantian then *his reaction to reason is, in a very real sense, strictly rational.*

Kierkegaard and the Transformation of Reason

My second reason for emphasizing the notion of *reaction* is that there is, to my mind, in Kierkegaard's work a significant development of what might be called a philosophy after Christianity. I hesitate to call it a Christian philosophy; but I want to suggest that underlying his struggle against the distortion of Hegelian philosophy of religion and dogmatics, on the one hand, and, on the other, their disastrous consequences on Christian living is the revelation of faith's *transformation of reason*.

I have already shown the way in which he is the heir to the critical philosophy and what I am now saying is that in a context which spoke of "going further than Hegel" Kierkegaard's aim was indeed to go further than Kant. The tension in Kant between his avowal of faith and the agnosticism of the critical outlook is, for Kierkegaard, overcome because he applies the paradigm of the Christian story. What is, after all, so noteworthy that it must be something of a key to understanding Kierkegaard is that he clearly *rejects irrationalism*. If that is so then his reaction to reason is an advocacy of *a new view of what reason is and can do*.

Perhaps the significance of the Christian paradigm becomes clear if we reflect that *Philosophical Fragments*, the first critique of rationalism, follows *Fear and Trembling*. In the latter the story of Abraham had been retold not simply so as to show that faith was a leap that was discontinuous with speculation and ethics but also to emphasize that Isaac was restored to Abraham. The paradox that Abraham believed was more than the assertion that the command of God was to break the moral law. It was, in fact, that God would fulfill his promise of blessing Abraham's seed though the only son was to be murdered. From this Kierkegaard derived the theme of *Repetition* and his view that repetition is the category of faith, the mark of Christianity.

It would then, I think, be proper to characterize his reaction to reason as death and resurrection. What he contends is that if we grasp that the whole problem of belief is the issue of what we do with our sin we see that the work of reason is involved in this rather than being the lifeline that provides salvation. The mapping of faith in *Fragments* thus shows the paradoxical passion of reason that brings it to its self-destruction. Only so, according to Kierkegaard, can we believe. And it is to the *offended* reason that there is thus given an occasion for belief.

This view of things helps us understand *Fragments* where one of the puzzling features is the clever but wrong-headed argument that history is not knowledge. The puzzle is his exploitation of the ambiguity of belief—the Danish "*tro*," like the English "belief," can mean either a *weak* epistemological claim or faith. Perhaps, after all, Kierkegaard is not as confused as I have always thought this argument to be. It may be that what he is saying is that if reason can embrace the Absolute Paradox then there is a belief which is also rational because it also involves those rational processes of historical judgement. It is thus that I see him suggesting that for reason the pilgrimage to faith is indeed a matter of dying with Christ and rising again with him. That is certainly a more accurate view than irrationalism. We now need to look at the detail.

THE PLACE OF REASON IN KIERKEGAARD'S WRITINGS

Problems Interpreting Kierkegaard's Writings

Before going further I should point out the well-known fact that the interpretation of Kierkegaard's thought is difficult for several reasons. The most important of these is that it is a dialectical authorship produced, for the greater part, pseudonymously. The pseudonymous authorship began with *Either-Or* in 1843 and reached its climax with *Concluding Unscientific Postscript* in 1846, after which there were two works under a different pseudonym.

We do not need to discuss the issue here but we must be clear about how we understand this authorship. Roughly speaking the issue is whether we should take Kierkegaard to be expressing his own opinions *only* when he writes under his own name. That seems to be implied by what he said in *Concluding Unscientific Postscript* where he makes "A first and last declaration," saying, "There is therefore in the pseudonymous works not a single word of my own."[3] That the pseudonymous authorship is an instance of what Kierkegaard called indirect communication is obvious enough but one also needs to grasp what that means in terms of his own position. Clearly he saw the pseudonyms as some kind of ideal types. Thus he regards a pseudonym as being excellent for accentuating a point, a stance, a position, and that it makes a poetic person.[4] However, it cannot be the case that these pseudonyms never express Kierkegaard's opinion since there are several occasions when the pseudonyms agree with his own declared views. The difficulty, then, is quite simply so to expound Kierkegaard's works that we never ignore the possibility of his saying something in order to effect his Socratic midwifery while also seeking that elusive unity of thought which makes his whole output a single authorship. It has always been my belief that beneath the variety there is such a coherent intellectual standpoint, not indeed a system but still a consistent philosophy.

The Death and Resurrection of Rationality in Kierkegaard's Writings

To begin our exposition, then, we can look at what had been achieved in the very earliest of his works, *The Concept of Irony*, which, in any case, as an academic thesis, presents no problems of pseudonymity. The intention of that work was to show that Hegel's interpretation of irony was wrong. This was achieved by an ironic deployment of Hegel. Speaking fulsomely of Hegel he nevertheless makes clear that by considering only romantic irony Hegel has failed to grasp that irony can be a proper attitude.[5] One of the most interesting expressions of the rejections of Hegel is his earlier remark that in Hegel's *History of Philosophy* there is "absolutely nothing to illuminate the relation between the three distinct

---

3. Kierkegaard, *Postscript*, 551.
4. Kierkegaard, *Journals and Papers*, 6528; Kierkegaard, *Papirer* X2 A 184.
5. Kierkegaard, *Concept of Irony*, 282; S.V. 1, 279.

contemporary conceptions of Socrates'—and this despite the fact that Hegel said that 'with respect to Socrates there is not so much the discussion of philosophy as of individual life.'"[6] That is to say, if we are properly to grasp the nature of this teacher's standpoint then it will not do to offer a historical account of him without looking for the character behind these three different accounts.

What *Irony* makes clear is that the way in which life must be judged is by ethical standards, and aesthetic views are inadequate if they fail to do this. I begin there because it helps us make sense of the first of the pseudonymous works, *Either-Or*. In a note expanding a comment on the difference between Socrates and Christ that he had made in an earlier note on *Irony*, Kierkegaard remarks that Christ was the Truth.[7] This Socrates neither was nor knew—any more than he knew that the relation of Christ to the historically given reality was "absolutely real" while that of the ironist Socrates was purely negative.[8] That the negativity of irony makes it an inadequate life-view is what may be called the book's general point. Thus the eighth of the Latin theses asserts: "Irony, as infinite and absolute negativity, is the lightest and weakest meaning of subjectivity."

I suggested that this helps us to make sense of *Either-Or*; for this is no easy thing to do. It is one thing to appreciate the way in which the construction of the first half in particular matches the lack of unity that characterizes the "aesthetic" stage; but it is quite a different thing to expound the philosophical intention and achievement of the work. As Kierkegaard has obligingly expressed that intention in his usual oblique manner the task is to elaborate the significance of comment. This is what he says: "My special concern with the whole of *Either-Or* is to make it quite clear that the metaphysical meaning at the root of it all is to lead everything forward to the dilemma (either-or). The same thought lies also at the root of the little philosophical essay 'Tautology as the highest principle of thought.' Alas, how many people will understand me when I say that if the principle of contradiction is true (and it is expressed by the words either-or), then, tautology is the philosophical expression of this principle."[9]

6. Ibid., 243; S.V. 1, 245.
7. Ibid., 52.
8. Ibid., 242.
9. Kierkegaard, *Journals and Papers*, 405; Kierkegaard, *Papirer* III B 177.

The critical point here is the remark that "either-or" is an expression of the truth of the principle of contradiction. We recall that since 1839 there had been much discussion in Copenhagen of the Principle of Contradiction. The debate was between those who argued, with Hegel, that contradiction was to be resolved into a higher unity and those who maintained that only opposites could be harmonized and that there could be no mediation between contradictories (*modsigelser*). As Kierkegaard was to remark later in *Postscript*, the Hegelian philosopher had "taken away the principle of contradiction" and it had become "a favorite sport that as soon as anyone hints at an *aut-aut*, Hegelians have been on the warpath."[10] This is an interesting issue but we need not pursue it beyond saying that clearly this controversy was an important factor in confirming Kierkegaard's anti-Hegelian outlook.

The important point is that he had as great an interest in elevating logic as did Hegel; but unlike Hegel he was a formalist in his view of logic and he had no desire to collapse the distinction between logic and theology. What I mean by the latter comment is that whereas Hegel had achieved a translation, if I may so put it, of Christian Doctrine into logic Kierkegaard wanted to see logic remain a criterion of true theology. Thus he quotes with approval King Lear's remark, "Yes, and no at the same time: that is not good theology"[11] and echoes the sentiment in *Fragments*.[12] Nothing could be clearer evidence of Kierkegaard's distaste for a pure irrationalism and it suggests too that it is correct to see Kierkegaard's critique of rationalist theology on the model of death and resurrection. His *preparatio evangelica*, I am suggesting, is the rejection of the Hegelian view of logic.

Two points need to be made about this anti-Hegelian stance in relation to logic. The first is a specific one, namely, that because logic is to be understood in a formalist fashion the Hegelian claim about the logical nature of the System was false. I have shown in chapter 5 how this works. All I want to add to that now is that this marks an interesting reaction to the particular rationalizing of theology that Hegel had effected. The system was, for Hegel, very obviously a defense of the essential truth of Christianity against the rationalist dehistoricization effected by the

---

10. Kierkegaard, *Postscript* 1, 304.
11. Kierkegaard, *Journals and Papers*, 4773, II A 34.
12. Kierkegaard, *Fragments*, 46–47.

Enlightenment. Indeed he saw himself as a restorer of orthodoxy.[13] Yet, according to Kierkegaard, this very defense of the historicity of Christianity became a vicious confusion of logical and historical categories because for Hegel the truth of Christianity is something that is *necessarily* unfolded in history. This is precisely the kind of confusion which Barth in his discussion of Hegel was to single out as a serious flaw in Hegel's theology: "Hegel, in making the dialectical method of logic the essential nature of God, made impossible the knowledge of the actual dialectic of grace which has its foundation in the freedom of God."[14]

It is perhaps this perception of what is over-ambitious in Hegel's view of logic that motivated those early studies of logical issues, which can be seen in Kierkegaard's papers. To follow the confusion of logic and theology, as I have described it, in Hegel's system would be too much to attempt here. However, what is clear from what I have said already is that not only did Hegel offer a deceptively attractive logical formulation of the Christian doctrine of God, Trinity, and incarnation, but the whole nature of logic is that it is a science which is creative and is indeed the science of the spirit. My second point is the more general philosophical one that *logic is uninformative*. Here Kierkegaard seems to me to advocate a return to Kant's critical philosophy, which had made so fundamental a distinction between the *a priori* and the *a posteriori*. We have, I think, failed to see this critical spirit of Kierkegaard because the language in which the discussion is always couched is that of Hegel. Yet what, after all, is the nature of tautology except the annoying fact that it is, for all its emptiness, incontrovertible and certain truth? In saying, then, that tautology is the highest principle of thought Kierkegaard is reminding us that we delude ourselves if we imagine that a speculative system can yield for us the novelty of knowledge that anything called "science" holds.

Too often Kierkegaard's diatribes against the "science" of Hegelianism have been taken not simply as evidence of an irrationalism but more especially of a hostility towards modern science. That there is something very profoundly conservative about Kierkegaard's outlook I do not deny but I also think that it is wrong to ignore the many ways in which he was a spirit far ahead of his own age. One example of that, I suggest, is the very real enthusiasm he had for empirical science. Writing

13. Hegel, *History of Philosophy*, 200ff.
14. Barth, *From Rousseau to Ritschl*, 304.

to his brother-in-law, the scientist Peter Wilhelm Lund, on 1 June 1835, he speaks with knowledge and admiration of the natural sciences.[15] What he was interested in, however, was the mystery of the inner world of human existence and, even more than Kant, he was concerned to limit knowledge to make room for *glaube*.

My point at the moment is that an important preliminary step in the enterprise of limiting reason is this contention that *logic does not describe or define reality*. The relation of logic to reality is spoken of by Kierkegaard in terms that are strangely reminiscent of Kant's description of his categories. Logic, says Kierkegaard, predisposes reality for our knowledge but it does not itself stand in any relation to the actuality of reality.[16]

In this suggestion about tautology Kierkegaard can also perhaps be credited with an anticipation of Godel's theorem or proof, namely, that no set of axioms and rules for a system containing its own system is ever complete. That tautology is the highest principle of thought could thus be construed as asserting the improvability of any logical proof. What is said inside the system is indeed proof but there is no "outside" to any tautology which is its proof. Kierkegaard did not in fact see this very clearly and nowhere made any *clear* use of such an insight. Yet in his discussion of the distinction between logic and existence and his view of logic as concerned only with essences he was moving towards such a philosophy of logic. This rejection of the possibility of a system of existence as distinct from a system of logic[17] is a clear example as is the argument of *Fragments* about proof's presupposition of existence.[18]

The obvious relevance of this to theology shows all too clearly Kierkegaard's underlying motivation. However, before coming to his treatment of such issues let me look at the way in which this claim about tautology was shown by Kierkegaard to be a step forward from the Kantian and the Hegelian legacy. The interesting feature of the form "either-or" is that it can express a tautology as in the law of the excluded middle: Either p or *not p*. In the essay to which Kierkegaard referred

---

15. Kierkegaard, *Journals*, 16, 6–7. Cf. Hannay, *Kierkegaard: A Biography*, 98, on Kierkegaard's view of knowledge.

16. Kierkegaard, *Concept of Anxiety*, 13; S.V. 6, 112.

17. Kierkegaard, *Postscript*, 118ff.; S.V. 9, 100ff.

18. Kierkegaard, *Fragments*, 40; S.V. 6, 40.

in this *Journal* entry—the diapsalm "Either-Or: An ecstatic lecture"[19]—we are offered four tautologies: "Marry, laugh at the world's follies, believe a girl, hang yourself—or don't; and you will regret it, whatever you do." This is not at all clear because, in fact, not only are none of these statements (most being deontological statements) strictly a tautology but what Kierkegaard does is to operate with two sets of four tautologies—(a) four different values to the variable p in our abstract formula and (b) four implications of the form, "If for any value of both p and *not p* none is true then 'Either p or *not p*' implies none." If we now return to his discussion, Kierkegaard's point is that the difference between this kind of philosophical attitude and Hegel's is that it does not resolve the dilemma by some *final* movement but rather by an *initial* one. As Collingwood would have put it, it is a question of our absolute assumption. This is what Kierkegaard says:

> My philosophy is at least easy to understand, for I have only one principle, and I do not even proceed from that. It is necessary to distinguish between the successive dialectic in either/or, and the eternal dialectic here set forth. Thus, when I say that I do not proceed from my principle, this must not be understood in opposition to a proceeding forth from it, but is rather a negative expression for the principle itself, through which it is apprehended in equal opposition to a proceeding or a non-proceeding from it. I do not proceed from my principle; for if I did, I would regret it, and if I did not, I would also regret that. If it seems, therefore, to one or another of my respected hearers that there is anything in what I say, it only proves that he has no talent for philosophy; if it seems to have any forward movement, this also proves the same. But for those who can follow me although I do not make any progress, I shall now unfold the eternal truth, by virtue of which this philosophy remains within itself, and admits of no higher philosophy. For if I proceeded from my principle, I should find it impossible to stop; for if I stopped, I should regret it, and if I did stop, I should also regret that, and so forth. But since I never start, so can I never stop; my eternal departure is identical with my eternal cessation. Experience has shown that it is by no means difficult for philosophy to begin. Far from it. It begins with nothing, and consequently can always begin. But the difficulty, both for philosophy and for philosophers, is to stop. This difficulty is obviated in my philosophy; for if anyone believes that

---

19. Kierkegaard, *Either-Or*, I, 36; S.V. 2, 40.

when I stop now, I really stop, he proves himself lacking in the speculative insight. For I do not stop now, I stopped at the time when I began. Hence my philosophy has the advantage of brevity, and it is also impossible to refute.[20]

Resurrected Rationality and Ethics

What I want to go on to discuss is the place Kierkegaard gives reason in ethics. The doctrine of the stages is familiar to everyone as is the distinction between the aesthetic and the ethical being made in terms of choice. In *Either-Or* the advice of Judge William to his young friend who faces despair is that the latter should *choose* despair. Only thus can he break the syndrome of despair and advance to the higher stage of the ethical. Constantly the Judge repeats that point, that ethics is characterized by choice, choice of oneself in one's eternal validity. While the concrete nature of the ethical stage as a type of life is very much a Kantian and Hegelian morality Kierkegaard's analysis of ethics is very different from either. In a word, for Kierkegaard ethics has to do with my feelings and my will and it is *not born of reason*. Though it will be true that in regard to the morality of the Christian life—just as much as in the matter of Christian faith—there is a resurrection, what is at first obvious is the death of reason.

Ethics, according to Judge William, is better spoken of not as knowledge but as *choice*. He explains the matter thus: "The ethical individual knows himself but this knowledge is not a mere contemplation (for with that the individual is determined by his necessity), it is a reflection upon himself which itself is an action, therefore I have deliberately preferred to use the expression 'choose oneself' instead of 'know oneself.'"[21]

The limits of a resurrected reason are clear in the recognition of the cognitive nature of this judgment just as much as in the more metaphysical emphasis in the repeated use of the phrase "choose oneself in one's eternal validity." However, as I say, the first thing that strikes me here is that Kierkegaard is taking issue with any description of the ethical as a purely rational activity. Indeed what seems to be quite fascinating about *Either-Or* is the way in which this philosophical novel is able to show the inconsistency of a moral outlook that tries to present a bourgeois ethic

---

20. Ibid., 31–32.
21. Kierkegaard, *Either-Or*, II, 263; S.V. 3, 239.

but is forced by its own honesty to the moral consciousness to stress the non-rational.

There is a long passage in the second volume which discusses the paradox of a novel kind of existence that is yet said to be choice of something and so something that already exists. One of its most interesting features is the concluding contrast between choice and creation: "I do not create myself, I choose myself. Therefore while nature is created out of nothing, while I myself as an immediate personality am created out of nothing, as a free spirit I am born of the principle of contradiction or born by the fact that I choose myself."[22] This is interesting because it throws more light on the reason why Kierkegaard was so anxious to defend the Principle of Contradiction as the basis of logic; but it is even more interesting as a characterization of ethical judgment.

In the business of moral choice and action Kierkegaard does not think that we are entirely free. This is perhaps one of the ways in which he was so profoundly Kantian;[23] for the causal nexus is what inevitably limits freedom. Equally the whole Hegelian emphasis on the actualities of social existence is, I think, accepted by Kierkegaard, as in the person of Judge William he expounds what ethical existence is. Thus a comment which anticipates Freud's theory of ego-ideal also links with a *sittlichkeit*: "This self which the individual knows is at once the actual and the ideal self which the individual has outside himself as the picture in the likeness to which he has to form himself and which, on the other hand, he nevertheless has in him since it is the self."[24]

The weakness of the aesthete's life, according to the Judge, is that he does "not think historically."[25] Ironically it is this very historicity of the ethical life that makes for the tensions leading to its breakdown. In the first place, the view of ethics inspired by Kant stresses the nature of ethics as obligation; but what Kierkegaard brings out is the way in which duty forces me to acknowledge something that is hardly rational, namely, an *infinite* obligation and the consequent guilt that is similarly limitless. There is a sense in which Kierkegaard clearly views a relationship to God as growing out of duty. Thus Judge William speaks of duty

22. Ibid., 220; S.V. 3, 200.
23. In his *Kierkegaard: A Biography*, 224ff., Hannay shows clearly the similarities with and divergences from Kantian ethics.
24. Ibid., 220; S.V. 3, 200.
25. Ibid., 130; S.V. 3, 122.

as "an old friend, an intimate, a confidant" and yet "his commanding ... is a divine way of expressing" the realization of what is willed.[26] I am not now concerned with the content of the ethical stage but am merely pointing out that the way in which *Either-Or* raises the problem of its dissolution is by a very faithful account of what it is to fulfill any duty.

It is thus that we are brought to the concluding paradox of an *ethical* recognition that as against God we are *always* and *infinitely* in the wrong. Paradox it would be for Kant, if not indeed the kind of impossible superstition that he condemns in his *Revelation within the Limits of Reason Alone* and his *Lectures on Ethics*. However, it was precisely this problem of an exceptional morality that intrigued Kierkegaard—probably because he was aware that by any normal or ordinary standard of morality his break with Regine Olsen was reprehensible. To wait two years for a teenager to come of age before proposing to her, overwhelm her with a whirlwind courtship, and then jilt her within a matter of days—this was neither respectable nor indeed rational nor in any sense proper behavior. Yet his own reckoning of the matter was that it was obedience to the call, "Still further!" "A spy in higher service," he was under "sealed orders," and his duty was clearly that of obedience to the highest authority. The difficulty was that the highest authority was not available for any public appeal so that when the young, foppish but promising theologian—a future university professor and almost certainly the Archbishop of Denmark after the next—was being earnestly sought by Councillor Olsen to do the honorable thing by his fiancée he could only say that he must go now because he was on his way to the theatre.

This is the clue to the profundity of Kierkegaard's discussion of Abraham's story as he retells it in *Fear and Trembling*. One of the most telling features in the discussion is the contrast drawn between the biblical figure and the tragic hero. There can be few arguments in the whole history of theology that better illustrate the truth that Christianity moves beyond tragedy than this discussion of Agamemnon, Jephthah, and Brutus. The crucial point is that, as Kierkegaard says, "the tragic hero still remains within the ethical," with a higher ethical norm validating the rejection of the lower.

There are two ways in which, I think, Kierkegaard views the death of reason in ethics as a *prius* to its resurrection. The first is that in speaking of a teleological suspension of the ethical he makes clear that the

---

26. Ibid., 149; S.V. 3, 139.

ethical is not thereby destroyed or "abolished" but is rather preserved at a higher level.[27] How this works we shall have occasion to consider again; but for the moment suffice it to say that Kierkegaard insists that Abraham believes in God's goodness. To put the matter in Kantian terms, what Kierkegaard argues is that there can be moral reasons why what clearly follows as an implication of the universal rule is not duty and that this is to gain a higher moral viewpoint.

The particular point I am making is that if he does not challenge the view that the identification of the rule as *ethical* is rational then no more does he want to say that Abraham's belief in the absurd is irrational or a rejection of reason *simpliciter*. The role of the higher absolute *telos* in the argument of *Fear and Trembling* is very precisely distinguished from the comparatively simple agony of the tragic hero. There, for all its pathos and horror, it is in logic no more complicated than the lawyer's appeal to a wider framework of law or to the fact that "the major includes the minor."

However, the paradox of the teleological suspension of the ethical is that the ethical is restored by virtue of the absolute relationship with the absolute. This is why the end of the biblical story, though it receives less notice in *Fear and Trembling* than Abraham's radical break with the ethics of the Law and his strict obedience to the simple command to sacrifice Isaac, is nevertheless crucial to the picture of the "knight of faith." What I mean is that Kierkegaard wanted to say that faith was indeed the death of reason in ethics but that because the ethical is retained in its teleological suspension ethical reason is resurrected. Though the book's author declares that he does not understand Abraham he also recognizes that there is a category that will make such understanding possible.[28]

The second way in which I see my interpretation revealed in the authorship is that in the acknowledged works where Kierkegaard is presenting a Christian view of life he is concerned with what even Kant would recognize as matters of morals. Thus the work of *Purity of Heart* is specifically a discussion of "willing the ethical" and nothing demonstrates the rationality of that ethical more than the mode of argument employed here. Kierkegaard's first task is to *show* the ways in which people delude themselves that they are indeed behaving ethically when

---

27. Kierkegaard, *Fear and Trembling*, 54; S.V. 5, 51.
28. Ibid., 60; S.V. 5, 56.

in fact they are not willing one thing. Again, *Works of Love* is an argument about the nature of the highest value.[29]

Resurrected Rationality and Religion

I come finally to the problem which one might initially think of as the only sphere in which Kierkegaard takes issue with rationalism, that of religious belief. It is more or less accidental that, for the most part, our discussion has followed the chronological course of Kierkegaard's writings and we move now from *Fear and Trembling* to the next publication, *Philosophical Fragments*. Though I have been anxious to offer an accurate interpretation of Kierkegaard it is the thought rather than its development with which I have been engaged. So also it is not necessary for us to discuss the precise and complete definition of *the* problem of *Fragments*. I speak of *the* problem because it is part of Kierkegaard's *literary* method and art that he identifies for himself one major problem that then determines his manner of approach in that work. What is obvious about *Fragments* and is incontestably part of its problem is the relation between Christianity and speculative idealism; but what is even more obvious is that the problem is actually posed in the way Lessing had posed the problem of Christianity. Thus *Fragments* has on its title-page the question which could be said to be its sub-title: "Is an historical point of departure possible for an eternal consciousness; how can such a point of departure have any other than a merely historical interest; is it possible to base an eternal happiness upon historical knowledge?"

There are several interesting points about the composition of the work and not least this title page. Originally the problem was couched in more personal terms: "How do I arrive at an historical point of departure for my eternal consciousness; how can such a point of departure have more than historical interest; how can I base my salvation upon historical knowledge?—A dogmatic-philosophical problem."[30] The autobiographical style suggests the continuing influence of Romanticism, which would lead a commentator back to the anti-Hegelian development of idealism. More significant, however, is the definition of the problem as dogmatic-

---

29. M. Jamie Ferreira says well, "Without moving forward to *Works of Love* scholarship can only unfairly evaluate Kierkegaard's various contributions to ethics" (Ferreira, *Love's Grateful Striving*, 5) and again that in *Works of Love* Kierkegaard is relying on a notion of what God's love for us is like.

30. Kierkegaard, *Papirer* V B 1.

philosophical and this confirms my characterization of the problem. If we read on in the *Papers* we find Kierkegaard defining his problem more clearly: "This is and remains the main problem with respect to the relationship between Christianity and philosophy. Lessing is the only one who has dealt with this. But Lessing knew considerably more what the issue is about than the common herd of modern philosophers."[31]

So for our purposes in this discussion we can take the problem of *Fragments* to be that of revelation and reason or the role of reason in relation to a historical revelation. Thus Kierkegaard is posing a slightly different form of Kant's problem of the limits of rational knowledge in relation to faith because he sees that any proper discussion of the problem of Christian faith has to include within its scope the historical knowledge that can be said to be its basis. It is in this sense that Kierkegaard is linking Kant and the Enlightenment and is the first theologian to address the modern problem of history and faith. Let us now see the way he sets out his problem and answer.

The problem is set out as a problem of knowledge. What is it for someone to know the highest truth? If idealism is right then the truth is already within one; for whatever form an idealist philosophy takes, its epistemology is basically that of Plato, the Socratic theory that knowledge is recollection.

The next step is to point out that for an idealist the acquisition of knowledge is concerned with something essential rather than with any relation to the teacher as such. Once we know, then Socrates as the teacher is of no importance. The method of Kierkegaard's argument in *Fragments* is hypothetical in that he asks first, "If idealism is true then what?" and then, "If the case is quite different then what?" So he says that man does not already have the truth in him but is in untruth and the teacher then cannot show him the truth that lies in him but must show the untruth. Moreover the teacher has an extra task—not only putting the truth before man but also enabling man to grasp it—"he must also give him the condition necessary for understanding it."[32] Now if, therefore, the moment of learning is thus decisive the teacher must be God (I leave aside what seems to me the pointless discussion whether *Fragments*, by the peculiar expression "the God," is indeed expounding Christian faith; for I think that *"Guden"* is an attempt to repeat *ho theos*

31. Kierkegaard, *Journals and Papers* 2370; Kierkegaard, *Papirer* V B 1, 2.
32. Kierkegaard, *Fragments*, 17.

and show the classical nature of the problem) since God is both Teacher and Savior.

The next part of the book's argument that is relevant to our discussion is chapter 3 with its account of the paradox of reason, "the passion of reason" that wills a collision with something that cannot be thought, "the Unknown which is the limit to which the Reason repeatedly comes."[33] In the appendix to that chapter the specific revelation of the incarnation as a paradox and miracle is noted. Finally, the concluding chapters of the book are an attempt to map out the role of historical knowledge in the belief of a contemporary and a later disciple.

One of the difficulties of Kierkegaard scholarship is the strange confusion one encounters in the pastiche Kierkegaard creates from a rich scholarship and a brilliantly imaginative engagement with the interplay of various problems and concepts. At the risk of producing a crude over-simplification of this argument, I want to suggest that Kierkegaard is saying three or four things. First, he wants to show as clearly as Kant did the limit of reason in relation to religious faith. Secondly, he wants to say that the rational knowledge of history is likewise unable to provide what is needed for the assertion of faith. Then, third, he says something very different—that there can be a "happy" encounter of the reason and the paradox, "a mature understanding," so that one can see him advocating a recognition of the idiosyncratic rationality of faith, both as a speculative endeavor of thought and as the exercise of historical enquiry.

Let me try and spell out the points. In the first place, the polemic Kierkegaard offers against rationalist theology is well known and his brilliant analysis of the problem of theistic proof is perhaps the least fully understood as it is the best known example of this. "The idea of demonstrating that this unknown something exists," he says, "could scarcely suggest itself to Reason."[34] It is an irrational enterprise since it must either assume the existence of the unknown (in which case it is otiose) or its non-existence (in which case it is impossible). Then he makes the point that one is not in any case able to reason *to* existence. Also, he shows the kind of vicious logic that any causal proof of God would involve by his analogy of proving Napoleon's existence from Napoleon's deeds. So the case of a rationalist theism which would have proof of God's existence as its most dramatic and typical achievement is shown

33. Ibid., 55.
34. Ibid., 49.

to be wrong. *Reason's knowledge is confined to the finite* and even when any claim about the unknown's existence is made it will still be true that reason "cannot advance beyond this point."[35]

In the second place, in the discussion of both the contemporary disciple and the later one ("the disciple at second hand") Kierkegaard points out that any historical knowledge will fall short of the kind of knowledge that faith claims. That is, all the eyewitness accounts or immediate experience can offer is a publicly verifiable statement—that this man was like this or that. It cannot, by definition, give me the knowledge that I want—the Johannine declaration, for instance, that we have "beheld his glory, glory as of the only-begotten son of the Father." The knowledge that a later disciple has is even more suspect because the epistemological status of statements about the past raises doubts. They can only be probable and not certain and therefore one is even further removed from the kind of certain premises one seeks for the argument. In this way Kierkegaard drew the sting of Lessing's critique by acknowledging that the rationalist theism that sought to move from the suspect ground of speculation to what seemed the safe haven of history was guilty of a category mistake. However, he wants also to say that it would be quite wrong to think that faith is some kind of nonsense, however much we may want to move away from the disastrous compromises of the philosophy and theology of his time.

If I may begin at the end of his argument, I would want to insist most strongly on the error of construing the argument of *Fragments* as a rejection of history. There is no doubt in my mind that this argument is the most powerful single influence on Barth just as much as on Bultmann and Tillich in the coincidence of their probabilism in Christology. However, that is not what concerns us; for it is important to grasp how, here as elsewhere, Kierkegaard is operating with a more sophisticated logic than is seen in any of the three—the distinction between a necessary condition and a sufficient condition of truth. He has shown that neither speculation nor history is a sufficient condition and what he is saying is that the difference between faith statements and historical judgments is such that for the former what is a necessary condition is only a most modest historical claim. But that is the point—there *has* to be some claim.

35. Ibid., 55.

It is not possible to argue here what I have shown elsewhere, that Kierkegaard's Christology does in fact depend on a variety of historical claims. The important point is that, in his annoying fashion, Kierkegaard engages in almost a sleight of hand when he points out the match that is to be found between the status of history as belief and the similar status of faith. As I said earlier, in Danish as in English the same word is used: "*tro*" is "belief" (general) and "belief" (religious faith).[36] But what I have also been anxious to bring out is the way in which Kierkegaard sees a positive relation between reason and faith. It must not be forgotten that it was the very passion of reason itself that drove it into collision with the unknown. Moreover, in the discussion of the issue of theistic proof here and in *Postscript* he suggests the way in which the evidence of faith is within itself, that the divine revelation is self-authenticating.

A contemporary author, the theologian Magnus Eriksson, writing under the pseudonym Theophilus Nicolaus, criticized Kierkegaard as advocating that faith was belief *against reason*. In the *Papers* there is to be found an unpublished draft reply that takes up the argument point by point.[37] The upshot of this is that Kierkegaard wants to insist that there is a positive relation and that after the death of reason there is a second movement. Thus too in *Postscript* he speaks of a "*second* immediacy." The point can be put in the words of a *Journal* entry—"Christianity . . . always turns the normal man's concepts topsy turvy."[38] To put my thesis briefly, I could say that Kierkegaard's view of reason was post-Kantian but as resolutely Kantian in his insistence that faith demanded a place for reason which typical rationalism would not accept.

---

36. This is discussed by Alastair Hannay (*Kierkegaard*, 101–2) as he broaches the issue of whether Kierkegaard's notion of religious belief is subject to the charge of irrationality.

37. Kierkegaard, *Papirer* X6 B 68–81. The earlier reference to his Kantian desire to emphasize the limits of reason is relevant here. On this see C. Stephen Evans, *Passionate Reason*, 181.

38. Kierkegaard, *Journals and Papers* 2238; Kierkegaard, *Papirer* X2 A 519.

11

Kierkegaard and the Problem of Time

It could be argued that Kierkegaard's idea of time is one of the most decisive notions in his whole authorship, underlying as it does his view of human existence and even his understanding of philosophy itself. However, to look for the central or the most important idea is a very dangerous method of interpreting Kierkegaard, and it will be no part of my argument that this is a more important theme for Kierkegaard than any one of the other great ideas that he uses in his analysis of human existence. What I want to do is to undertake the more humble task of showing *how* the role played in Kierkegaard's thought by the category of time is decisive and then to show what he has to say in his authorship about the philosophical problem of the nature of time.

THE UBIQUITY OF TEMPORALITY IN KIERKEGAARD'S THOUGHT

Temporality and the Practice of Philosophy

It was well said by Theodor Haecker that the great achievement of Kierkegaard was to import the person of the philosopher into philosophy.[1] This is an interesting point with regard to time on which I shall later comment—that Kierkegaard sought to see time not so much as something subjective rather than objective but something that was real in virtue of its internality. For the moment let us concentrate on this description of the nature and method of philosophy. Kierkegaard's criticism of the Hegelian philosophy was that it pretended to be something

---

1. Haecker, *Søren Kierkegaard*, 29.

sub specie aeterni and not in time. There are four points involved in this protest at which the importance of time for Kierkegaard is evident.

In the first place it is a feature of Kierkegaard's self-appointed task in philosophy of providing a corrective for what he regarded as the system's obsessive concern or preoccupation with the world-historical. For Hegel the task of the philosopher was to contemplate world-history, but for Kierkegaard this was to pretend to do something the philosopher could not do. Every living person, he says, unless he is altogether *distrait*, must choose; but if he chooses this metaphysical attitude he commits intellectual suicide.² The world-historical is an abstraction that is not in fact the object of philosophy. Therefore the Hegelian characteristic of philosophy falsifies the relation of philosophy and life's temporal character. "One thing," Kierkegaard remarks, "has always escaped Hegel—what it means to live. He knows only how to represent life, and if he is a master in this art it is also certain that he is the most striking contrast to a maieutic thinker."³

In the *Concluding Unscientific Postscript* Kierkegaard devotes considerable space to his contention that the speculative product of idealist philosophy is an illusion in so far as it pretends to this position of being able to view things *sub specie aeterni*.⁴ With his mordant wit he constantly contrasts the advantage such a philosopher would have over mere existing individuals. Unlike these poor characters who are always in the process of becoming, the speculative philosopher knows the secrets of providence, gazing as he does at the eternal and not the temporal. The very title of the *Postscript* is meant to make this humorous point. It is an unscientific (*uvidenskabelig*) postscript, unpedantic as opposed to the pretentious works of the professors who, so Kierkegaard argues, offer a mirage for the reality of philosophical understanding of existence. Again, the work emphasises the temporal character of the problem it poses. Instead of attempting the impossible, *viz*. an objective description of Christianity, it concerns itself with the treatment of the subjective problem of how to become a Christian—"How may I, Johannes Climacus participate in the happiness promised by Christianity?"⁵ There is an important contrast between the *Postscript* and the *Fragments* in

2. Kierkegaard, *Papirer* VII A 153.
3. Ibid.
4. Kierkegaard, *Postscript*, 1, 85–87, 133–36; S.V. 10, 69–72, 111–14.
5. Ibid. 15–16.

this respect. The *Fragments* poses a formal problem of the nature of Christianity but the *Postscript* makes the problem a personal one of how an individual is to relate himself to the objective revelation.

Temporality and Anthropology

The second area where I see the theme of time is in Kierkegaard's view of the nature of the human person. This has not been much discussed, and indeed it is a subject on which what he has to say is difficult to reconstruct. What is clear, however, is that his whole treatment of the subject is determined by the recognition that the human self is a *temporal* phenomenon. In several places he speaks of man as a synthesis of the temporal and the eternal. Clearly such a view has as its background the notion of man as a creation of God, and this has some very definite implications for Kierkegaard. The eternal provides the point of contact between past and the future because it is defined by Kierkegaard in terms of God's relationship to humanity in creation.

As early as 1843 this idea of humanity as a synthesis of the temporal and eternal had been expressed in *Four Edifying Discourses* where the last discourse, "To Acquire One's Soul in Patience," describes man's existential situation. The soul is described as a relation between the temporal and the eternal.[6] If the soul tries to escape the tension of this duality by turning either to mere worldly finitude or mere transcendent infinitude it violates its own nature.

A year later in *Concept of Anxiety* the same theme is again taken up, and it is this synthetic character of humanity which is seen to be the presupposition of anxiety. To experience anxiety is to be anxious over the possibilities of the future, to experience misgivings over one's uneasy relation to the eternal. Only a free spirit has such possibilities of existence and so anxiety is a mark of humanness. "If a man were a beast or an angel he would not be able to be in dread. Since he is a synthesis he can be in dread, and the greater the dread, the greater the man."[7] The synthesis of which Kierkegaard here speaks is precisely the synthesis of the temporal and the eternal.[8] The analysis of anxiety as a *human* phenomenon therefore lays great stress on the theme of time.

---

6. Kierkegaard, *Upbuilding Discourses*, 163; S.V. 4, 149.
7. Kierkegaard, *Concept of Anxiety*, 155; S.V. 6, 234.
8. Cf. ibid., 88; S.V. 6, 176.

In the *Four Edifying Discourses* of 1844 there is the same characterization of human existence as a tension between the temporal and the eternal. This synthesis is seen as the creation of God and as constituting the uniqueness of man. On the basis of this, man can either turn his face in love and joy to the Creator or reject true selfhood and God. The self is a "relation" between heaven and earth, eternity and time, and more specifically it is a relation that willingly accepts itself in this strange and burdensome tension.[9] When man wills to be himself, as a mixture of finite and infinite, he also wills to be what God ordained and is in relationship to God; when he refuses to be himself he is disobedient to God.[10]

It is not necessary here to discuss how this view is linked with the Romantic philosophical anthropology current in the nineteenth century, but it is worth stressing that despite the real connection between the two positions there is a decisive difference between Kierkegaard's anthropology and that of the Romantics. For both it is impossible to understand man purely in terms of his animal nature. To be human is to be that strange creature which awkwardly but marvelously synthesizes time and eternity. The decisive difference is that while for the Romantics this contact between man and eternity constituted religion, for Kierkegaard this is no more than what marks him off as human. (To become religious demands a radical change in this normal human consciousness, and the difference between a religion of immanence and a Christian faith is another point to be borne in mind here.)

Temporality and Ethics

Kierkegaard's understanding of ethics is the third area where the importance of time for his thought can be appreciated. It would be true to say that Kierkegaard wants to portray ethics as essentially a historical matter. Though he speaks in *Either-Or* in ways that suggest that he regards existence as the product of necessity as well as freedom, the main thesis of the book must be admitted to be that personal existence is decision-making in acts of freedom.[11] Man has to choose between the aesthetic existence with its self-destructive pursuit of pleasure and the despair

---

9. Kierkegaard, *Four Edifying Discourses*, 308; S.V. 4, 275.
10. Ibid. 326; S.V. 4, 289.
11. Kierkegaard, *Either-Or* 2 (1959 edition), 174ff.; S.V. 3, 160ff.

that issues in ethical existence. This kind of existence is characterized as the life of duty and responsibility.

Yet this is not a mere echo of the Kantian theory of the categorical imperative. There is one all-important difference in the way in which Kierkegaard views the inwardness of ethics. The characteristic of the aesthetic life is that it is ultimately determined from without. It is basically a passive attitude towards the world which is a surrender to forces other than the agent's own will. One of Kierkegaard's contributions as a moral philosopher lies in his ability to show how much that passes as ethics is an attempt to shake off the burden of personal decision and responsibility. *Choice* is what he is concerned to show as the typically ethical act, and ethical choice involves for him two kinds of movement—free self-development and obedient fulfillment of divine purpose. First, the person is realized only by his own self-development. Self-identity comes into existence in the very act of choice. Second, the self that is chosen somehow already exists; for a person does not create himself but only chooses himself. "He repents himself back into himself, back into the family of the peace, until he finds himself in God."[12] Repentance is man's own final and honest response to personal failure, a final negative element in the unsuccessful human quest for the eternal.

The moral man's basic relationship is to the law and not to God despite the fact that the moral law is the law of God. I am not now concerned with this analysis of the theological ground of ethics but simply with the fact that though this is how Kierkegaard would have tackled the metaphysical problem of the basis of ethics, his phenomenology of morals lays a massive emphasis on the category of time. As choice is an act in time so is repentance. So it is true to say that though Kierkegaard's main concern was with the inward rather than the outward character of ethics he does see ethics as very largely concerned with the temporal.

Temporality and Existence

Finally, in his analysis of the relation between necessity and existence Kierkegaard points out that what comes into being has nothing to do with necessity. Though this was a subject to which Kierkegaard devoted much thought, the references in the *Works* are few. However, the discus-

---

12. Kierkegaard, *Either-Or* 2, 219; S.V. 3, 201.

sion in *Philosophical Fragments* makes the specific point that is relevant to our discussion. These are the relevant passages:

> The necessary is a category entirely by itself. Nothing ever comes into existence with necessity: likewise the necessary never comes into existence and something which comes into existence never becomes the necessary . . . The change involved in coming into existence is actuality; the transition takes place with freedom. No coming into existence is necessary. It was not necessary before coming into existence, nor after the coming into existence, for there could not have been the coming into existence . . . Everything that has come into existence is *eo ipso* historical. For even if it accepts no further historical predicate, it accepts nevertheless the one decisive predicate: it has come into existence.[13]

This is the metaphysical problem of becoming or the possibility of change, and it is interesting that a category that is very significant for Kierkegaard's theology, the category of repetition, is what he here invokes as the best explanation of becoming. The historicity of the contingent is not established merely with relation to human life; for Kierkegaard points out that there is "much in nature that takes place in time. Thus when a brook ripples and continues to ripple there seems to be in it a qualification of time."[14] Life, he says, is repetition; and by contrast with the Greek doctrine of recollection, which simply asserts that it has been, repetition asserts that "existence which has been now becomes."[15] The existing self is characterized not only by the necessity of the past but also by the possibility of the future that it will become.

In both these types of historical existence Kierkegaard finds Hegel's logical categories of mediation and reconciliation bankrupt explanations. Logic cannot admit movement because logic belongs to the eternal world of being. "In logic no movement can *come about* for logic *is*, and everything logical simply is."[16] Kierkegaard regards Hegel's treatment of movement and becoming as illusory; for Hegel interprets reality as the expression of a logical necessity and so a timeless process. Once again then the underlying theme in Kierkegaard's thinking is that of time. Any

---

13. Kierkegaard, *Philosophical Fragments* (Thulstrup Edition), 92–93; S.V. 6, 69.
14. Kierkegaard, *Either-Or* 1, 55; S.V. 2, 55.
15. Kierkegaard, *Repetition*, 149; S.V. 5, 131.
16. Kierkegaard, *Concept of Anxiety*, 13; S.V. 6, 112.

adequate theory of the nature of existence will emphasize the temporality of existence.

Temporality and Christianity

Before turning to a discussion of what Kierkegaard offers as his own analysis of the concept of time let me conclude this survey of his thought as involved with the category of time by showing a similar emphasis in the more theological concern of what is sometimes called the religious authorship. Here two points are crucial. In the first place, Kierkegaard's Christology demands a clear emphasis on the temporal aspect of the Incarnation. Secondly, his view of Christian existence as an achievement or process leads him to emphasize time as the category of human existence.

INCARNATION

It is impossible here to do more than simply state dogmatically that Kierkegaard's Christology is misinterpreted when it is presented as a denial of any connection between the revelation of God in Christ and history. Reading Kierkegaard in this way is only possible because he was just as anxious to show that there was a difference between the assertions of Christian faith and those of history; but it is woefully wrong because it ignores the centrality of the theme of the God-man in his Christology. In the Christ God and man came together, and Christian belief is defined by Kierkegaard as baldly as this: that to believe is to believe the divine and human together in Christ. He speaks of Jesus as a "wholly ordinary man"[17] whose sympathy and capacity for sympathy depend on his having endured what others endure rather than on any formal characteristic of a common nature. Jesus himself experienced hunger and thirst, suffered, and died.[18] Nowhere perhaps does he make this clearer than when in *The Works of Love* he speaks of Jesus participating in all that is human:

> He who loved the whole race, our Lord Jesus Christ, yet humanly felt the need to love and be loved by an individual man . . . He was an actual man and can therefore share in all that is human; he was not an airy form which beckoned in the sky, without understanding or wishing to understand what humanly happens to a man. Oh no, he could have pity over the multitudes which

---

17. Kierkegaard, *Papirer* IX A 101.
18. Kierkegaard, *Christian Discourses*, 11; S.V. 13, 252.

needed food, and that in a purely human sense, he who had himself hungered in the wilderness.[19]

Similarly, when he is concerned to show how Jesus was tempted in all things, he points to Jesus' human experience. Thus in a journal entry he writes: "One of the outbursts where the human in Christ comes to the fore most strongly is in his word to Judas, 'What thou doest do quickly' . . . this human unrest, this vacillation as the decisive moment approached also found its place."[20]

The theme of *imitatio christi* has an important place in Kierkegaard's understanding of Christian ethics, and the logic of this is that he must therefore acknowledge the importance of time for this ethical model. So he says, "He who was the truth, and the way and the life, he who needed to learn nothing, yet he learned one thing: he learned obedience. In so close a relation does obedience stand to the eternal truth that he, who is the truth, learns obedience."[21] As I have argued elsewhere, the main thrust of Kierkegaard's Christology is its critique of Hegelian translation of Christology into a metaphysic with the result that all emphasis on history in Christology is lost.[22] It is the actuality of Christ that matters for Kierkegaard so that he insists that Christology finds its subject matter not in the union of God and humanity but in *this union as a historical fact in an individual.*

> Offence relates itself essentially to the setting together of God and man, or to the God-Man. Speculation naturally has thought that it could "comprehend" the God-Man—that one can well enough comprehend, for speculation takes away from the God-Msn the determination of temporality, contemporaneity, and actuality . . . No, the situation belongs with the God-Man, the situation that an individual man, who stands beside you, is the God-Man. The God-Man is not the unity of God and Man . . . the God-Man is the unity of God and an individual man.[23]

---

19. Kierkegaard, *Works of Love*, 125–26; S.V. 12, 150–51.

20. Kierkegaard, *Journals*, 221.

21. Kierkegaard, *Gospel of Sufferings*, (Swenson and Swenson edition), 54; S.V. 11, 237.

22. See Heywood Thomas, *Philosophy of Religion in Kierkegaard's Writings*, chapter 5.

23. Kierkegaard, *Practice in Christianity*, 81–82; S.V. 16, 85–86.

One final point can be made here. There could be no understanding of a *work* achieved by Christ in Kierkegaard's Christology if that Christology ignored the category of time. But central to his Christology is the view that Christ had a mission that he freely fulfilled and that this fulfillment was an achievement of work. From the beginning Christ's life is a story of temptation[24] and his resistance of it is quite specific.[25] Kierkegaard insists that Christ came to the world out of love, took upon himself the form of a humble servant, and lived only for one thing—to love and help humanity.[26]

It is not only in its demand for the recognition of the historicity of Christ that Kierkegaard's Christology makes use of the notion of time. There are two other respects in which this is true. First, there is the emphasis on this revelation as having occurred at the fullness of time. "The concept around which everything turns in Christianity, the concept which makes all things new is the fullness of time, is the instant as eternity, and yet this eternity is at once the future and the past."[27] Already in *Fragments* the concept of the fullness of time had been singled out as a decisive difference between the Socratic and the Christian understanding of how we learn our eternal happiness. It is true that the Moment is unique as history; but as far as the lesson is concerned that might be said to be irrelevant. However, the whole point of the Christian message is that this piece of time is unique: "And now the moment. Such a moment has a peculiar character. It is brief and temporal indeed, like every other moment; it is transient as all moments are; it is past, like every moment in the next moment. And yet it is decisive, and filled with the Eternal. Such a moment ought to have a distinctive name; let us call it the Fullness of Time."[28]

The other feature of Kierkegaard's Christology to which we refer here involves the notion of time in a rather paradoxical fashion. In *Fragments* Kierkegaard describes the character of true Christian belief in terms of contemporaneity and so he discusses what is for faith the dialectic of time. There is no advantage that those who were the histori-

---

24. Kierkegaard, *For Self-Examination*, (1946 edition), 79; S.V. 17, 96–97.
25. Kierkegaard, *Christian Discourses*, 366–67; S.V. 14, 179–80.
26. Kierkegaard, *Practice in Christianity*, 20–21; S.V. 16, 25.
27. Kierkegaard, *Concept of Anxiety*, 90; S.V. 6, 178.
28. Kierkegaard, *Philosophical Fragments* (Thulstrup edition), 22, cf. 24; S.V. 6, 22, cf. 23.

cal contemporaries of Christ have over us who are their successors. If the event of his incarnation were a historical event purely and simply then that contemporaneity would be an advantage; but since it is the Absolute Paradox this cannot be the case. Therefore in the *Fragments* Kierkegaard, besides denying the relevance of contemporaneity, asserts that Christianity gives this concept a new significance or use.

> When the believer is the believer and knows the God through having received the condition from the God himself, every successor must receive the condition from the God himself in precisely the same sense, and cannot receive it at second hand; for if he did, this second hand would have to be the hand of the God himself. And in that case there is no question of a second hand. But a successor who receives the condition from the God himself is a contemporary, a real contemporary; a privilege enjoyed only by the believer, but also enjoyed by every believer.[29]

Christianity is therefore defined in *Practice in Christianity* as "absolute contemporaneity with Christ"—"as Christ is the absolute it is easy to see that with respect to Him there is one situation: that of contemporaneousness."[30] Actually, it is not easy to understand this because Kierkegaard here makes both a literal and a quasi-metaphorical use of the term "contemporaneous." In the literal sense this is said not to be relevant to faith whereas in the quasi-metaphorical sense it is the very term that we must use of the relation of faith. It is very interesting and instructive to see Kierkegaard here showing how time is irrelevant to faith and *also* adopting a temporal relation as the model for talking of faith. Faith is in one important sense a non-historical relation to its object: but it is also a real relation. Because of the nature of our existence this reality can only be modeled on the temporal relation of contemporaneity. The relation is neither memory nor hope but co-presence. In all these ways then the notion of time is vital for Kierkegaard's Christology.

Temporality and Christian Existence

The second point has to do with Kierkegaard's understanding of *existence*, a word that he used in a novel way. That this novel use is not the simple opposition of authentic and inauthentic existence is seen if we recall Kierkegaard's view of the human being as a synthesis of time and

---

29. Ibid. 85; S.V. 6, 64.
30. Kierkegaard, *Practice in Christianity*, 82; S.V. 16, 86.

eternity. This thought is basic in all Kierkegaard's description of existence. To exist means to realize the task that the synthesis presents, that is to bring the eternal into the temporal.[31] "Existence is the child born of the infinite and the finite, the eternal and the temporal."[32] Existence is the highest interest of the individual and this constitutes his reality.[33] In his great work on Kierkegaard, the Danish scholar of a former generation, E. Geismar, illustrates this existing attitude towards life in this diagram.[34]

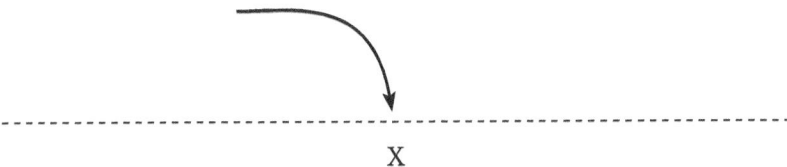

Here the top line signifies the eternal which is to be expressed in time and the bottom dotted line signifies the moments in time, with X representing the particular moment when the eternal is brought into the temporal. The speculative attitude is the very opposite of this.

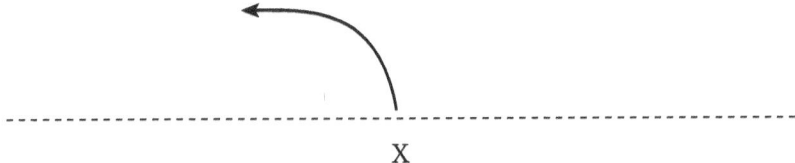

Instead of regarding the eternal as the future (as "Becoming"), which is to be realized as a task, the concern for the eternal in the speculative is abstract, directed towards the past (that is, the eternal is viewed as "being"). By these diagrams Geismar illustrates the difference Kierkegaard sees between Greek and Christian religion.[35] Socrates saw the God-relationship in terms of the past, as is evident from his doctrine of eternal recollection. For Christianity, this God-relationship is to be seen

31. Kierkegaard, *Postscript*, 1, 92, 394; S.V. 9, 71, 10, 85.
32. Ibid., 85; S.V. 9, 80.
33. Ibid., 314.
34. Geismar, *Lectures on the Religious Thought of Søren Kierkegaard*, III, 67–68.
35. cf. Kierkegaard, *Repetition*, 131–33; S.V. 5, 115–17, 130–41; Kierkegaard, *Concept of Anxiety*, 82–93; S.V. 6, 170–81. In *Philosophy of Symbolic Forms*, 120, Cassirer remarks on the Hebrew consciousness of time as future.

in the "repetition," which makes the eternal a task to be realized. The Greeks had the eternal behind them while Christianity faces the eternal.

This distinction between the past and the future reference to eternity becomes in the *Postscript* the decisive point in every differentiation between "speculation" and "existence." Here then the category of existence has a double significance. Not only is it invoked in the characterization of the ethical dimension of Christianity but it also provides the idiom for the distinction that Kierkegaard wants to make between this and other styles of life. That is, the eternal, which is the background of human existence, is not only to be realized in *time* but our attitude towards it is Christian in so far as it shows a particular aspect of temporality, namely *facing the future*.

KIERKEGAARD'S UNDERSTANDING OF TIME

It is clear then that the category of time plays a varied and crucial role in Kierkegaard's thought. What now does he have to say about time? It is in *The Concept of Anxiety* that he presents his view, but it is noteworthy that already in the second part of *Either-Or* this view is adumbrated. He attacks the view of time that makes the present the only reality, the past a mere "no-longer-now," and the future a "not-yet-now." This kind of view is echoed in Elizabeth Anscombe's insistence that the past is real only if we can have a present criterion of its reality.

For Kierkegaard, as for Bergson later, *duration* is the basic presupposition for an understanding of time. He sees that experienced time is a unity in which the modalities are distinguished by reference to human purposes and decisions. A phenomenological account of time is not of a succession of past, present, and future but of a past held in memory and a future that is projected in my decisions. Both past and future are relevant to my present existence and are thus interrelated.

It was this connection that was at the heart of the criticism Kierkegaard made in *Either-Or* of the Hegelian idea of the unhappy consciousness. The unhappy person, says Hegel, is a person who is never present to himself, being absent from himself either in the past or in the future. With this Kierkegaard largely agreed but he insisted that Hegel understood the matter abstractly rather than existentially. By this I take him to mean that Hegel was content with the merely formal description of the relation to the temporal modes whereas he, Kierkegaard, is concerned with the content. Thus we can distinguish two types of unhappiness. One type is the individual who is absent from himself because he has no hope and for him the future is a threat to be feared. Another type of unhappiness is the individual who cannot find himself in the past because the past is his unfulfilled possibilities. Happiness is found only in acknowledging the reality of past and future and appropriating their present relevance. So time is experienced as an inter-related unity rather than a series of discrete moments.

This helps us to put into proper perspective Kierkegaard's talk about the time of internal history. The existing subject has a personal history which is his very being and which further, as we have seen, is what distinguishes him from natural objects. This is why Kierkegaard tends to speak of the time of nature as spatially qualified. It is also why he distinguishes two kinds of history: external and internal.[36] External history is history as observed from the outside, the stuff of written history, whereas internal history is history as experienced by the individual as he exists. Kierkegaard takes as an example a knight who slays five bears, four dragons, and delivers three princes, the brothers of his beloved princess. The external and internal histories are quite different. Kierkegaard goes further than saying that they are different; it is the internal history that is for him the only true history: "Internal history is the only true history; but true history contends with that which is the life principle of history, i.e., time. But when one contends with time, then the temporal and every little moment of it acquires immense reality."[37]

The same problem is treated in *Stages of Life's Way*[38] in Frater Taciturn's psychological experiment entitled, "Guilty/Not Guilty?" where the truth of the matter is seen only as we uncover the internal history. The relevance of this to our theme is what Kierkegaard pointed out in the words just quoted: internal history is related to existential time in which the three modes are given in the unity of immediate experience.

What has been said about internal history may become clearer if we consider its relevance to the problem raised by the obvious truth that we cannot have any observational criteria for statements in the past tense. However, to assert that the past cannot be known strikes one as not only paradoxical, but manifestly untrue. The problem which the knowledge

---

36. Kierkegaard, *Either-Or* 2, 112; S.V. 3, 127.
37. Ibid. 113; S.V. 3, 128; cf. the discussion of the ideal husband and of courage in the succeeding pages.
38. Kierkegaard, *Stages on Life's Way*, 187ff.; S.V. 8, 13ff.

of the past poses for the empiricist is one of which Kierkegaard was clearly well aware, though his discussion of the issue in *Philosophical Fragments* was unfortunately a victim of his own keen sense of polemic. For the empiricist the only test of the reality of X is that it is presently observed and it is obviously a contradiction in terms to say that a past event X is presently observed. In order to make his point about the necessity of faith for any claim that Jesus Christ is the Savior Kierkegaard exploited this problem and was able to make the exaggerated assertion that faith needed only the bare statement that the contemporary disciple had so believed. This is, I suggest, most unfortunate not only because of the theological confusion it generated but more particularly because the account of historical knowledge he gives in this section of *Fragments*, for all its probabilism, emphasizes the possibility of historical knowledge and the reality of the past. It is not fanciful to compare the skepticism there expressed with the claims of a Russell that we could know what is meant by the past while doubting its reality. It seems to me, however, that what Kierkegaard wants to say about the past is very much like Wittgenstein's insistence that "man learns the concept of the past by remembering."[39]

It is, then, against the background of his discussion of the stages on life's way that Kierkegaard's discussion of time is to be viewed. He first of all urges that we define time as "infinite succession" but then immediately alerts us to the problems that arise from such a Zeno-like definition and the division of time into past, present, and future. No matter how plausible this division may seem to be it is false, because we are assuming that they are distinctions within time itself. This clearly cannot be the case. Past, present, and future arise only when we try to see time in terms of our own finite experience. "If in the infinite succession of time a foothold could be found, i.e., a present which was the dividing point, the division would be quite correct. However, precisely because every moment, as well as the sum of the moments, is a process (a passing by), no moment is a present, and accordingly there is in time neither present, nor past, nor future."[40]

The question of the present arises, of course, as soon as we begin to think of one moment succeeding another. There is a past moment that preceded that moment which is racing by and so on. But the present is

---

39. Wittgenstein, *Philosophical Investigations*, 231.
40. Kierkegaard, *Concept of Anxiety*, 85; S.V. 6, 175.

not "the concept of time unless precisely as something infinitely void, which again is the infinitely vanishing." This argument is like the problem that J. J. C. Smart raises in the essay "The River of Time" whether the speaker who constitutes himself as the norm and indicator is regarded as stationary with the timeline moving or whether he himself is in motion.[41] Such a difficulty reveals the problem with regard to the model of time as a flowing river—at what rate does it flow and so on? However, that problem is quite simply the problem of regarding models as descriptions rather than figurative expressions. What Kierkegaard had noted was not so much this kind of paradox, which might be said to be obvious and insignificant, as the more profound point that this non-moving present can be given sense only by seeing that "the present is the eternal or rather that the eternal is the present and the present is full."[42]

It is particularly interesting to seek some light on Kierkegaard's position by considering McTaggart's celebrated attempt to eliminate time because both sought to understand time by finding some point of reference outside what might be called the ordinary "flow" of time. It so happens that I write this on my birthday and I am therefore all too sensitive to the problem he raised about the paradox of a present past at different times. What Kierkegaard did was to confront the Zeno-like paradox produced by talking of time as an infinite succession with the *experience* of time, which, after all, is the only entrée we have to the understanding of time's passage. We need not labor the point that he was as keenly aware of the resulting anxiety as Marlowe's Faustus when he cries, "Stay, thou fleeting moment, stay!"

The remarkable thing is the way in which Kierkegaard showed himself alive to the way in which abstract nouns are systematically misleading. So it is that he is not tempted to some paradoxical juxtaposition of a present experience of time and the fact of change. Rather, as he had shown in *Repetition*, it was not the past event that was repeated but the past fact of that event which is now my present experience. I can recall the earliest birthday I celebrated; and after all these years it is a present experience, not the past being now still alive but the memory being still alive. That is what is expressed in the common phrase, "I remember it as if it were yesterday." That there is indeed such a present experience led

---

41. Smart, "The River of Time," 213.
42. Kierkegaard, *Concept of Anxiety*, 86; S.V. 6, 175.

Collingwood to utter the paradox that history is the re-enactment of a past thought.

Yet the point of *Repetition*, as far as Kierkegaard's own thinking was concerned, was that it showed the reality of what might be called the arithmetic of the past such as Plato had shown when thinking of comparing ages in *Parmenides* 154B–155D. The decisive notion here is the infinite, for, if one does not understand that infiniteness is a characteristic of the present one has posited the present as something finite, something that does apparently and quantitatively exist between past and future, a wholly untenable position. The point Kierkegaard wants to make is that the eternal is the present or better that the present is the eternal. In conceptual terms we say that the "eternal is the annulled succession." If we try to visualize it, we say that the eternal is "a going-forth, yet it never budges from the spot, because for visual representation it is the infinitely present."

What is Kierkegaard saying here? In the first place, he is attempting a critique of models. We are tempted to use as our model for talking of time the picture of a sequence because our thinking is dominated by the hidden model of time as a spatial relation. We are "visualizing time instead of thinking it."[43] Secondly, he wants to show that in any infinite series there can be no finite quanta because each quantum is infinitely divisible. This is especially clear when we consider time, for time has the quality of an infinite series in two ways. First, it makes an infinite reference both forwards and backwards. Secondly, the specious present of which Kierkegaard is thinking is specious precisely because it is infinitely divisible within itself. But another characteristic peculiar to time is that it seems to possess direction: it has the appearance of going from one point to another. We can make sense of this infinite flight of succession in one of two ways. First, we can think of the infinite flight of succession as fundamentally a finite flight of succession. In making this move one is endowing each moment with finitude just as the beats of a clock mark off the finite intervals. But it also gives each period an equal value so that all periods are equally robbed of any claim to a unique value. Further, there are no rhythmical climaxes. There is, in short, no moment. Alternatively one may annul the successiveness by summing up all time in the providential foreseeing care of God, in the same way as a person at last grasps or completely understands his own plans. The

---

43. Ibid.; S.V. 6, 176.

way in which we talk of the expression of the will of God, that is, the use of such phrases as "the Alpha and the Omega," "from age to age," "Thy Kingdom come," shows how this notion can sum up all time. The Incarnation is that intersection of mere successiveness and succession annulled and is the earnest of this providential summing-up. The eternity that is present is a summation that is yet characterized by succession, still full with the future, a fulfillment of realized expectations.[44] There can be moments because there is a Moment. Don Juan is a creature of the first solution for whom the second is not yet a possibility inasmuch as the second is grounded in faith.

As I have emphasized, Kierkegaard's most illuminating comments on time are in the context of this kind of analysis of human existence. Thus, resuming the point already made about the view he holds of the human being, for him it is true to say that the life which is in time and is merely a temporal existence has no present. Further, if one defines time in terms of the instant and that instant is the purely hypothetical exclusion of past and future, "then the instant is not the present, for that which in purely abstract thinking lies between the past and the future has no existence at all."[45] One's life is never present so long as one lives only for the moment and has no relation to the eternal. On the other hand, the fact that "the present as the eternal" has no past or future either is what constitutes its perfection. Therefore when we say that someone has presence we mean that he is carried away by neither the flux of instantaneity nor the abstraction of temporality.

In order to find the true present, time must be defined eschatologically. That is, the true present is the point of intersection of time and eternity.

> Thus understood, the moment is not properly an atom of time but an atom of eternity. It is the first reflection of eternity in time, its first attempt, as it were, at stopping time. For this reason, Greek culture did not comprehend the moment, and even if it had comprehended the atom of eternity, it did not comprehend that it was the moment, did not define it with a forward direction. Because for Greek culture the atom of eternity was essentially eternity, neither time nor eternity received what was properly its due.[46]

---

44. Ibid., 86; S.V. 6, 177.
45. Kierkegaard, *Concept of Anxiety*, 87; S.V. 6, 175.
46. Ibid., 88; S.V. 6, 176.

The modern understanding of the instant becomes possible, Kierkegaard thinks, because of the destruction of the psychically determined cosmos of Hellenism by the Spirit. "No sooner is the spirit posited than the instant is there." Before man rested in nature or fate and was unable to have the perspective on himself to grasp what is meant by instant. If the Greeks spoke of time, this was as time passed, "defining it like the definition of time in general, as a going by."[47]

Thus understood, the Greek idea of recollection shows that eternity is viewed as behind us, and this is in marked contrast to the Christian notion of eternity as something that lies ahead of us. Though repetition is not then equivalent with the Christian notion of eternity it does come close to the eternal that has been fulfilled, the realized eschatology. Eternity for Kierkegaard is the present.

> Repetition is the new category that will be discovered. If one knows anything of modern philosophy and is not entirely ignorant of Greek philosophy, one will readily see that this category precisely explains the relation between the Eleatics and Heraclitus, and that repetition proper is what has been mistakenly called mediation . . . There is no explanation in our age as to how mediation takes place, whether it results from the motion of the two factors and in what sense it is already contained in them, or whether it is something new that is added, and if so how . . . When the Greeks said that all knowing is recollection, they said that all existence, which is, has been; when one says that life is a repetition, one says: actuality, which has been, now comes into existence.[48]

But just as repetition becomes a possibility when the instant is posited so the distinctions of the modality of time become possible. As Kierkegaard says, the future may indeed be understood as "the whole of which the past is a part." Further, we see the future as the disguise in which the eternal is to make its appearance, though eternity is not the same as the future. For us eternity has a relation to time but it is a paradoxical relation whereas the Greeks could have no concept of the future or the eternal. The very notion of time then is to be explicated by reference to the point in time where eternity meets it in the Incarnation.

---

47. Ibid., 89; S.V. 6, 177.
48. Kierkegaard, *Repetition*, 148–49; S.V. 5, 130–31.

Kierkegaard and the Problem of Time

What we have been following in these considerations is Kierkegaard's remarkable attention to the great tradition in philosophy of the relation of time to eternity, following Plato, together with the very different understanding that philosophical reflection in the Christian tradition yields. Thus Plato had said of eternity in *Timaeus* (37 E6–38 A6), "We say that it was and will be; but in truth 'is' applies to it while 'was' and 'will be' are properly said of becoming in time." So powerful was the influence of Plato's dialogues on Kierkegaard that this thought became a foundation of his thinking about time, motion, and the role of eternity in Christian thinking about history and salvation. Having portrayed human life as determined by time and subject to the varying determinants of time, Kierkegaard had a very sharply defined notion of eternity.

Though showing little knowledge of St. Thomas, he would probably have accepted Thomas' odd definition of eternity: "The simultaneously whole and perfect possession of indeterminable life." The implications of this definition are developed in *Summa Theologiae* thus: "There are two things to be noted about time, namely, that time itself is successive, and that an instant of time is imperfect. To deny that eternity is time Boethius uses 'instantaneously whole'; to deny temporal instaneity the word 'perfect.'"[49] Thomas is here distinguishing between the notion of temporal extension (which involves the idea of succession) and that of temporal location such as involved in stating that X exists at this particular moment. What Kierkegaard sought to develop was an interiorization of both these notions, but an interiorization very different from that of Kant's view of time as a form of our sensibility. For him, the proper way of understanding time, which in a way unites the two notions, distinguished itself as a qualitative view that takes as its starting-point man's experience of his spiritual existence. It might be objected that in his argument that it is the instant of the Incarnation that finally gives time meaning Kierkegaard limited his own view of time; and indeed the way in which his radical thinking on time was developed by Heidegger would seem to support such a view. However, even if one were to agree that his philosophical achievement here can be quite properly appreciated without following him into his distinctively Christian conclusion, one must admit that faith in that Incarnation is a classic example of how time is essentially an existential fact.

49. Aquinas, *Summa Theologiae* 1:10; 137.

12

Kierkegaard and the Problem of Death

THE PROBLEM I WANT to discuss is posed by Wittgenstein's remark in the *Tractatus*: "As in death too the world does not change but ceases. Death is not an event in life. Death is not lived through." The discovery of an almost identical point in Kierkegaard's *Journal* is very interesting. Referring to Christian Scriver's *Seelen-Schatz* he comments: "Scriver says that it is good to have business with death—the advantage is ours ('to die is gain'). This is a more splendid way of tricking death than that of Epicurus. Death cannot get hold of me, because when I am, death is not, and when death is I am not."[1]

This seems to suggest that it is not possible to talk of my death as an event. To any unsophisticated reflection on the fact of death this must seem an intolerable paradox and one is tempted to dismiss the point as mere verbal quibble, especially as one considers the subjective reference of the concept of "the world" in the *Tractatus*. Yet it is clear that in much the same honest way as Kierkegaard, Wittgenstein too thought about the mystery of living and dying. That Anglo-Saxon philosophy in recent years has been so shy of talk about death and so prone to dismiss out of hand the talk of existentialist philosophers about the personal significance of death is another reason for going back to Kierkegaard. What I shall attempt to do here is to gather together something of what Kierkegaard has to day about death and, having set out these thoughts more or less systematically, to see how they illumine the problem of death as an event and related problems.

---

1. Kierkegaard, *Journals and Papers*, 726; Kierkegaard, *Papirer* X4 A 60.

KIERKEGAARD'S SCATTERED REFLECTIONS ON DEATH

Reflection on Death Outside of Concluding Unscientific Postscript

Apart from *Concluding Unscientific Postscript* there is no extensive treatment of the problem of death. There are, however, two hundred references, often only fugitive ones, in the Collected Works; and there are some twenty entries on the theme in the Papers, almost all of them being in the *Journal*. Yet, for all its comparative paucity the material is rich and sets out the problem very clearly. Indeed it seems to me that this is one of the clearest revelations of his philosophical power because what he achieved was the exposition of a transcendental metaphysics. He spoke of three problems as being especially difficult: that of freedom and motion, "one of the most difficult in all philosophy"; that of the implications of the Christ-relationship to the situation of human life which is where "we meet by far the most difficult of all problems"; and finally that of the sense in which we can speak of individual immortality.

I think it can be taken as read that for Kierkegaard the doctrine that all men are immortal was a point of departure. That is, he did not here, any more than anywhere else, want to question what he regarded as part and parcel of the Christian doctrine of humanity; for this is surely what he means when he speaks of humanity as a synthesis of time and the eternal. It is interesting that this is a position common to all the pseudonyms and I suggest that this confirms one's suspicion that for Kierkegaard rationalist metaphysics of immortality rested on a mistake—that of not asking what we mean when we say that a person dies. Death and immortality go together and immortality is life *after* death, which, as Wittgenstein so secularly put it, is after my world ceases.

The very first indication of Kierkegaard's interest in this problem is an undated entry in the *Journal* of 1837: "When in the hour of death it grows dark for a true Christian, it is because the sunlight of eternal happiness shines too brightly in his eyes."[2] Apart from bearing out what I described as his point of departure this entry has very little significance.

The first significant clue is the entry of 28 March 1839, which expresses dissatisfaction with the tendency to make immortality problematic: "With regard to the immortality of the soul, the real question will certainly be as to the nature of immortality rather than immortality."[3]

---

2. Kierkegaard, *Journals and Papers*, 712; Kierkegaard, *Papirer*, II A 213.
3. Kierkegaard, *Journals*, 265.

Cryptic the entry certainly is; but it can be said, I think, that already there is a shift of emphasis away from the speculative approach to the problem. The discussion, he suggests, should not be whether the term "immortal" is a predicate to be used of human beings or whether there is a certain state of affairs or kind of existence called "immortality" but, rather, how one conceives of this kind of experience called immortality of the soul. This is the period of Kierkegaard's theological studies and so this is a reaction against the tradition of metaphysical rationalist theology.

In 1844, the year in which *The Concept of Anxiety* was published, there were three entries in the *Journal*, two of which deal with grave inscriptions. The first of these is especially interesting: "There is a shocking eloquence . . . when one reads the brief words which a deceased person has had placed over his grave, the last words . . . into which he has poured his whole soul. What is this preacher-prattle compared with this commentary? . . . Thus does the grave call out to one—Death's last struggle, when there is no time anymore to select widely or to chatter about categories or about the difference between paganism and Christianity."[4] This point about the graveyard's eloquence is repeated in another of the entries: ". . . out there everything preaches; for just as nature declares God, so every grave preaches."[5] The eloquence of the grave's inscription lies precisely in the fact that all the dying person's soul has gone into it: there is a sense then in which this literary expression exemplifies what it means to die; for it is the achievement of an urgent task.

If we now turn to the *Concept of Anxiety* it is the temporal nature of this urgency that is in the forefront of the discussion. The view of time here expounded is that "temporality is sinfulness."[6] Kierkegaard then points out in a note that from this it follows that death is seen as punishment. The "more highly we value man the more terrible death appears."

> The beast does not really die, but when the spirit is posited as spirit, death shows itself as the terrifying. The anxiety of death therefore corresponds to the anxiety of birth, yet I do not wish to repeat here what has been said, partly truly and partly cleverly, partly enthusiastically and partly frivolously, that death is a metamorphosis. At the moment of death, man finds himself

---

4. Kierkegaard, *Journals and Papers* 714; Kierkegaard, *Papirer*, V A 36.
5. Ibid., 715; Kierkegaard, *Papirer*, V A 56.
6. Kierkegaard, *Concept of Anxiety*, 92.

at the uttermost point of the synthesis. It is as though spirit cannot be present, for it cannot die and yet it must wait, because the body must die. Because the pagan view of sensuousness was more naïve, its temporality more carefree, so the pagan view of death was milder and more attractive, but it lacked the ultimate.[7]

One of the most significant features of this discussion is the rejection of the category of metamorphosis as inapplicable to death. Kierkegaard is keenly aware of the way in which death is regarded as the end. So here is the paradox; it is indeed something temporal, something that is not only a result of time but something that has a temporal location and even some kind of temporal duration. Yet it is not like the sleep I had last night from which I rose refreshed (i.e., changed) this morning. It is interesting to see that a *Journal* entry of 1846 comments on the modern preference for a quick and sudden death: "What does this mean? It means that we want to shove away the thought of death and *shove death out of life* as much as possible."[8] The spirituality commended, namely, the prayer that one is spared the evil of a sudden death, is by no means insignificant or irrelevant; but the most obvious point is the way in which Kierkegaard wants to locate death within time, my time. Yet he saw it as the result and the end of time. As he was to say in *Sickness unto Death* some years later so in a *Journal* entry of 1847 he says: "Over against sickness, all physical suffering and the distressing misrelationships between soul and body rooted therein, there is that consolation: death is the sickness that puts an end to all others."[9] Four years later he notes the point as a sophistry of Epicurus, his main interest being now much more existential. However, it is worth emphasizing that he had uncovered a philosophical problem about death that faces us all, believers or unbelievers: can one understand death?

Reflections on Death in Concluding Unscientific Postscript

As I have indicated, there is a reasonable quantity of material for an exposition of Kierkegaard's view of death; but, though it is a topic to which he returns in what is now called the acknowledged or second literature, his fullest discussion occurs in *Concluding Unscientific*

---

7. Ibid., 92n; S.V. 6, 180n.
8. Kierkegaard, *Journals and Papers*, 717, my italics, VII1 A 145.
9. cf. Kierkegaard, *Sickness unto Death*, 150ff., and Kierkegaard, *Papirer*, VIII1 A 87.

Postscript.[10] With characteristic subtlety he distinguishes the various ways in which one knows about death and argues that this does not add up to an understanding of death if our problem is that of understanding what it means to die. He distinguishes six situations in which one speaks of knowing about death: (a) prediction of fatal effects, (b) history of culture, (c) fictional death, (d) evaluation of death in suicide, (e) social status and tragic drama, (f) poetic attitudes and liturgical notes. That is, knowledge about death can be, first of all, a scientific or clinical matter that is no different from any other scientific prediction such as "If you do not put fuel in your car it will stop" or "If you play about with nuclear reactors you can cause explosions." That there is such a complete analogy is precisely why Kierkegaard wastes no time on this because there is a difference between talking about *people* dying and mechanical or even biological effects. So he points out the difference within the former class of statements between talk about historical persons and talk about fictional characters. Talk about Napoleon's death is not the same as talk about Juliet's death in *Romeo and Juliet*. Even so, when we visit Verona or see a performance of Romeo and Juliet it is hard to see any difference (as is so well brought out by Nancy Mitford). However, when I say, "I know that the Stoics regarded suicide as a courageous deed and that others consider it a cowardly act,"[11] there is, as far as my knowing is concerned, not a great deal of difference between this kind of knowledge and my knowledge of likely effects. There is indeed one significant difference, namely, that this is talk that expresses attitudes and is not merely talk about effects. Talk about death can thus be valuational; the Stoics meant to commend suicide while other people mentioned meant to denigrate it.

This sense in which talk about death is valuational is made the more complicated when we reflect on the circumstances of death: "I know that death may result from so ridiculous and trivial a circumstance that even the most serious-minded of men cannot help laughing at death."[12] Then there is the very different kind of valuation that is involved in the consideration of a literary intention or dramatic technique where there is no such possibility of an unintentional incongruity: "I know that the tragic

---

10. Kierkegaard, *Concluding Unscientific Postscript to Philosophical Fragments*, 1, 165ff.; S.V. 9, 138ff.

11. Ibid., 165; S.V. 9, 138.

12. Ibid.

hero dies in the fifth act of the drama and that death here has an infinite significance in pathos; but that when a bartender dies death does not have this significance."[13] Finally, when poetic and liturgical references to death are examined we see the same kind of evaluative language. With a rather self-consciously modest air of assurance, Kierkegaard says that he could produce the same variety of effects as the poet or say what the clergy are accustomed to say on this subject.[14] Yet all this falls short of what he regards as the paradigm of understanding death: "I had better think about this, lest existence mock me because I had become so learned and highfalutin that I had forgotten to understand what will some time happen to me as to every human being—sometime, nay, what am I saying: Suppose death were so treacherous to come tomorrow! Merely this one uncertainty . . . generates inconceivable difficulties."[15] Notice the way in which the business of understanding death is brought back again and again to *my* understanding something about me. That is why the mere uncertainty of whether it happens tomorrow is enough to make *general* predictions and even general evaluations highfalutin nonsense. Since it is something uncertain then it is, Kierkegaard says, a possibility of any time that is my time.[16]

It was precisely this self-reference that led Wittgenstein to his pronouncement; for what he saw, just as Kierkegaard had done, was that it was ridiculous to say of death, "Never mind, if it happens it happens" or as the surgeon tells me, "All operations like this are rather unpleasant and you will have quite a lot of pain as you recover; but then it will all be over and you'll feel like a new man."

It might be thought that Kierkegaard is here confusing the uncertainty of death with its personal significance or self-reference; but that is not so. His argument is not based on the fact that I happen to be so vain as to regard my death the most important of all events. It could be that I just live for the day when the newspapers will carry my obituary and so the uncertainty whether it will be tomorrow or the day after or the next week is an irritation and so *I* want to know. His point, however, is that there is a necessary relation between this uncertainty and the kind of significance my death has for me. It is not that the predictability of

13. Ibid.
14. Ibid., 105–6.
15. Ibid.
16. Ibid., 166; S.V. 9, 139.

death contains within it the inevitable difficulty of a contingent future but that this contingency makes death a framework within which I see my future events.

The personal significance of death as something self-involving—that is to say, almost any statement I make about my death involves my taking up certain attitudes—is what Kierkegaard discussed next. He insists that "the lofty thinker" cannot escape the problem of saying "what it means to die."[17] Is it possible to have an idea of death? Can death be apprehended beforehand? Or does it have no other existence than its occurrence? If it is some kind of non-being what then is it to say that it exists? These epistemological dilemmas and logical problems are, however, meant to be an introduction to the crucial way of stating Kierkegaard's difficulty: *whether it is absolutely impossible for the living individual to approach death in any sense whatsoever* since, to use Wittgenstein's pithy précis of Kierkegaard's grandiloquence, death is not lived through.

The negative answer to the abovementioned question is just as tantalizing as the affirmative; for the necessity of that negative answer demands a metaphysic that once again is understood as self-involving. As for the affirmative answer, this too Kierkegaard treats in a Kantian fashion, involving the distinction between the existing thing and the idea of it.[18] How, then, can I prepare for my death? This, he says, is the relevance of ethics and religion: we need "an ethical expression for the significance of death and a religious expression for the significance of death and a religious expression for the victory over death."

What makes his idea of the language of death as self-involving clearest of all is the next step in the argument. As so often, after all the clever sophistry there comes a plain statement that is the point he wants to make. Clearly, he says, "when the subject thinks his own death, this is a deed."[19] The whole passage is a nice example of what Austin called performative meaning, as Kierkegaard talks of the gap between intention and action and the difficulty of deciding whether someone is genuine in his declaration that he has thought about death. "If a man is a deceiver he will contradict himself precisely when he is engaged in offering the

---

17. Ibid., 167; S.V. 9, 140.
18. Ibid., 168; S.V. 9, 141.
19. Ibid.

most solemn assurances."[20] The contradiction is not direct but simply in the incongruity of the behavior and the profession.

The Peculiarity of Saying That We Understand What Death Means

I do not want to proceed further with *Postscript* for the moment because the next theme is immortality and I shall return to this. Let me try to summarize, then, what I have said so far. It seems to me that Kierkegaard understood the idea of "death as an event" to be puzzling since death is something that I cannot understand as an experienced fact about myself. Secondly, the language about death is self-involving language not only because it demands that I assume attitudes but because it is a word-act. Thirdly, talk about death is evaluative as the trivial example of the drama reveals. Finally, death raises the question of ethics and religion.

I want now to consider these four points and show how it is that Kierkegaard illumines for us the peculiarity of saying that we understand what death means. As I have said, he was well aware of the kind of comment which Wittgenstein makes; but the fact that he has so little to say on this suggests that he saw how intolerable a paradox it is to say that death is not an event in my life. The old conundrum of Aristotle's—"Are there more living than dead?" with the answer "Living because the dead are not"—shows how there seems to be a problem of reference in statements about dead people. If a man is dead he does not exist and if he does not exist then it could be said that there is not a person of whom any predication is made. A man who has died is not the subject of his death. However, as Wittgenstein pointed out in *Philosophical Investigations*, this is to confound the reference (*bedeutung*) of the name with the bearer of the name.[21] When Mr. N. N. dies, we say that the bearer of the name dies not that the reference dies. And it would be nonsensical to say that; for if the name ceased to have reference, it would make nonsense to say, "Mr. N. N. is dead." Legal cases afford relevant examples, especially as we are now seeing cases concerning the switching off of life-support machines both as such and connected with the issue of murder.

20. Ibid., 170.
21. Wittgenstein, *Philosophical Investigations*, 140.

Of the latter there is an interesting example reported authoritatively in the second volume of the *All England Law Reports* for 1981.[22] The case concerned the prosecution of a man who had stabbed his wife. She was treated by being put on a life-support machine and died when the life-support machine was switched off. At his trial the husband's defense was that he had not caused his wife's death because the cause in law must have been the switching off of the life-support machine. The judge in the Winchester Crown Court rejected this plea and, when the case went to appeal, the judge's verdict was upheld by the Court of Appeal. So once again we have what is rather like an antimony: If the stabbing was at time t1 and the death at time t2 then at what time could the murder have taken place? It cannot be at t1; but, as the husband rightly enough argued, he was not involved, he did nothing, at time t2. Therefore there was no time at which he killed his wife. Yet the judges were clear that whatever might be said about the temporal location of the killing, the stabbing was the substantial and operating cause of death. This legal example shows how moral language demands a capability of referring to what is not and this means that it entails second-order language. It is here that I am reminded of the old logical dogma that existence is not a predicate and of Frege's useful concept of a second-order predicate. What I mean is that the only way one can make sense of all this discussion is to talk of existence as a predicate.

To express the logical form of our language about death in the way in which Kierkegaard has tried to do we need, I suggest, a different kind of logic. If, as Wittgenstein argued, the reference remains, then it will be true that individuals are eternal in the sense that once existing they exist forever. Yet the logic we need is one that is capable of talk about coming into and going out of existence. It hardly needs to be pointed out that such talk was a matter that concerned Kierkegaard throughout his life. Just as much as St. Thomas Aquinas,[23] he was anxious to distinguish the *esse* of anything—and in particular persons—from any abstract quality. And this was his complaint about the prevalent Hegelianism: that these were confused. As he says in *The Present Age*, "The individual ... realizes ... he belongs to an abstraction in which reflection subordinates him."[24]

22. *All England Law Report* (1981), 422.
23. Cf. Aquinas, *Summa Theologiae* 1, 3, 5.
24. Kierkegaard, *Two Ages*, 85; S.V. 14, 68.

One thing which has come out of this analysis of Kierkegaard's discussion is the centrality of the notion of time to any elucidation of the language about death. For instance, the point about reference being difficult here is simply due to the fact that this kind of reference was possible only in the *time* before death. Again it might be said that he sees fear of death as irrational because there *is* nothing of which we can be afraid. This, as Kierkegaard himself makes clear, is a matter of the difference between my attitude *now* and my condition at some future date.

It seems to me that Kierkegaard's philosophy was very much colored by his concern with time and that in his thinking on death he was very much impressed by the direction of time. He does not, in fact, discuss the issue of the time before a man's birth but I would be surprised if he was unaware of Lucretius' thoughts on that topic. No one, said Lucretius, finds it disturbing to contemplate the eternity preceding his own birth and since death is merely the other end as it were of that pole there can be no reason why we should fear it rather than show the same equanimity. Kierkegaard saw that this backward reference does not entail the possibilities that the prospect of death precludes. Keats' sonnet "When I have fears that I may cease to be" is something that we can understand and accept in a way in which Hamlet's cry "O cursed spite that I was ever born" is not; for part of the tragedy is the belief that all possibilities are open to his free-ranging thought. The point I want to make then is that Kierkegaard was calling our attention to the *mystery* of death when he reminded us of the difficulty of understanding what it is to die. It is no accident, in my view, that his own understanding of time is based on the model of the Incarnation.

I mentioned the way in which the issue of death for Kierkegaard involved ethics and religion. This is the burden of most of his entries in the *Journal* from 1847 onwards. The thought of death is what makes living bearable[25] and it is only some aesthetic reduction of ethics that can so eliminate the self-involvement of death as to utter "the nonsense about whether it is more painful to lose another or to die oneself."[26] The ethics of the matter is that "I shall die and then go up for judgment"[27] and so there is an urgency about achieving "every good work."[28] In 1850–51 he

25. Kierkegaard, *Journals and Papers*, 720; Kierkegaard, *Papirer*, VIII1 A 406.
26. Ibid., 721; Kierkegaard, *Papirer*, X1 A 233.
27. Ibid.
28. Ibid., 724; Kierkegaard, *Papirer*, X3 A 340.

mocks the same Christian attitude to death, which shows an idolatry of the sensuous,[29] and, using the comparison of contributions to a burial society, describes people's expectations to become Christian in death as a relationship of possibility.[30] Finally, under the date 2 July 1855, he pictures being a Christian as being kept alive in the state of death.[31]

What Does It Mean to Be Immortal?

This talk of judgment with its presupposition of immortality leads us on to that theme and takes us back to *Postscript*. The question, "What does it mean to be immortal?" is an example Kierkegaard there takes of the earnestness that relates death to my whole existence.[32] In the course of a dismissive comment to the effect that some believe there is an immortality and some do not, he wonders whether Hegel's system can contain immortality. Not even his revered teacher Møller could convince him that it does.[33] The question is wrongly put by Hegel and his followers, which will make it a matter of abstractions; and just as in the matter of understanding death so here one makes no progress except by realizing that it is something that concerns the individual. It is "essentially not a learned question, rather it is a question of inwardness, which the subject by becoming subjective must put to himself."[34] As it is not then a task of elaborating some hypothesis about a matter of fact neither is it that of establishing something about social terms: "in social terms it cannot be expressed, inasmuch as only the subject who wills to become subjective can conceive the question and ask rightly, 'Do *I* become immortal or am *I* immortal?'"[35]

From this insistence on the privacy of my awareness of my immortality Kierkegaard goes on to argue that proofs are not to the point. It is not that proofs turn out to be false but that the notion of proof is a misrepresentation of the logic of belief in immortality. "Systematically, immortality cannot be proved at all. The fault does not lie with the proofs,

---

29. Ibid., 723; Kierkegaard, *Papirer*, X3 A 250.
30. Ibid., 725; Kierkegaard, *Papirer*, X3 A 710.
31. Ibid., 731; Kierkegaard, *Papirer*, XI2 A 422.
32. Kierkegaard, *Concluding Unscientific Postscript*, 1, 171; S.V. 9, 142.
33. Ibid., 171–72; S.V. 9, 143.
34. Ibid., 173; S.V. 9, 144.
35. Ibid.; S.V. 9, 144.

but in the fact that people will not understand that viewed systematically the whole question is nonsense so that instead of seeking outward proofs, one had better seek to become a little subjective. Immortality is the most passionate interest of subjectivity; precisely in the interest lies the proof."[36]

It is worth emphasizing in passing that the argument is not a simple one. Kierkegaard contends that asking the objective question is like asking about the location of the beauty in my favorite beautiful picture or poem. Secondly he maintains that the only use of the concept of proof in talk about immortality is the interest of subjectivity. We shall come back to this point; but for the moment let us follow the argument.

It is clear that a great part of what he has to say replicates the insistence on the self-involving nature of language about death. The distinctive feature of the existing subject's question is that it concerns his or her own immortality and not "immortality in general, for such a phantom has no existence."[37] This existential question includes, for Kierkegaard, four questions:

(i) What significance does it have in relation to immortality that time has not been properly used?

(ii) What does it mean for the whole of existence that this most prized achievement or prize is in fact something which if real is *given* us?

(iii) How can we talk at one and the same time from the standpoint of infinity and of finiteness?

(iv) How can I prevent the metaphysical conception of immortality confusing the ethical and reducing it to an illusion?[38]

The thrust of all the questions is decidedly towards the importance of the ethical and it is not too much to say that Kierkegaard suggests that one of the primary uses of the concept of immortality is the moral regulation of our life. He returns to the error of making it a question about a general state of affairs because the corollary would be that the individual is our such state of affairs. Interestingly enough that rejection leads him straight to a condemnation of the ludicrous state of affairs when people

---

36. Ibid., 174; S.V. 9, 145.
37. Ibid.
38. Ibid., 174–75; S.V. 9, 145–46.

whose lives are a complete disorder and who have never achieved any degree of steady purpose "one day ask the clergyman with deep concern whether in the beyond they will then really be the same—after never having been able in their lifetime to be the same for a fortnight."[39] The existential question about immortality is for the existing subject a deed; and once again we see the replication of points about death: "So he asks how he is to behave in order to express in existence his immortality, whether he is really expressing it; and for the time being, he is satisfied with his task which surely must be enough to last a man a lifetime since it is to last for an eternity."[40] The issue of immortality thus becomes a matter not of the future but of the present, of ethics and not metaphysics. Or is that not perhaps an over-simplification?

Certainly it is not true that for Kierkegaard whether or not a man is immortal is a question decided by the man's attitude. In a *Journal* entry of 1847 he remarks, "We are all immortal. If someone immerses himself completely in this thought and lives into it he does not thereby become more immortal than all of us are."[41] A sermon entitled "There Will Be a Resurrection of the Dead—Both of the Righteous—and of the Unrighteous"[42] emphasizes the difference between mere speculation about immortality and the existential earnestness which ought to stop thinking about immortality. Instead of talking of the possible proofs of the immortality of the soul the religious speaker uses a completely different language. He or she says, "Do not doubt that you are immortal. Tremble that you are immortal."[43]

Man's immortality means that man cannot escape his responsibility for his life. Immortality, says Kierkegaard, is the judgment that "You are immortal, and you must make an accounting to God, immortal one, how you have lived! Precisely because you are immortal you will not be able to escape from God; you will not be able to mislay yourself in a grave and appear as if nothing were the matter, and the measure by which you will be judged by God is this—that you are immortal."[44]

---

39. Ibid., 175; S.V. 9, 146.
40. Ibid., 176; S.V. 9, 147.
41. Kierkegaard, *Journals*, VIII B 81.
42. Kierkegaard, *Christian Discourses*, 210ff.; S.V. 13, 192–94.
43. Ibid., 220; S.V. 13, 202.
44. Ibid., 214; S.V. 13, 196.

This is a very interesting development of the traditional argument for immortality from human nature because it unites the kind of argument that, in form at least, goes back to Plato with an essentially moral argument. It is also interesting to notice that Kierkegaard does not make any radical distinction between resurrection and immortality. He distinguishes between immortality and resurrection by saying that they are on different planes and that immortality is a matter of *anamnesis* whereas the resurrection faith looks always towards a future. Yet so far is he from being tempted to say that resurrection has nothing to do with immortality that he suggests that only a being who has the possibility of immortality within him- or herself and who, in relationship to God, reserves the possibility of individual immortality, can win against an eternal life.

The ethical quality of immortality once more comes to the fore in a *Journal* entry of 1857 which is headed "Immortality":

> Cicero writes (in *De Natura Deorum* Bk 11 towards the end) that the gods have no superiority over men except that they have immortality, *but this is not necessary for leading a happy life.* To be sure, it's very confusing the way people in Christendom force immortality onto men, making them believe that they feel a deep need for immortality. After all, didn't immortality first come with Christianity—and why? Because immortality demands that one must die to the world. To be able to die to the world—the Eternal and immortality must stand fast. Immortality and dying to the world are correlatives. In the suffering of dying to the world the hope of the infinite is born. But in Christendom men will cheat to get everything—immortality as well.[45]

The contribution of Kierkegaard then to this traditional problem of philosophy is two fold. (a) He has modified the traditional argument from human nature in important ethical and theological directions. (b) He continues this modification by raising the question of the proper way of approaching this problem, a way that elevates it from the status of problems to what we might call a policy. If I am not concerned with the self-involving character of this language then I have not begun to understand what it means to say that anyone is immortal.

I am very conscious of not even having covered all the ground and especially of not having done full justice to Kierkegaard's insights. This is, of course, an abiding problem and I shall never be able to do all that

45. Kierkegaard, *Journals and Papers*, 1952; Kierkegaard, *Papirer*, X4 A 440.

I want to do. I hope, however, that I have shown the philosophical and theological riches that are there for others to continue the task of harvesting them and making them available for our appropriation.

13

Kierkegaard and the Philosophy of Education

It is a truism that philosophical discussion of Kierkegaard has been very limited and such as there has been has concerned itself with him as a precursor of existentialism or phenomenology. Slight as is the interest shown in him by professional philosophers, it is even so a good deal greater than that shown by educationists. Happily, one of the few papers on Kierkegaard by educationists is a British contribution, that of W. R. Niblett,[1] but it remains generally true that educationists pay little attention to Kierkegaard. Thus there has been no paper since Niblett's published in 1954. I should add that this chapter is written not so much as a piece of philosophy of education but merely because I am sure that it is a useful exercise to discuss the relevance of Kierkegaard's thought to philosophy of education and I do what I can in the hope that some philosopher of education will take up the story.

PHENOMENOLOGY AND EDUCATION

As I said, Kierkegaard has been linked with phenomenology and in a volume of papers on phenomenology and education there are two papers devoted to Kierkegaard. In the first, Ronald Grimsley, talking of "Kierkegaard and the Educative Function of the Imagination," made a most useful point when he called attention to the "broadly educative emphasis" in Kierkegaard's authorship, which results from the religious purpose that Kierkegaard himself understood it to have.[2]

If I can use a fashionable word, it could be said with justice that what Kierkegaard offers us is neither a theology nor a philosophy but an

1. Niblett, "On Existentialism and Education," 101–11.
2. Grimsley, "Kierkegaard and the Educative Function," 13.

ideology. His authorship sprang from the conviction that he was singled out by Providence for the task of instructing his age in the business of "becoming a Christian"—a different matter from its self-description as "being Christian." The way Kierkegaard fulfilled this task seems to me important for the purpose of this discussion of philosophy of education and I shall return to some points that were not made by Ronald Grimsley. However, Grimsley's point here does raise the question of how the authorship can be described as religious. How is a collection of disparate writings to be seen as serving a single kind of purpose? It is a collection that ranges from diaries to large-scale quasi-philosophical works through sermons and short stories. More particularly one can ask in what sense all this can be spoken of as a religious education.

Two answers can be made to this. In the first place, one could explore the analogy between this kind of working and the search for complementarity between religious education in the narrow sense and education as a whole. It is this kind of search and the resultant discovery of a high degree of complementarity between religious education and other studies that has led educationists to argue that religious education should be integrated with more liberal studies than a narrow emphasis on either biblical instruction or even instruction on religion in isolation. Sometimes this kind of argument is put as a matter of saying that religious education is a feature of any aspect of education and that the whole business of the three Rs (Reading, [W]riting, and [A]rithmetic) is to be viewed from the perspective from this fourth R. A very different answer is to call attention to the unity of Kierkegaard's method in all these writings, a method which can be rightly called phenomenological. Kierkegaard was no Husserl before his time; but there is ample evidence of the same method being employed, the same desire to "get back to the facts."

That method was employed by Kierkegaard in an effort to make clear what kind of life-style Christianity involved. In that sense the whole of the authorship was an exercise in religious education. At the close of Grimsley's paper another important point was made—that Kierkegaard was no narrow Puritan.[3] How often one is given a portrait of Kierkegaard as a gloomy misanthrope and pathological ascetic. Misinterpretations these clearly are; but the real difficulty in correcting these misrepresentations is doing justice to the evidence of this complicated and enigmatic

3. Ibid., 21.

life. There is no doubt that towards the end of his life Kierkegaard did develop a stricter view of Christian morality than he had earlier. Several commentators have reminded us that whereas in the early works the emphasis is on the Knight of Faith who cannot be distinguished from the Knight of Infinite Resignation, in the last years the emphasis is on the theme of the imitation of Christ.[4]

Grimsley was, of course, concerned with the particular questions of the attitude towards the imagination and he rightly emphasizes the affinities with and the differences from the Romantic attitude to the imagination. Iconoclasm is indeed only one feature of the whole Puritan ethic; but there is a certain inevitability about this attitude in that context. It is for this reason that I think we should be offering a deceptively simple view of Kierkegaard if we resolutely refuse to apply the label of "Puritan" to our characterization of him.

Incidentally, the influence of his father could be adduced as evidence to support this; for in both his exercise of imagination and in the ascetic view of Christianity Kierkegaard was indebted to his father. Indeed the argument of Josiah Thompson that Kierkegaard was a neurotic who opted for the world of dreams is very dependent on the "crazy upbringing" (significantly the phrase is Kierkegaard's), in particular the imaginary walks through Copenhagen which father and son took in the drawing room.[5] Thompson's argument and his view of Kierkegaard are, I think, mistaken; but the evidence he uses serves to give greater force to my argument at this point.

EDUCATION AND KIERKEGAARD'S THEORY OF SUBJECTIVITY

It is unnecessary for me to show the importance of the principle of subjectivity in Kierkegaard's philosophy.[6] However, it is worth insisting, as Pojman did in his contribution to the volume mentioned above, in the paper entitled "Kierkegaard's Theory of Subjectivity and Education,"[7] that the principle does have a place in the history of philosophy. To appreciate Kierkegaard's significance one must recall that the period be-

---

4. For example, Lindstrøm, "La théologie de l'imitation de Jesus-Christ."
5. See Thompson, *Kierkegaard*, 39–40.
6. Cf. Heywood Thomas, *Philosophy of Religion in Kierkegaard's Writings*.
7. Pojman, "Kierkegaard's Theory of Subjectivity and Education," 1ff.

tween 1830 and 1850 was the great flowering of the Hegelian school in Denmark. This is not to say that there was no critic of Hegel in Denmark. Indeed the more one reads of philosophers such as Niels Treschow (1751–1833), F. C. Sibbern (1785–1872), and P. M. Møller (1794–1838) the more one realizes that the principle of subjectivity can be viewed as the climax of a Danish critique of Hegelianism. Therefore the obvious point to be made about this principle is that it represents Kierkegaard's polemic against Hegel. The Hegelian philosophy is criticized as a confusion of thought and being, logic and existence. By contrast, Kierkegaard views philosophy as beginning and ending in existence. The rationalism of Hegel dehumanized existence.

But the principle of subjectivity is no irrationalism or subjectivism. Kierkegaard was eager to criticize reason only in the same sense as Kant did in the *Critique of Pure Reason*. He was filled with admiration for Hegel's logical genius but saw that philosophy is not logic, as is very clear from the well-known *Journal* entry: "Had Hegel written the *Logic* and then said in the preface that it was merely an experiment in thought in which he had even begged the question in many places then he would certainly have been the greatest thinker who had ever lived. As it is, he is merely comic."[8]

I have referred to Møller's influence on Kierkegaard and Pojman may well have been thinking of this when he spoke of Kierkegaard as a nineteenth-century Socrates; for Møller was an ardent Platonist.[9] However, he is concerned with Kierkegaard's explicit use of Socrates as a model and in this I feel there are some matters for comment. It seems to me that Pojman tended to take too narrow a view of the philosophy of Socrates as well as of that of Kierkegaard. Neither of them seems to me to be exclusively concerned with morality. It is not because it was, for instance, any more a moral than a religious task that Kierkegaard pleaded for an existential philosophy. He sought indeed a philosophical idea and so in one sense the quest was neither moral nor religious. However in so far as the idea he sought was one for which he could live and die[10] it was related to both morality and religion. Socrates was

---

8. Kierkegaard, *Journals*, 497; Kierkegaard, *Papirer* V A 73; cf. Kierkegaard, *Postscript*, 93; S.V. 9, 80, "If a man occupied himself all his life with logic he would nevertheless not become logic; he must therefore himself exist in different categories."

9. Pojman, "Kierkegaard's Theory of Subjectivity and Education," 2-3, 11.

10. Cf. Kierkegaard, *Journals*, 22; Kierkegaard, *Papirer* I A 75.

his model of a philosopher because Socrates wanted to *be* what he was thinking. This may seem to be nothing more than a verbal quibble; but it is a good deal more than that. For instance, there is doubtless some relic here of the Romantic idealization of the Hellenic world which had captured Kierkegaard's imagination and which, through Møller, influenced his thinking quite considerably. Nevertheless, the essential importance of Socrates for Kierkegaard was that he bridged the gap between thought and being; and this is not synonymous with Romanticism.

Again the precise character of Kierkegaard's conception of Socrates has important implications for our understanding of his moral theory. Clearly this cannot be fully discussed here; but equally clearly if it were true that Kierkegaard's use of the Socratic model was an ethical concern then we should expect that he would hold that virtue is knowledge. In fact, Kierkegaard's view of morality owes more to Kant: and the understanding of moral action which is discussed and elaborated in *Fear and Trembling* in the paradigm of Abraham's sacrifice is deontological. This is but one strand in Kierkegaard's ethical thinking, it is true; but the other strands are just as alien to a Hellenistic theory—the sense that as against God we are always in the wrong, the obligation to imitate Christ and the necessity of works of love.

The difficulty of understanding Kierkegaard's principle of subjectivity was well illustrated by Pojman's sensitive treatment of it in his paper. Despite the sensitivity of his approach he seemed to me to reduce the meaning of "subjectivity is truth" to a distinction between general statements and particular ones.[11] He illustrated this by taking as examples the statements "All men are mortal" and "You are going to die." Now it is not at all clear from this example that there is any essential difference between these propositions, and indeed a Russellian analysis of the general proposition would yield something that would be very much like the prediction. It might be said that the general statement does not in fact function as a prediction; but this does not seem a convincing way of making a *distinction* between the two. Further, it might be said that the second statement cannot be in the form of a third-person assertation; but again this seems to suggest a very distinctive contextualization for the assertion. In short, the second can only be distinguished from the general assertion if we give the use of the second-person some quality of first-person language. As we saw, a basic point that Kierkegaard makes

11. Cf. Pojman, "Kierkegaard's Theory of Subjectivity and Education," 3f., 6f.

about the language of death is that it is properly understood only when we appreciate that it relates to ourselves.[12] The distinction is therefore one between statements which are self-involving and those which are not. This is why it is a matter that involves decision.

A PRESUPPOSITIONLESS SYSTEM?

This is also why I should want to distinguish between learning by experience and Kierkegaard's concept of appropriation. Appropriation is very much a matter of *self-involvement*, and I "inwardly digest" what I "read, mark, and learn" only by seeing myself as this or that. However, there is a great deal that I learn from experience which is not thus self-involving, as, for instance, when I learn from experience what sweeping a chimney is like or what it is to hammer the finish on a silver bowl. I am fond of my roses and I learn from experience that the soil in my borders is impoverished but this is not subjective knowledge. That is indeed of more profound significance to educational theory than the matter of experiential learning.

I have spoken of the philosophical significance of Kierkegaard's principle of subjectivity. One of the main arguments he develops in this connection is that an existential system is impossible.[13] The point of the argument is that Hegel and his followers are wrong to imagine that they can derive existence from the abstract movement of the logical dialectic. There is an impressive development of logical theory involved in this argument, as I have tried to show in chapter 5, and it needs to be said again and again that the proper context for understanding his view is the debate between the Hegelian and non-Hegelian logicians in Copenhagen. Kierkegaard's concern was to show the peculiar complexity of the assertions we make about human existence.

In *Fragments* and *Postscript* he stresses the way in which historical assertions introduce a second complexity into the process of becoming. He characterizes this further by saying that there is a task for the existing human and this task is existence—a task that can be called ethical in a broad sense of the word. This is not therefore any anti-intellectualism and his critique of science makes this very clear. In the letter to P. W. Lund, Kierkegaard reveals his enthusiasm for natural sciences whilst at

---

12. See earlier, chapter 12.
13. See Kierkegaard, *Postscript*, 118–25; S.V. 9, 100–106.

the same time making it clear that he cannot make science his own life's work.[14] The point is made with clarity and force in the *Postscript*, the very work that elaborates the theme of subjectivity: "All honor to the pursuit of science and all honor to everyone who assists in driving the cattle away from the sacred precincts of scholarship. But the ethical is and remains the highest task for every human being."[15]

It is interesting to note that in the International Institute of Philosophy Colloquium held in Copenhagen in 1966 and devoted to Kierkegaard and contemporary philosophy, there was a paper by A. Naess entitled "Kierkegaard and the Educational Crisis."[16] Especially interesting is the fact that he approached the subject from this same general concern with the shape and character of Kierkegaard's thought. One theme that he takes up is the opposition to system, and this seems to me a very clear example of the relevance of Kierkegaard's thought to a philosophy of education. This is an area of philosophy where there is an even greater tendency to systematization than in metaphysics.[17] Any belief in the possibility of such a system, however, is misguided because it is an attempt to encapsulate human existence in an illusory pre-existing world of thought. What is interesting and what proved influential in Kierkegaard was his opposition of the personal and the system. His critique of the Hegelian system was in part logical; but his main concern in rejecting it was to preserve a proper appreciation of the person in philosophy. The relevance of this for philosophy of education is put thus by Naess:

> It is the choices of the individual, the process of finding himself, which gradually illuminates the world he is living in. Kierkegaard teaches us that there is a source of inner life, which, if not stopped, generates values and sets of value priorities, that is, in short, an inwardness; and truth in the abstract, as mere agreement with external observation, has no place for the individual if not related to that inwardness. In our time we

---

14. P. W. Lund (1801–80) was a cousin of Kierkegaard's on his mother's side and he achieved some distinction as a geologist, anthropologist, and botanist. He discovered some fossils in Brazil. He and Kierkegaard corresponded regularly and the letter in question shows the philosophical character of Kierkegaard's interest in science. The letter is in Kierkegaard, *Journals*, 16; Kierkegaard, *Papirer* I A 72.

15. Kierkegaard, *Postscript*, 151; S.V. 9, 125.

16. Naess, "Kierkegaard and the Educational Crisis."

17. Cf. Curtis and Boultwood, *A Short History of Educational Ideas*.

stress the difference between results that can be recorded and stored in a machine, and a result incorporated in the personal world view of an individual. The aim of the educator cannot be to multiply the former, but the latter.[18]

Another aspect of the opposition to the Hegelian system was Kierkegaard's rejection of the claim that it was a presuppositionless system. There are various ways in which this theme can be taken up (e.g., by comparison with Collingwood's "absolute presuppositions"); but let us pursue this emphasis on the person and the personal. If we understand Kierkegaard aright then he is saying that the philosopher can never leave himself behind when he begins on his philosophical exploration.

De Omnibus Dubitandum (1842/3), an incomplete work of Kierkegaard's youth, is the story of a young man who discovers that philosophical doubt is unrelated to real doubt. The value of the Cartesian method as a critique to be applied to Hegel was quite clear to Kierkegaard;[19] but he refused to be seduced into the illusion that philosophy was value-free. And at this point he is saying something very relevant to philosophy of education, where it is often asserted dogmatically that educational theory contains no normative element and is quite neutral.[20]

Perhaps the most significant way in which the valuational function of philosophy was made clear by Kierkegaard was in his insistence that there was an integral connection between an individual's philosophizing and his existence. The proper model for a philosophy was a house in which we live. The rationalist-system-builders, however, presented a very different picture: "In relation to their systems most systematizers are like a man who builds an enormous castle and lives in a shack close by; they do not live in their own enormous systematic buildings. But spiritually that is a decisive objection. Spiritually speaking, a man's thought must be the building in which he lives—otherwise everything is topsy-turvy."[21] Like Kant, Kierkegaard had a very clear understanding of how the human being is involved in the nexus of cause and effect but

---

18. Naess, "Kierkegaard and the Educational Crisis," 66; cf. ibid., 67, "Through the artistic use of paradoxical terminology Kierkegaard has provided us with a rich store of expressions stressing the personal aspect of knowing."

19. See Kierkegaard, *Journals and Papers*, 736; IV C 14.

20. Cf. O'Connor, *Introduction to the Philosophy of Education*, 109.

21. Kierkegaard, *Journals*, 583; Kierkegaard, *Papirer* VII A 82; cf. Kierkegaard, *Sickness unto Death*, 68; S.V. 11, 215.

is, even so, not explicable in these terms.²² Therefore he would want to insist that the knowledge a person seeks in philosophy cannot be neutral like scientific knowledge.

KIERKEGAARD'S OWN INTEREST IN EDUCATION

It might be thought that what I have done is to show that there are themes in Kierkegaard's thought that can be applied to any area of philosophy, and, in a sense, this is indeed true. However, the justice of pressing Kierkegaard into the service of philosophy of *education* lies in Kierkegaard's own indubitable interest in education. Though few in number, there are some explicit references in his works and papers. He deplores the contemporary tendency of "practical education to make people into functional human beings."²³ This early impatience with and distaste for contemporary education remained, and he bemoaned the hypocrisy he saw here, as elsewhere in Danish society: "The modern hypocrisy with respect to the whole educational system and upbringing—instead of working in earnest, parents and teachers assure one another how important this matter is and what they are doing—in order to get new window ventilators."²⁴ The general confusion of the age was thus all too obvious in its educational system and policy.

I mentioned earlier the importance of bearing in mind Kierkegaard's dates, and this is very clear when one recalls that from 1840 onward Grundtvig was active in education.²⁵ Kierkegaard was

---

22. See Kierkegaard, *Concept of Anxiety*, 65; S.V. 6, 163.

23. Kierkegaard, *Papirer* II A 6.

24. Kierkegaard, *Papirer* VIII 1 A 257. This refers to reports in the *Berlingske Tidende* that the principal of the Børgenrdydshole (literally the civic virtue school—where Kierkegaard himself attended) had planned to add window ventilators that would be a move towards a free rather than an enclosed educational system. Kierkegaard thought the whole thing called for ironical comment. However, Bishop Mynster comments frequently in his visitation diaries (*Visitationsboger* 1835–53, vol. I) on the misery of overcrowded schools.

25. For the study of Grundtvig (1783–1872) the best guide is the renowned Danish church historian and educationist, Hal Koch. Besides his German book *Grundtvig, Leben und Werk* he also published an English study the following year, *Grundtvig*. Also useful is Johannes Knudsen, *A Danish Rebel*, which could be described as a "search to find what his message means to us" (p. xi) and chapter 10 of which deals with Grundtvig's contribution to education. Grundtvig's work as the "founder" or "father" of the Danish Folk Schools has been studied by F. S. Skrubbeltrang in his book *The Danish Folk High Schools*. A more recent study of this is Rordam, *The Danish Folk High Schools*.

so thoroughly opposed to Grundtvig that it is not surprising to find some sharp comments on his educational views. Grundtvigianism was a liberal movement that had considerable influence not only in Denmark but also in other parts of Scandinavia and even in America. Grundtvig believed that both church and state would be best served by an instructed populace. His ideal of education was something more practical than intellectual. Grundtvig's educational aims have been well described by J. Novrup thus:

> Against the concept of an academic culture he advanced the idea of a *folkelig* culture. *Folkelig* education, or, as he called it, education and efficiency for life, must come from a new school where "our native country's natural and historical qualities, expressed in real life and in the demands of the present time" became the midpoint. Such a school must emerge from learning and maintain vital connection with it, but at the same time it must be *independent*. Here real life and the present must assert their rights.[26]

The term *"folkelig"* is an obviously appropriate word to use of Grundtvig's educational ideas and indeed they could be summed up in the two words *"folkelig"* (national) and *"menneskelig"* (human). What was needed was a "fatherland education based on the mother tongue."[27] The aim of education should be that of producing a unified nation with a sense of historical continuity. However, all this would result, as Kierkegaard thought, merely in mediocrity: "In the next generation the parents will probably be so mediocre that they themselves will be in need of upbringing—and they are the ones who are supposed to aid the schoolmaster in bringing up the children! Especially when Grundtvig prevails and introduces the new education . . . When the time comes I trust I shall be dead, although I could wish that Grundtvig might still be living then."[28]

What I have tried to show by this historical contextualization is that there is a real interest on Kierkegaard's part in the educational discussion of the day. There is, then, matter here for another tale—and some other narrator. It is now time to consider the more general question of

---

26. Novrup, *Scandinavian Adult Education*, 20.

27. Grundtvig, *Grundtvigs Erindringer*, 143.

28. Kierkegaard, *Papirer* VIII1 A 258. This may be a reference to Grundtvig's view of the responsibility of the various organs of society—see Gronbaek, *Psykologiske Taenken og Teorien hos Grundtvig*, 149.

his relevance for us as we face the challenge of a determined and drastic revision of our educational system.

KIERKEGAARD AS A PHILOSOPHER OF EDUCATION FOR THE TWENTY-FIRST CENTURY

As I have maintained, Kierkegaard is to be seen as a philosopher in the tradition of Kant and therefore it is most likely that his contribution to the general themes of philosophy of education will lie in the perception that morality occupies a crucial place in the life of man. We hear much these days about individual freedom and individual responsibility and yet what is so obvious in education is the drive towards central authority and collectivization. Here is Kierkegaard's first area of relevance. No mere intellectual aristocrat or elitist, he foresaw this kind of crisis and understood the nature of the problem. He rejected the concept of culture that he saw in the new democracy that was emerging in his society. It was, he thought, the introduction of the mass man: "'The masses': that is really the aim of my polemic," he says.[29] His essentially theological conception of humanity and the nature of human moral responsibility implied that human existence is a matter of individuality. As all life is to be viewed as "before God" so there is no point at which I am absolved from my responsibility for myself. It might be argued that this has echoes of Kant and certainly there are links with Kant's moral philosophy in his view of the nature of morality as distinguished from what is natural or empirically true. Thus he distinguishes spirit-man from animal-man:

> Between existence as spirit-man and existence as animal-man there is a whole difference of quality. However, in our sense perception there is nothing to be seen of this difference. The collision lies in the fact that the animal-men pounce upon the spirit-man or are goaded into fury by him. If I were to talk about it in the Greek manner I would have to say that the spectacle amuses the gods exactly as a hunt amuses men . . . From a Christian point of view, this thing has to be considered in a different way; this collision is the education of the spirit-man, his examination, also his mission, in so far as he has the task of bearing witness to the fact that man is a spirit—a task which, in the course of the centuries, in relation to an increasingly polished bestiality, has become more and more urgent, but also more and more strenuous.[30]

29. Kierkegaard, *Papirer* VIII1 A 23.
30. Kierkegaard, *Papirer* XI1 A 225.

With such a view of the nature of man and the mission of moral man Kierkegaard will inspire argument about the nature of education in relation to culture to fasten on the issue of morality as a task. Part of the argument will be the kind of sociological analysis which has illuminated the pervasive influence and devastating effect of mass culture in our society. However, the essential point will be the recapture of a fundamental understanding of human development and educational goals as moral activities.

I want to move on to consider Kierkegaard's relevance to a general understanding of education and then to two different kinds of more specific education—aesthetic and religious. Since I can claim no special competence in any of the fields, these remarks are perforce very sketchy; but they will, I hope, suffice to establish the point that philosophers of education will find in Kierkegaard something to interest and inspire them.

In the first place, it will surely be a truism that education is a process whereby the pupil is engaged in self-discovery and self-fulfillment. The Aristotelian overtones of this latter concept were music to Kierkegaard's very Hellenistic soul and, as his view of the human being generally is that a person's quest of the self is the nature of existence, so he specifically views education in this light. Treating children like battery-hens is, he points out, nobody's idea of education.[31] Thus it seems to me that his typical view of the ideal of human existence has just as natural an application to education.

What concerns me at the moment is not the claim that the religious is the highest sphere of existence but the more general claim that no existence is real unless it is self-aware, self-involving, and committed. This idea of subjectivity is, I repeat, a subtle and complex notion and, as Pojman argued,[32] it certainly has relevance to the epistemology of the learning process. My argument at the moment is that the very character of a life lived in its fullness is what Kierkegaard described as its existential nature and that this is what education is recognized to involve. Therefore it seems to me desirable to turn from philosophies that offer very different models of humanity to this philosophy with its constant emphasis on the existential. It is not enough to reject mechanical models when we are content to operate with assumptions that are part and parcel of such in-

---

31. Kierkegaard, *Papirer* II A 12.
32. Pojman, "Kierkegaard's Theory of Subjectivity and Education," 4f.

animate models as the empiricist *tabula rasa*. Nor again will it suffice to protest that we are operating with dynamic models if what we assume is that the aim of education is some technological competence rather than a character of existence. My point, then, is quite simply that Kierkegaard showed himself to be a reliable guide and that in his view of humanity he has provided a central concept of a philosophy of education.

Having said much already about ethics, I must comment on the nature of aesthetics and religion. Any aesthetic response will involve two features of what can be said to be Kierkegaard's theory of knowledge—its self-involving nature and the role of emotion, especially in knowledge that has the Platonic character of *eros*. Kierkegaard's interest in aesthetics dates certainly from his student days, if not before, and it is not always remembered that he was a master of the Danish language and a literary craftsman of outstanding distinction. He had made history by his request that he should present his dissertation in Danish rather than in Latin—and because his classical competence was well known he was allowed to do so and thus forged a literary philosophical style. *The Concept of Irony* is as much a literary masterpiece as it is a philosophical tour de force. Kierkegaard's literary production proper—which he regarded as initiated by this work—is equally a work of art and it would be very easy to be tempted into an exposition of its literary worth. However, while Kierkegaard achieved something unique by his oeuvre and his manifestation of a genius for metaphor and parable, these points do not concern us now, though it is certainly true that his work is a veritable model for anyone who wants to bring home the lesson that communication is basically the telling of a story. Rather, the point is the kind of thing that has been argued by Duke Madenfort, that Kierkegaard is an important figure in any historical account of the *concept* of the aesthetic.[33]

Though Kierkegaard called the most elementary stage and sphere of life "aesthetic" and saw this as a kind of life that was doomed to a shipwreck on the rocks of despair, he was far from advocating some iconoclasm or puritanical reflection of art. Probably his reason for using the term for this purpose was the way in which etymology and his own argument showed the immediacy of awareness in such situations. The young aesthete is the hero of *Either-Or* and the first part of the book is composed of "a number of attempts to formulate an aesthetic philoso-

---

33. Madenfort, "The Aesthetic as Immediately Sensuous—An Historical Perspective," 5–17. It is interesting that Kant is another example chosen to exemplify this view.

phy of life,"[34] the theory which is instantiated in his hedonism. What I want to emphasize is that there is here a view of the aesthetic phenomenon as something immediate because it has to do with the realm of sense and so a quite different view of beauty from Ruskin's moralist and intellectual views. Thus it seems to me that Kierkegaard is reminding us that we can talk till doomsday and unless we bring the pupil to the point of seeing, hearing, and feeling the work of art we have achieved no aesthetic education.

Finally, I turn to religious education, where Kierkegaard is perhaps most helpful precisely because he is so typically negative in what he has to say about religious communication. One can introduce a breed of sheep into a country, but one cannot introduce Christianity. To claim this judgment as an illumination of the problem of religious education may seem a paradox worthy of Kierkegaard himself. Yet it seems to me that so much has been said about the need to avoid indoctrination and the importance of making children aware of the pluralist situation, I feel that we lose sight of the essential mystery of religion. We are so anxious to avoid indoctrination that religious education becomes a matter of informing children *about* Christianity and it will inevitably be that kind of education that we achieve with regard to our multicultural context.

There are two respects in which Kierkegaard's paradox does show the weakness of this kind of religious education. In the first place, as I said, the religious affirmation is emptied of mystery as it is made synonymous with some kind of information, important though that remains. Secondly, the student is passive—and this will be the case however much the teacher strives to introduce activities and experiential methods; but the activity essential to a religious growth lies beyond the reach of such methods. This, then, is where Kierkegaard's advocacy of a Socratic maieusis, an indirect communication, can serve as a criterion of what religious education should be.

---

34. Kierkegaard, *Either-Or* I, 11; S.V. 2, 19.

Epilogue

I HAVE BEEN CONCERNED to show what kind of legacy Kierkegaard left us, all of us, because I am very much aware that the lessons I have learned from him relate to the main features of modern philosophy and theology. As a young scholar breaking his milk teeth in Kierkegaard research I used to think that what I should do was to produce a portrait of Kierkegaard the thinker comparable with the great Lowrie's portrait of Kierkegaard the man. It did not take me many years to realize that I could not achieve such an ambition. I know too little of him and life is too short to discover all that one needs for such a task. Even the great scholars of the twentieth century—such as Thulstrup, Diem, and Fabro—contented themselves with only *aspects* of his thought or *part* of his work. A great deal more needed to be said than what I have done but I have called a halt in order to say a little.

I have tried to look at him and his work in the round. There have been times when I have been all too conscious how difficult it is to plumb the depths of his thought. There have been times too when, driven to irritation by his subtle craftiness, one bursts out, "This is too clever by half!" Yet I have tried to take him on his own terms and let the literature unfold into a unity and coherence of thought that seem to me still to challenge philosophy, theology, and religion.

In these concluding pages some autobiographical references such as these will be perhaps a proper "repetition." On all three of the topics I have just mentioned, I have found inspiration as well as challenge in my reading of Kierkegaard. My upbringing in philosophy was in the empiricist tradition and to a very large extent that attitude was reinforced by my encounter with linguistic analysis as I listened to John Wisdom. The methods and insights that I learned did indeed prove important as tools for my understanding of Kierkegaard and more generally in philosophy of religion. However, there are two things in my understanding of what philosophy is that I owe to Kierkegaard. First, I have never been able to rid myself of some sense that if I philosophize my task is to be a "subjective thinker." Anselm was quite clearly a very subjective thinker in more ways than one, as his beautiful exposition of the ontological argument in chapter 2 of *Proslogion* shows. He was happy to talk of existing in thought but he knew that the existence of the believer and that of God is existence as reality. Similarly Kierkegaard teaches one how one is inevitably drawn into what Keats called "a life of thought," which for him, as he told his brother George, was so poor a thing by comparison with "a life of feeling." However, again like Anselm, Kierkegaard could see that philosophy should not be content with that absorption into thinking but must recognize the interest in existence that, he says, characterizes the subjective thinker.

In *The Republic* Plato makes Socrates exclaim at the end of the dialogue that the answer to the question the group had been discussing was there "tumbling" at their feet. This immediately reminds us of Kierkegaard's recurring thesis that philosophy is not a matter of results, which is the second of these inter-related lessons I have learned from him. The philosopher at the end of a discussion such as described in *The Republic* does not have any result that he did not have at the beginning. Yet when we read Plato we are made aware of *what* it is that we knew from the beginning: there is a peculiar sense of knowing my own mind, grasping how it is that I know, what it is that I know and for what I think.

It is over fifty years ago since I heard the Danish logician Jørgensen giving a lecture on Kierkegaard and I still remember being struck by the way he summed up the whole of Kierkegaard's thought by saying that he sought and advocated honesty. At the time, I admit, I reacted with youthful impatience and I thought that Jorgensen had trivialized Kierkegaard. Fortunately I have never forgotten the remark and now see it to be profoundly true in its rich ambiguity. Honesty of thought is the kind of single-mindedness that Wittgenstein had in mind when he remarked that the difficulty in philosophizing is to remember everything. It is also that attitude to self and the world which is perhaps the most morally difficult thing about philosophy and which made those who knew him well describe Wittgenstein as a religious thinker in his devotion. This is the recognition that as I think I form myself, and that I am a self only in my social existence. Struggling with Kierkegaard is to discover behind and beneath his onslaught on idealism there is a profound debt to the contributions of Fichte and Schelling. The vocation of the scholar that he or she shares with every person is to become a self-in-interrelation. What I have sought to describe and to illustrate is the nature of the claim that Kierkegaard's achievement was to bring the philosopher's existence into philosophy. Freud said that the opposite of play was not work but reality: in that sense it could be said that Kierkegaard taught us that philosophy was too prone to become play. What he meant by "reality" may seem far removed from a discussion such as that of a G. E. Moore; but I rather fancy that he would have applauded Moore's appeal to common sense and the limitations of experience.

The word "limitations" reminds me all too clearly of the limitations of my exposition and my failure to spell out all the philosophical themes in Kierkegaard's thought. Fortunately there are now not only the outstanding contributions of the second half of the twentieth century but also a fresh new scholarly harvest in the twenty-first. All this is ample evidence of the rich and fruitful legacy Kierkegaard bequeathed to philosophy.

What is wonderful about Kierkegaard is the way in which his thinking, with its variety of concerns, was a seamless garment. The contempt that he expressed for the ridiculous jobbing builders (which he thought the fashionable amongst his contemporary philosophers to be) was mirrored in his analysis of what passed for (and will often pass for) Christian communication. Nor was it only "parrot-like talk" that struck him as at once comic and tragic. In *The Fatherland* article of 28 May 1855 he argues that from the Christian point of view the silence of Bishop Martensen is both inexcusable and comic, as comical as Countess Orsini's shouting whisper in Lessing's *Emilia Galotti*: "It shouts so clearly that it can be heard not only by men of superior understanding, but that the people, the plain man, can understand it; and it shouts so loud that it can be heard in a neighboring kingdom."[1]

This is why I said that the "Wittgensteinian Kierkegaard" is so often found in his discussion of what the church is. For clearly what is at issue here is whether Martensen's *behavior* was consistent with what must be said about Christianity as a *form of life*. My point in referring to this is that just as Kierkegaard was at pains to make the philosophical point that the Christian's believing is not the application of some understanding or theory, so he was primarily concerned to awaken his readers to the challenge of appropriating faith. One of the great achievements of

---

1. Kierkegaard, *Attack on Christendom*, 68; S.V. 19, 84.

Paul Holmer was his grasp of that double point when he insisted that the only proper way to "understand" Kierkegaard is to take to heart the instruction "Go thou and do likewise." As he puts it so eloquently:

> Kierkegaard believed that the glory of being human was to realize in one's own personality the most pervading of passions and enthusiasms. Among these, those of Christian quality were the truth for him. It is well to have the reminder (which all of us who write in this volume ought to be able to give ourselves) that Kierkegaard's entire writing career was expended not to make us scholars but to help us use our scholarly aristocratic abilities to grasp the possibilities which his aristocratic talents so deftly described.[2]

To list those possibilities would be to repeat our tale; but suffice it to say that there is nothing in the whole complex of Christian worship and life where one of these does not confront us as a task.

In conclusion, I would make a similar point very briefly about the importance of his legacy to theology. It is impossible here even to begin the account of his tremendous influence on the development of twentieth-century theology; but it is not too much to say that both the Barthian revolution and the very different impact of Bultmann's demythologizing program do in fact reflect that. Even so idealist a theologian as Tillich was very ready to recognize his debt to Kierkegaard. It hardly needs to be said that the greatest modern discussion of the doctrine of original sin, namely Reinhold Niebuhr's, takes Kierkegaard as a starting point.

A theologian, then, he certainly was: whether he would ever have been happy to become a professional theologian I would not like to say. Had he done so I am sure that he would have noted the rather odd way in which the theologian is both marginalized and also expected to be the conscience of society. He would also have reflected unhappily again and again on the way theology is tempted to a concern with itself rather than the reality that gives rise to it. In his own oeuvre he left a legacy of the honest conversation that he found lacking in Martensen. Indeed what he disapproved of most in Martensen was not just the silence condemned in the article mentioned above but the way that was characteristic of Martensen's thinking. The silence, he remarked, was not simply dumb but "dumb by wanting to be clever"; "It is when there is something a

---

2. Johnson and Thulstrup, eds., *A Kierkegaard Critique*, 53.

teacher doesn't know—which may perfectly well occur—and he then does not himself say straightforwardly 'I don't know it,' but shrewdly wants to make as if he knew it."[3] This was the impression he had formed of Martensen's *Christian Dogmatics*, as he records in his *Journal* of 1849: "it is the old sophistry of being able to talk—but of not holding a dialogue."[4]

I finish my story indeed by saying that characteristic of Kierkegaard's legacy to theology is the fact that his discussion of doctrine has brought us back to the issue of communication. His own choice of a method of *indirect* communication was the artistic creation that made the man and his work one whole. As for myself, I am content if I have done no more than call attention to a legacy that makes Kierkegaard a thinker for the twenty-first century.

---

3. Kierkegaard, S.V. 19, 84.
4. Kierkegaard, *Journals and Papers* 673, X1 A 566.

Bibliography

Adorno, Theodore W. *Kierkegaard: Konstruktion des Aesthetischen.* Tübingen: Mohr, 1962.
Ammundsen, V. *Søren Kierkegaard's Ungdom.* Copenhagen: Gad, 1912.
Aquinas, Thomas. *Summa Theologiae: Latin Text and English Translation, Introduction, Notes, Appendices, and Glossaries.* 2 vols. Edited by T. C. O'Brien. London: Blackfriars, 1963.
Arilsden, Skot. *Biskop Hans Lassen Martensen, hans Liv, Udvikling og Arbejde.* Copenhagen: Gad, 1932.
Aristotle. *Complete Works of Aristotle.* The Revised Oxford Translation. Edited by J. Barnes. Princeton: Princeton University Press, 1992.
Andersen, Vilhelm. *Tider og Typer af Dansk Aands Historie.* First series, part II, volume II. Copenhagen: Gyldendalske, 1916.
Barth, Karl. *Anselm: Fides Quaerens Intellectum.* Translated by Ian W. Robertson. London: SCM, 1960.
———. *Protestant Theology in the Nineteenth Century: From Rousseau to Ritschl.* London: SCM, 1959.
Bejerholm, Lars. *Meddelelsens Dialektik: Studier i Søren Kierkegaard teorien om sprak, kommunikation och pseudonymitet.* Copenhagen: Munksgaard, 1962.
Billeskov Jansen F. J. "The Literary Art of Kierkegaard." In *A Kierkegaard Critique*, edited by Howard A. Johnson and Niels Thulstrup, 11–21. New York: Harper, 1962.
———. *Studier i Søren Kierkegaards litteraere Kunst.* Copenhagen: Rosenkild and Bagger, 1951.
Blattner, William D. *Heidegger's Temporal Idealism.* Cambridge: Cambridge University Press, 1999.
Bohlin, Torsten. *Kierkegaards Dogmatiska Aaskaadning.* Stockholm: Diakonistyr, 1925.
Boyer, Alain. *Hors du Temps, un essai sur Kant.* Paris: Vrin, 2001.
Blattner, William D. *Heidegger's Temporal Idealism.* Cambridge: Cambridge University Press, 1999.
Brandes, G. *Søren Kierkegaard, En Kritisk Fremstilling in Grundriss.* Copenhagen: Gyldendal, 1877.
Bruaire, Claude. *Logique et religion chrétienne dans la philosophie de Hegel.* Paris: Seuil, 1964.
Capel, Lee. "Historical Introduction." In *The Concept of Irony*, by Søren Kierkegaard, 1–16. London: Collins, 1966.
Caputo, John D. "Heidegger and Theology." In *The Cambridge Companion to Heidegger*, edited by Charles Guignon, 270–88. Cambridge: Cambridge University Press, 1993.
Cassirer, Ernst. *Kant's Life and Thought.* New Haven, CT: Yale University Press, 1982.
———. *Philosophy of Symbolic Forms.* 3 vols. New Haven, CT: Yale University Press, 1923–29.

Clausen, H. N. *Optegnelser om mit Levneds og min Tids Historie*. Copenhagen: Gad, 1877.
Collins, James. *The Mind of Kierkegaard*. London: Secker and Warburg, 1954.
Come, Arnold B. *Trendelenburg's Influence on Kierkegaard's Modal Categories*. Montreal: Inter Editions, 1991.
Croxall, T. H. *Glimpses and Impressions of Kierkegaard*. London: Nisbet, 1959.
———. *A Kierkegaard Commentary*. London: Nisbet, 1956.
Curtis, S. J., and M. E. A. Boultwood. *A Short History of Educational Ideas*. London: University Tutorial Press, 1956.
Diem, Hermann. *Kierkegaard's Dialectic of Existence*. Translated by Harold Knight. Edinburgh: Oliver and Boyd, 1959.
Dunning, Stephen. *Kierkegaard's Dialectic of Inwardness*. Princeton: Princeton University Press, 1985.
Dupré, Louis. *Kierkegaard as Theologian*. London: Sheed and Ward, 1963.
Elrod, John W. *Kierkegaard and Christendom*. Princeton: Princeton University Press, 1981.
Evans, C. Stephen. *Kierkegaard's Fragments and Postscript: The Religious Philosophy of Johannes Climacus*. Atlantic Highlands, NJ: Humanities, 1983.
———. *Passionate Reason: Making Sense of Kierkegaard's Philosophical Fragments*. Bloomington, IN: Indiana University Press, 1992.
Fabro, Cornelio. *Søren Kierkegaard: Diario*. Brescia, Italy: Morcelliana 1948–51.
Ferreira, M. Jamie. *Love's Grateful Striving: A Commentary on Kierkegaard's Works of Love*. Oxford: Oxford University Press, 2001.
Fenger, Henning. *Kierkegaard, the Myths and Their Origins: Studies in the Kierkegaardian Papers and Letters*. Translated by George C. Schoolfield. New Haven: Yale University Press, 1980.
Fichte, J. G. *Attempt at a Critique of all Revelation*. Translated by Garret Green. Cambridge: Cambridge University Press, 1978.
———. *The Science of Knowledge*. Translated by Peter Heath and John Lachs. Cambridge: Cambridge University Press, 1982.
———. *The Vocation of Man*. Edited by R. M. Chisholm. Indianapolis: Bobbs-Merrill, 1956.
Findlay, J. N. *Kant and the Transcendental Object*. Oxford: Clarendon, 1981.
Forsyth, P. T. *The Work of Christ*. London: Independent Press, 1958.
Gallagher, M. P. "Wittgenstein's Admiration for Kierkegaard." *The Month* 39 (1968) 43–49.
Geismar, E. *Lectures on the Religious Thought of Søren Kierkegaard*. Minneapolis: Augsburg, 1937.
———. *Søren Kierkegaard, Hans Livsudvikling og Forfattervirkshomed*. Copenhagen: Gad, 1927–28.
Gill, Jerry. "Kant, Kierkegaard and Religious Knowledge." *Philosophy and Phenomenological Research* 27 (1967) 188–204.
Green, Ronald M. "Kierkegaard's Great Critique: *Either-Or* as a Kantian Transcendental Deduction." In *International Kierkegaard Commentary*, vol. 4, edited by Robert L. Perkins, 139–54. Macon, GA: Mercer University Press, 1995.
Grimsley, R. "Kierkegaard and the Educative Function." In *Phenomenology and Education*, edited by B. Curtis and W. Mays, 13–27. London: Methuen, 1978.
———. *Kierkegaard and French Literature*. Cardiff: University of Wales Press, 1966.

Grundtvig, N. F. S., Steen Johansen, and Henning Høirup. *Grundtvigs Erindringer og Erindinger om Grundtvig*. Copenhagen: Gyldendal, 1948.
Haecker, Theodor. *Journal in the Night*. Translated by Alexander Dru. London: Harvill, 1949.
———. *Søren Kierkegaard*. London: Oxford University Press, 1937.
Hannay, Alastair. *Kierkegaard*. London: Routledge and Kegan Paul, 1982.
———. *Kierkegaard: A Biography*. Cambridge: Cambridge University Press, 2001.
Hannay, Alastair, and Gordon D. Marino, editors. *The Cambridge Companion to Kierkegaard*. Cambridge: Cambridge University Press, 1998.
Harris, H. *David Friedrich Strauss and His Theology*. Cambridge: Cambridge University Press, 1973.
Heiberg, Johan L. "Letter to Orsted, No.126." In *Breve og Akstykker vedrørende Søren Kierkegaard*, edited by Martin Borup. Copenhagen: Gyldendal, 1946-50.
———. *Prosaisk Skrifter*. 2 vols. Copenhagen: Reitzel, 1862.
Hegel, G. W. F. *Aesthetics*, vol. 1. Translated by T. M. Knox. Oxford: Clarendon, 1975.
———. *Lectures on the History of Philosophy*. 3 vols. Translated by E. S. Haldane and F. H. Simson. London: Routledge and Kegan Paul, 1892-95.
———. *Philosophy of Religion*. 3 vols. Translated and edited by Peter C. Hodgson. Berkeley, CA: University of California Press, 1984-87.
———. *Science of Logic*. Translated by A. V. Miller. London: Allen & Unwin, 1969.
Heywood Thomas, John. "J. G. Fichte and F. W. J. Schelling." In *Nineteenth Century Religious Thought in the West*, vol. 1, edited by Ninian Smart, John Clayton et al., 41-80. Cambridge: Cambridge University Press, 1985.
———. "Lukác's Critique of Kierkegaard." In *Faith, Knowledge, Action: Essays for Niels Thulstrup*, edited by G. L. Stengren, 184-98. Copenhagen: Reitzel, 1984.
———. "Paradox." *Bibliotheca Kierkegaardiana* 3 (1980) 192-219.
———. *Philosophy of Religion in Kierkegaard's Writings*. Lampeter: Mellen, 1994.
———. Review of *Kierkegaard* by Josiah Thompson. *Religious Studies* 13 (1977) 101-4.
———. Review of *Parables of Kierkegaard*, edited by Thomas C. Oden. *Religious Studies* 16 (1980) 368.
Himmelstrup, J. *Søren Kierkegaards Opfattelse af Sokrates. En Studie i dansk Filosofis Historie*. Copenhagen: Busck, 1924
Hirsch, Emmanuel. *Kierkegaard-Studien*. 2 vols. Gütersloh, Germany: Bertelsmann, 1933.
Höffding, Harald. *Den Store Humor*. Copenhagen: Gyldendalske, 1916.
Holmer, Paul. "On Understanding Kierkegaard." In *A Kierkegaard Critique*, edited by Howard A. Johnson and Niels Thulstrup, 40-54. New York: Harper, 1962.
Hutcheson, Peter, ed. *All England Report 1981*. London: Butterworth, 1981.
James, William C. "Anthropological Poetics: Auden's Typology of Heroism." *Kierkegaardiana* 10 (1977) 239-45.
Johnson, Howard A., and Niels Thulstrup. *A Kierkegaard Critique: An International Selection of Essays Interpreting Kierkegaard*. New York: Harper, 1962.
Kant, Immanuel. *Critique of Pure Reason*. Translated by Kemp Smith. London: Macmillan, 1953.
Khan, Abraham H. *Salighed as Happiness?: Kierkegaard on the Concept Salighed*. Waterloo, ON: Wilfred Laurier University Press, 1985.

Kierkegaard, Søren. "Also a Defense of Women's Superior Talents." In *Early Polemical Writings*. Kierkegaard's Writings, 1. Edited and translated with introduction and notes by Julia Watkins. Princeton: Princeton University Press, 2009

———. *Armed Neutrality and an Open Letter*. Edited and translated by Howard V. Hong and Edna H. Hong. New York: Simon and Schuster, 1969.

———. *Attack upon Christendom, 1854–1855*. Translated with an introduction by Walter Lowrie. London: Oxford University Press, 1946.

———. *Breve og Akstykker: Vedrørende Søren Kierkegaard*. 2 vols. Edited by Niels Thulstump. Copenhagen: Munksgaard, 1954.

———. *Christian Discourses: The Crisis and a Crisis in the Life of an Actress*. Kierkegaard's Writings, 17. Edited and translated with introduction and notes by Howard V. Hong and Edna H. Hong. Princeton: Princeton University Press, 2009.

———. *The Concept of Anxiety: A Simple Psychologically Orienting Deliberation of the Dogmatic Issue of Hereditary Sin*. Kierkegaard's Writings, 8. Edited and translated by Reidar Thomte. Princeton: Princeton University Press, 1981.

———. *The Concept of Irony*. Translated by Lee M. Capel. London: Collins, 1966.

———. *Concluding Unscientific Postscript to Philosophical Fragments*. 2 vols. Kierkegaard's Writings, 12. Edited and translated by Howard V. Hong and Edna H. Hong. Princeton: Princeton University Press, 1992.

———. *Either-Or*. 2 vols. Kierkegaard's Writings, 2. Edited and translated by Howard V. Hong and Edna H. Hong. Princeton: Princeton University Press, 1988.

———. *For Self-Examination / Judge for Yourself!* Kierkegaard's Writings, 21. Edited and translated by Howard V. Hong and Edna H. Hong. Princeton: Princeton University Press, 1991.

———. *Four Edifying Discourses*. In *Eighteen Upbuilding Discourses*. Kierkegaard's Writings, 5. Edited and translated by Howard V. Hong and Edna H. Hong, 103–76. Princeton: Princeton University Press, 1992.

———. "From the Papers of One Still Living." In *Early Polemical Writings*. Kierkegaard's Writings, 1. Edited and translated with introduction and notes by Julia Watkins. Princeton: Princeton University Press, 2009.

———. *Gospel of Sufferings*. Translated by A. S. Aldworth and W. S. Ferrie. Cambridge: James Clarke, 1955.

———. *The Journals of Søren Kierkegaard*. Edited by Alexander Dru. London: Oxford University Press, 1938.

———. *Journals 1853–55: The Last Years*. Translated and edited by Ronald Gregor Smith. London: Collins, 1965.

———. *Letters and Documents*. Kierkegaard's Writings, 25. Edited and translated by Henrik Rosenmeier. Princeton: Princeton University Press, 2009.

———. "Open Letter." In *Armed Neutrality and an Open Letter*, edited and translated by Howard V. Hong and Edna H. Hong, 47–55. New York: Simon and Schuster, 1969.

———. *Philosophical Fragments, or, A Fragment of Philosophy by Johannes Climacus*. Translated with an introduction by David Swenson, new introduction and commentary by Neils Thulstrup, and translation revised and commentary translated by Howard V. Hong. Princeton: Princeton University Press, 1962

———. *Point of View*. Kierkegaard's Writings, 22. Edited and translated by Howard V. Hong and Edna H. Hong. Princeton: Princeton University Press, 2009.

———. *Practice in Christianity*. Kierkegaard's Writings, 20. Edited and translated by Howard V. Hong and Edna H. Hong. Princeton: Princeton University Press, 1991.

———. *Repetition*. In *Fear and Trembling/Repetition*. Kierkegaard's Writings, 6. Edited and translated by Howard V. Hong and Edna H. Hong. Princeton: Princeton University Press, 1983.
———. *Samlede Vaerker*. 3rd ed. Copengagen: Gyldendal, 1964.
———. *Sickness unto Death: A Christian Psychological Exposition for Upbuilding and Awakening*. Kierkegaard's Writings, 19. Edited and translated by Howard V. Hong and Edna H. Hong. Princeton: Princeton University Press, 1983.
———. *Søren Kierkegaard's Journals and Papers*. Translated and edited by Howard V. and Hong and Edna H. Hong. Bloomington, IN: Indiana University Press, 1967.
———. *Søren Kierkegaards Papirer*. VB 24. Edited by P. A. Heiberg and V. Kuhr. Copenhagen: Gyldendal, 1909-48.
———. *Stages on Life's Way*. Kierkegaard's Writings, 11. Edited and translated by Howard V. Hong and Edna H. Hong. Princeton: Princeton University Press, 1988.
———. *Two Ages: The Age of Revolution and the Present Age. A Literary Review*. Kierkegaard's Writings, 14. Edited and translated by Howard V. Hong and Edna H. Hong. Princeton: Princeton University Press, 1978.
———. *Works of Love*. Kierkegaard's Writings, 16. Edited and translated by Howard V. Hong and Edna H. Hong. Princeton: Princeton University Press, 1995.
Kirmmse, Bruce H., editor. *Encounters with Kierkegaard: A Life as Seen by His Contemporaries*. Translated by Bruce H. Kirmmse and Virginia R. Laursen. Princeton: Princeton University Press, 1996.
———. *Kierkegaard in Golden Age Denmark*. Bloomington, IN: Indiana University Press, 1990.
Kneale, W., and M. Kneale. *The Development of Logic*. Oxford: Oxford University Press, 1964.
Knudsen, Johannes. *A Danish Rebel: The Life of N. F. S. Grundtvig*. Philadelphia: Muhlenberg, 1955.
Koch, Hal. *Grundtvig*. Yellow Springs, OH: Antioch, 1952.
———. *Grundtvig: Leben und Werk*. Berlin: Schmidt, 1951.
Kollegie til Schellings Forelaesninger I Berlin, Pk 4 Laeg 4 in Kierkegaard Arkivet C.
Kuhr, Victor. *Modsigelsens Grunsaetning*. Copenhagen: Gyldendal, 1915.
Lash, Nicholas. "Theory, Theology and Ideology." In *The Sciences and Theology in the Twentieth Century*, edited by A. R. Peacock, 209-28. Oxford: Oxford University Press, 1986.
Lawson, Lewis A., editor. *Kierkegaard's Presence in Contemporary American Life: Essays from Various Disciplines*. Metuchen, NJ: Scarecrow, 1970.
Leibniz, Gottfried. *Theodocy: Essays on the Goodness of God, the Freedom of Man, and the Origin of Evil*. Translated by E. M. Huggard. London: Routledge and Kegan Paul, 1952.
Lindstrøm, V. "La théologie de l'imitation de Jesus-Christ selon Søren Kierkegaard." *Revue d'histoire et de philosophie religieuses* 35 (1955) 379-92.
Lovejoy, Arthur O. "On the Discrimination of Romanticisms." In *English Romantic Poets*, edited by M. H. Abrams, 6. Oxford: Oxford University Press, 1960.
Lowrie, Walter. "Introduction by the Translator." In *Attack upon Christendom*, by Søren Kierkegaard, xi-xviii. London: Oxford University Press, 1946.
———. *Johann Georg Hamann*. Princeton: Princeton University Press, 1950.
———. *Kierkegaard*. Oxford: Oxford University Press, 1938.
Lowy, Michael. *Pour une sociologie des intellectuels Revolutionnaires*. Paris: Presses Universitaires de France, 1976.

Mackey, Louis. *Kierkegaard: A Kind of Poet*. Philadelphia: University of Pennsylvania Press, 1971.

MacKinnon, Donald M. *Themes in Theology: The Threefold Cord*. Edinburgh: T. & T. Clark, 1987.

Madenfort, D. "The Aesthetic as Immediately Sensuous—An Historical Perspective." *Studies in Art Education* (1975) 5-17.

Martensen, H. L. *Af mit Levnet*. 3 vols. Copenhagen: Gyldendal, 1882-83.

———. *Berlingske Tidende*, December 28, 1854.

Medina, Angel. *Reflection, Time and the Novel: Towards a Communicative Theory of Literature*. London: Routledge and Kegan Paul, 1979.

Møller, L. P. M. *Efterladte Skrifter*. Vol. 5. 3rd ed. Copenhagen: Reitzel, 1856.

Mynster, J. P. *Blandede Skrifter*, Vol. 1. Copenhagen: Gyldendal, 1852.

Naess, A. "Kierkegaard and the Educational Crisis." *Danish Yearbook of Philosophy*. Copenhagen: Munksgaard, 1971.

Niblett, W. R. "On Existentialism and Education." *The British Journal of Educational Studies* (May 1954) 101-11.

Novrup, Johannes. *Scandinavian Adult Education*. Copenhagen: Det Danske Forlag, 1948.

O'Connor, D. J. *Introduction to the Philosophy of Education*. London: Routledge and Kegan Paul, 1958.

Patrick, Denzil G. M. *Pascal and Kierkegaard*. London: Lutterworth, 1947.

Pattison, George. "Art in an Age of Reflection." In *The Cambridge Companion to Kierkegaard*, edited by Alasdair Hannay and Gordon D. Marino, 76-100. Cambridge: Cambridge University Press, 1998.

———. *Kierkegaard: The Aesthetic and the Religious*. London: Macmillan, 1992.

———. *Kierkegaard's Upbuilding Discourses*. London: Routledge, 2001.

Phillips, D. Z. *The Concept of Prayer*. London: Routledge, 1965.

Pike, James, ed. *Modern Canterbury Pilgrims*. New York: 1956.

Pojman, Louis. "Kierkegaard's Theory of Subjectivity and Education." In *Phenomenology and Education*, edited by B. L. Curtis and W. F. Mays. London: Methuen, 1978.

Poole, Roger. *Kierkegaard: The Indirect Communication*. London: University Press of Virginia, 1993.

———. "The Unknown Kierkegaard: Twentieth-Century Receptions." In *The Cambridge Companion to Kierkegaard*, edited by Alasdair Hannay and Gordon D. Marino, 48-75. Cambridge: Cambridge University Press, 1998.

Praz, Mario. *The Romantic Agony*. Oxford: Oxford University Press, 1970.

Przywara, E. *Das Geheimnis Kierkegaards*. Munich: Oldenburg, 1929.

Ramsey, Frank. "Facts and Propositions." In *Foundations of Mathematics and Other Logical Essays*, 138-55. London: Routledge and Kegan Paul, 1931.

Ramsey, I. T. *Religious Language*. London: SCM, 1957.

Reardon, B. M. G. *Hegel's Philosophy of Religion*. London: Macmillan, 1977.

Rodway, Allan. *The Romantic Conflict*. London: Chatto and Windus, 1963.

Roos, Heinrich. *Kierkegaard and Catholicism*. Translated by Richard M. Brackett. Westminster, MD: Newman, 1954.

Roos, Karl. *Kierkegaard og Goethe*. Copenhagen: Gad, 1955.

Ryan, Robert. *The Romantic Reformation*. Cambridge University Press, 1997.

Rudelbach, A. G. *Om det borgerlige Aegteskab*. Copenhagen: Schwartz, 1851.

Bibliography

Russell, Bertrand. "Dr. Schiller's Analysis of *The Analysis of Mind*." *Journal of Philosophy* 19 (1922) 645–51.
Santayana, George. *Egotism in German Philosophy*. London: Dent, 1916.
Schelling, F. W. J. *On University Studies*. Translated by E. S. Morgan. Athens, OH: Ohio University Press, 1966.
Schwanenflugel, H. *J. P. Mynster*. Vol. 2. Copenhagen: Gyldendal, 1901.
Sibbern, F. C. S. *Maanedskrift for Litteratur* 19 (1838) 283ff., 424ff., 546ff.
Sillem, E. A. *Ways of Thinking about God*. London: Darton, Longman and Todd, 1961.
Skrubbeltrang, F. S. *The Danish Folk High Schools*. Copenhagen: Danish Information Handbooks, 1947.
Smart, J. J. C. "The River of Time." In *Essays in Conceptual Analysis*, edited by Anthony Flew, 213–27. London, Macmillan, 1969.
Smith, R. Gregor. *Kierkegaard's Relation to Hegel*. Princeton: Princeton University Press, 1980.
———. "Commentary on *Philosophical Fragments or a Fragment of Philosophy by Johannes Climacus*." In *Philosophical Fragments or a Fragment of Philosophy by Johannes Climacus*, by Søren Kierkegaard, translation and introduction by David Swenson, new introduction and commentary by Neils Thulstrup, and translation revised and commentary translated by Howard V. Hong. Princeton: Princeton University Press, 1962.
Stark, W. "Kierkegaard on Capitalism." In *Kierkegaard's Presence in Contemporary American Life*, edited by L. A. Lawson, 120–50. Metuchen, NJ: Scarecrow, 1970.
Stirling, James H. *Lectures on the Philosophy of Law*. London: Longmans, 1873.
Stobart, M. A. "New Lights on Ibsen's 'Brand.'" *The Fortnightly Review* 66 (1896) 227–28.
Strauss, David F. *Ausgewählte Briefe*. Edited by Edward Zeller. Bonn: Strauss, 1895.
———. *Die Christliche Glaubenslehre in inrer geschichtlichen Entwicklung und im Kampfe mit der modernen Wissenschaft*. 2 vols. Darmstadt: Buchges, 1973.
Sundby, Thor, "Kierkegaard og Pascal." *Blaise Pascal*. Copenhagen, Gyldendal: 1877.
Tennemann, Wilhelm Gottlieb. *Geschichte der Philosophie*. Leipzig: Barth, 1810.
Thomas, R. S. *Selected Poems 1946–68*. Newcastle upon Tyne, UK: Bloodaxe, 1980.
Thompson, Josiah. *Kierkegaard*. New York: Knopf, 1973.
Thomte, Reidar. *Kierkegaard's Philosophy of Religion*. Reprint. Eugene, OR: Wipf and Stock, 2009.
Thulstrup, Niels, editor. *Breve og Akstykker: Vedrørende Søren Kierkegaard*. Copenhagen: Munksgaard, 1953.
Tilliette, Xavier. *Schelling une philosophie en devenir*. 2 vols. Paris: Vrin, 1970.
Tisseau, P. H. "La *Confession* de Musset et le *Banquet* de Kierkegaard." *Revue de litterature comparée* 13 (1934) 491–511.
Trendelenburg, Friedrich A. *Erläuterungen zu Platos Menexenus*. Berlin: Weidmann, 1905.
———. *Outlines of Logic: An English Translation of Trendelenburg's Elementa Logices Atistotele*. 2nd ed. Translated by R. Broughton. London: Simpkin, Marshall, Hamilton, Kent, 1898.
Wallace, William, editor. *The Logic of Hegel*. Oxford: Oxford University Press, 1925.
Waage, O. *J. P. Mynster og de philosophiske Bevaegelser paa hans Tid I Denmark*. Copenhagen: Reitzel, 1867.
Watkin, Julia. *Nutidens Religieuse Forvirring, Bogen om Adler*. Copenhagen: Reitzel, 1983.

Weiss, Paul. *Modes of Being*. 2 vols. Carbondale, IL: Southern Illinois University Press, 1958.

Westphal, Merold. "Kierkegaard and Hegel." In *The Cambridge Companion to Kierkegaard*, edited by Alasdair Hannay and Gordon D. Marino, 101–24. Cambridge: Cambridge University Press, 1998.

———. *Kierkegaard's Critique of Religion and Society*. Macon, GA: Mercer University Press, 1987.

White, Victor. *God the Unknown*. London: Harvill, 1956.

Wisdom, John. "Moore's Technique." In *Philosophy and Psycho-Analysis*, 120–48. Oxford: Blackwell, 1969.

Wittgenstein, Ludwig. *Philosophical Investigations*. Translated by G. E. M. Anscombe. Oxford: Blackwell, 1958.

www.ingramcontent.com/pod-product-compliance
Lightning Source LLC
Chambersburg PA
CBHW031725230426
43669CB00007B/249